Literary Biography

Literary Biography

An Introduction

Michael Benton

WILEY Blackwell

This paperback edition first published 2015

Edition history: Blackwell Publishing Ltd (hardback, 2009)

Registered Office
John Wiley & Sons, Ltd, The Atrium, Southern Gate, Chichester, West Sussex, PO19 8SQ, UK

Editorial Offices
350 Main Street, Malden, MA 02148-5020, USA
9600 Garsington Road, Oxford, OX4 2DQ, UK
The Atrium, Southern Gate, Chichester, West Sussex, PO19 8SQ, UK

For details of our global editorial offices, for customer services, and for information about how to apply for permission to reuse the copyright material in this book please see our website at www.wiley.com/wiley-blackwell.

Library of Congress Cataloging-in-Publication Data

Benton, Michael, 1939–
Literary biography: an introduction / Michael Benton.
p. cm.
Includes bibliographical references and index.
ISBN 978-1-4051-9446-4 (hardcover: alk. paper) ISBN 978-1-1190-6011-6 (paperback)
1. Authors, English–Biography–History and criticism–Theory, etc. 2. English prose literature–History and criticism–Theory, etc. 3. Authors–Biography–Authorship. 4. Biography as a literary form. I. Title.
PR756.B56B46 2009
820.9′492–dc22

2009009386

A catalogue record for this book is available from the British Library.

Cover image: Dickens Dream

Set in 10/12.5pt Sabon by SPi Global, Pondicherry, India

1 2015

Those parallel circumstances and kindred images, to which we readily conform our minds, are, above all other writings, to be found in narratives of the lives of particular persons; and therefore no species of writing seems more worthy of cultivation than biography, since none can be more delightful or more useful, none can more certainly enchain the heart by irresistible interest, or more widely diffuse instruction to every diversity of condition.

Dr Samuel Johnson, *The Rambler*, No. 60, Saturday, October 13, 1750

As everybody knows, the fascination of reading biographies is irresistible. No sooner have we opened the pages ... than the old illusion comes over us. Here is the past and all its inhabitants miraculously sealed as in a magic tank; all we have to do is to look and to listen and to listen and to look and soon little figures – for they are rather under life-size – will begin to move and to speak, and as they move we shall arrange them in all sorts of patterns of which they were ignorant, for they thought when they were alive that they could go where they liked; and as they speak we shall read into their sayings all kinds of meanings which never struck them, for they believed when they were alive that they said straight off whatever came into their heads. But once you are in a biography all is different.

Virginia Woolf, 'I am Christina Rossetti', in *Collected Essays*, IV, 1967: 54

The trawling net fills, then the biographer hauls it in, sorts, throws back, stores, fillets and sells. Yet consider what he doesn't catch: there is always far more of that. The biography stands, fat and worthy-burgherish on the shelf, boastful and sedate: a shilling life will give you all the facts, a ten pound one all the hypotheses as well. But think of everything that got away, that fled with the last deathbed exhalation of the biographee. What chance would the craftiest biographer stand against the subject who saw him coming and decided to amuse himself?

Julian Barnes, *Flaubert's Parrot*, 1985: 38

Contents

Illustrations

Acknowledgements

I am grateful to the editors of the following journals who have granted me permission to reproduce revised versions of articles that have appeared in their publications.

The *Journal of Aesthetic Education* for 'Literary Biography: The Cinderella of Literary Studies', which originally appeared in Vol. 39, No. 3, Fall 2005 and now features in parts of Chapters 1 and 2; and for 'Reading Biography', which originally appeared in Vol. 41, No. 3, Fall 2007 and now forms the bulk of Chapter 3. Both are used with the permission of the University of Illinois Press.

Auto/Biography for 'Literary Biomythography', which was first published in Issue 13, No. 3, 2005 and is reprinted as Chapter 4.

I am also indebted to the following galleries for permission to reproduce paintings and engravings from their collections:

The National Portrait Gallery, London for illustrations 6.1, 6.2, 6.3, 6.5, 6.6, 6.7, 6.9, 6.10, 6.11.
The Estate of Patrick Heron and DACS for 6.10.
The Charles Dickens Museum, London, for 6.8.
The British Museum, London, for 11.1.

I am especially grateful for the kindness of friends in helping me to complete this book. My thanks go to Dominic Hibberd for his willingness and patience in being interviewed about his biography of Wilfred Owen and for the fascinating insights into his ways of working; and to Geoff Fox and Pam Barnard who read each chapter in draft form and whose detailed marginalia and general comments have both sharpened the text and saved me from a number of errors and obscurities; any that remain are my own. Finally, my biggest debt is to my wife, Jette Kjeldsen, for her unmatchable combination of scrupulous reading, trenchant criticism and strong support.

Introduction

No-one, it seems, has a good word to say for biographers, not even the biographers themselves. That their subjects are often critical, even abusive, is only to be expected: 'biografiends' Joyce called them; 'a disease of English literature' was George Eliot's diagnosis of their work (quoted in Salwack, 1996: 37). But for biographers to turn upon themselves is uniquely odd. Perhaps the current spate of self-vilification was triggered by guilt stirred by Janet Malcolm's analysis of the Plath biographies in which she describes the biographer as a 'professional burglar' and accounts for the popularity of the genre by its prurient and 'transgressive nature' (Malcolm, 1995: 9). Whatever the cause, Dale Salwack's (1996: 6) book on literary biography begins with a catalogue of quotations from writers disgusted by biography; Michael Holroyd (2003: 3–9) plays devil's advocate in his entertaining 'The Case Against Biography'; and Mark Bostridge's (2004) collection of essays by practitioners is replete with self-conscious masochism. His Preface describes biography, in a tone of nervous playfulness, as a 'vice' and acknowledges that the biographer is often spoken of 'as a scoundrel'. Then, successive biographers indulge themselves in bouts of literary flagellation. Here are half a dozen of them. They see themselves as 'voyeurs' (pp. 7, 44), as 'vultures' (pp. 9, 54) and, in a string of equally nasty names, as 'scavenger, jackal, vampire, garbage-collector' which, Hilary Spurling concedes, are 'all of them valid up to a point' (p. 68)! They are seen, too, as guilty of a 'biographical love' between biographer and subject that is 'obsessive, possessive, irrational and perverse' (p. 38), which, in turn, may lead to 'a narcissist's wedding' (p. 12). It is little wonder that the issue of such a marriage is likely to be a malformed parasite: 'intrusive, trivial, irrelevant and somehow immoral' (p. 50).

Faced with the practitioners' lack of self-confidence, their subjects' frequent abuse, and the scepticism of academia, this defensiveness is understandable. However, by definition, anyone writing or reading a biography assumes the relevance of the life to the works as part of the historical and cultural context of literature. But it is an assumption that begs basic questions about the nature of the genre and what it offers the reader. It is these questions that this book sets out to explore. *Literary Biography: An Introduction* has two purposes: the main one is to discuss the principal generic issues in a literary form of ambiguous nature and uncertain status; the subsidiary and complementary aim is to show how the biographical context can enrich the study of familiar canonical authors whose lives and works mutually illuminate each other. As the title indicates, the book is intended as an introduction for students and general readers. It is not an attempt to theorise biography. This would require consideration of the genre both from a historiographical point of view and, in a literary perspective, from a historicist stance. Such an exploration would, no doubt, be revealing in its complementary concerns for the textuality of historical representation and the historicity of biographical texts. But it is an exploration beyond the scope of this book. Where I have drawn upon literary theory – especially in Chapters 2 and 8, for example – I have aimed to do so in language that is accessible without oversimplifying the ideas.

The book is selective, concentrating on those authors and biographers whose writings open up the key generic issues. My principal examples are taken from the mainstream literary canon – Shakespeare, Dickens, Blake, Wordsworth, the Brontës, and a range of twentieth-century authors. Major biographers from Dr Johnson, Boswell and Woolf to Holroyd, Holmes and Lee are also drawn upon extensively. The book is selective also in that the majority of subjects and biographers are British or Irish. I have found no place to discuss the distinguished 'Lives' of Henry James by Leon Edel, or of Edith Wharton by Hermione Lee, let alone biographies from European or Commonwealth sources. There are, of course, losses here; but in the competition for space, my aim has been to illustrate different aspects of literary biography with examples that will be most familiar to readers coming new to the genre. There are also practical reasons for the selections I have made. First, there are many more biographies about these subjects, stretching over different historical periods, making the study of the genre richer, more demanding, and more amenable to the teasing out of its characteristics. Secondly, the works of these writers are both well known to the wider reading public and specified on course programmes year after year, so that readers are likely to find more points of contact and interest in these 'Lives' than in any others.

How far can information about a poet or novelist be expected to clarify the source of the works and illuminate the nature of the poetry or fiction that we read? T. S. Eliot discussed this question in 'The Frontiers of

Criticism' (1957), distinguishing between the '*explanation*' of origins and context, seeing it as 'preparation' for the '*understanding* and *enjoyment* of literature' which, he emphasises, is unique to each individual reader: 'There are ... many facts about which scholars can instruct me which will help me to avoid definite *mis*understanding; but a valid interpretation, I believe, must be at the same time an interpretation of my own feelings when I read [a poem]' (pp. 49–50, Eliot's italics). Eliot acknowledges the uses of biography but also sees the danger of it becoming a barrier to the appreciation of the works, either through information overload, or through falsely 'explaining' poems or novels in non-literary, biographical terms (p. 52). The biographical context of Eliot's remarks is itself significant. They occurred in a lecture to some 14,000 (!) people in a baseball stadium at the University of Minnesota in Minneapolis and, as Eliot's biographer comments, no doubt with the memory of an interpretation of *The Waste Land* in mind that provoked him to warn 'against too much psychological or biographical conjecture in the explication of poetry' (Ackroyd, 1985: 317). Reading the life in the works or reading the works through the life are the Scylla and Charybdis between which literary biographers must navigate. Unlike their counterparts in political or military fields, they sail in uniquely dangerous waters. To one side, they face the hard rocks of historical data which they ignore at their peril; to the other, a whirlpool of imaginative literature which, for biographical purposes, is of uncertain depth and relevance. Maintaining a steady, discriminating course which acknowledges the importance of both bodies of evidence, without being subsumed by either, is the special skill demanded of the literary biographer.

* * *

The twelve chapters which make up this book exist in a federal relationship – independent essays that set out to give a sense of the historical development of the genre, to describe and account for its main characteristics, and to illuminate its connections with the arts of fiction and portraiture. Given the variations in the genre, any attempt to update the efforts at a typology, made in the past by Clifford (1962) and Edel (1984) among others, seems inappropriate. Instead, the diversity is best served by viewing literary biography from a range of perspectives – historical, comparative, inferential, auto/biographical and so on. As in any federation, there are not only different roles but also contrary emphases, and occasional dissenting voices. So, here, the roles of the first three chapters are to sketch the evolution of the genre, to introduce the principal traits of a hybrid form that lies between history and fiction, and to look at the consequences for the reader. In subsequent chapters, there are contrary emphases, for example, in listening to a biographer speaking about his practice, while others struggle with the dearth of hard evidence in their search for Shakespeare, or read the lives of their subjects alongside, behind or against the autobiographical images projected in the works. And, in Chapter 4, there is a measure of dissent from the whole biographical project in the subversive argument for the inevitable mythologizing of literary subjects. Yet, implicit in the notion of biomythography is the view that the genre is an art supported by elements of craft, rather than vice versa. It is this that holds this federal relationship together and is the stance adopted throughout this book.

Chapter 1 begins with a discussion of the ambiguous status of literary biography – a genre in vogue with the reading public yet still treated with a mixture of suspicion and disdain in many academic circles. It offers a historical sketch, identifying three phases of particular importance in the mid-eighteenth century, the early twentieth century and the present day. The contributions of the two major figures, Dr Johnson and Virginia Woolf, are then considered both for their theoretical essays and in two key works, *The Life of Savage* and *Orlando*, in order to show where the main issues in literary biography originate and how they have developed.

Using concepts drawn from narratology, Chapter 2 shows how biography's handling of life stories is both like and unlike that of fiction. Narrative is not neutral but imposes a shape on 'real life histories' involving selection, continuity, coherence and closure. These four elements are discussed with particular reference to examples of the beginnings, middles and endings of biographies of the Brontës, Thomas Hardy and Jane Austen. Two features unique to reading *literary* biography are identified: how readers must accommodate the image of the 'implied author' constructed from the author's works with that presented by the biography; and the asymmetrical time-lines of the author's 'life narrative' and 'literary narrative'. Literary biography is then shown to occupy an uncomfortable position between factual and fictional truth, illustrated in different ways from Thomas Hardy's self-ghosted biography and from Mrs Gaskell's *Life of Charlotte Brontë*.

Chapter 3 considers the dualistic nature of the genre from the point of view of the problems and benefits it presents for the reader. The first part conceptualises the communication between biographer and reader that is represented in the text. It argues that the hybrid character of biography, a cross between verifiable historical information and aesthetic narrative, is also reflected in the twofoldness of the writer's task and the reader's role. The second part shows how this model works in practice through examining two recent biographies of William Blake, one by G. E. Bentley, Jr with a 'documentary' emphasis, the other by Peter Ackroyd with an 'aesthetic' emphasis. It exemplifies the differences, in particular by contrasting how these two accounts deal with one of Blake's central concepts, the 'Two Contrary States of the Human Soul', which provides the theme for his *Songs of Innocence and Experience*. The third part considers two potential problem areas that derive from biography's hybrid form: the handling of historical data within the time-frame of the subject's life; and the difficulties of dealing with the 'inner life' of the subject's mind and feelings. A brief final section weighs up the problems and benefits of studying literary biography and concludes that this genre offers readers uniquely important reading lessons.

Myth-making is endemic in the life histories of novelists and poets. Literary biographies are complicit in the process even when they seek to demythologise their subjects. Chapter 4 outlines a five-phase development in the Brontë myth as the paradigm of 'biomythography'. Life-writings about Byron, Dickens and Sylvia Plath are then shown to follow a similar pattern and to exemplify, respectively, the characteristics of celebrity, idolatry and martyrdom which typify myth-making and which literary biography both helps to create and attempts to expose. The chapter concludes with ten brief reflections on the notion of biomythography which substantiate its claim to subvert any concept of life-writing based on a simplistic account of supposed 'facts'.

Chapter 5 is untypical in the prominence it gives to explicit discussion of a writer's works. To a greater or lesser extent, all literary biographers draw inferences from their subject's writings; but Shakespeare's invisibility as a man means that his plays and poems become the prime source of insight into the mind that created them. Accordingly, the chapter summarises the evidence for the 'life', such as it is, and then discusses what recent biographers infer about the thinking of their implied author in a representative selection of his works. A final section assesses the patterns of thinking in Shakespeare's works which modern biographies reveal, in particular, the increased sophistication in language and thinking around the middle of his career, and his typical mode of representing ideas through the dialectical conflict of characters and situations.

Chapter 6 on the relationship between biography and portraiture consists largely of a gallery of ten portraits of poets and novelists, each with an accompanying commentary which links these images to the lives, works or times of the writers and to the artistic conventions of the period when the paintings were created. Portraiture is seen as veering uneasily between aesthetic and referential values. The chapter questions the common notion of these 'sister arts', finding some similarities in the cultural motivation behind them and in the uncomfortable position which both occupy within the literary and visual arts while, at the same time, recognising their role in canon formation within literary history, as well as their broad cultural appeal.

Chapter 7 develops the theme of 'lives and times', acknowledging that each age rewrites the biographies of its favoured authors in ways which reflect the mores and literary conventions of the period. Any of the major nineteenth-century novelists could be the focus, but Dickens is taken as a particularly interesting example since not only have there been recurring 'Lives', but there is also a fascinating biographical conundrum to be explored in the relationship between the private, domestic family man, the even more private literary man at his writing desk, and the public man of affairs recognised by all (and not least by himself) as a giant of the Victorian Age. These relationships are discussed in respect of three major biographies: the Victorian Dickens of John Forster, the Modern Dickens of Edgar Johnson, and the Post-modern Dickens of Peter Ackroyd.

Self-representation in autobiographical literary works requires the biographer of the author to discriminate between the subject as a historical person and the persona projected into the text and mediated by literary technique. The difficulties are particularly acute when the author's self-creation is dedicated to accounting for the growth and development of an artistic life. Chapter 8 focuses upon William Wordsworth's *The Prelude* and James Joyce's *A Portrait of the Artist as a Young Man* as the two seminal texts and considers the implications for biographers who must view the lives of their subjects through an autobiographical screen. Following suggestions by Paul de Man, it argues that autobiographical writing is both 'mask' and 'metaphor' and it draws some conclusions about literary auto/biography, concentrating particularly upon the gaps and temporal qualities of narrative, the synthetic operation of memory, and the effect of literary forms and language in the self-creation of the subject.

In the interview recorded in Chapter 9, we can listen to a biographer's reflections upon the practice of his craft – or, should one say, his art? For one of the issues that arises from the conversation with Wilfred Owen's biographer, Dominic Hibberd, is his role in relation to his subject, in this case, one that lies somewhere between the detached historian and the ardent storyteller. The conversation covers three broad areas: first, the development of the biographer's initial interest in the subject, the handling of sources, the management of data and the process of composition; secondly, the main themes that emerge in the portrait of Owen – his reading, his religious upbringing, his sexual orientation, his class-consciousness – and how they bear upon his writing; and thirdly, some wider generic issues such as the justification for a new biography, and the relationship that develops between the biographer and the subject.

Chapter 10 considers five modern biographies of twentieth-century subjects – Graham Greene, Bernard Shaw, T. S. Eliot, George Orwell and Philip Larkin. It gives a critical pen portrait of each writer as seen through the eyes of their biographer and sets each 'Life' in the context of the literary estate that has (or in one case, has not) sanctioned its publication. Some tentative conclusions are then drawn about how biographers respond to their subject's literary persona and about the different relationships biographers forge with authors and their literary estates.

Chapter 11 revisits the relationship between history and fiction in life-writing initiated in the opening two chapters. It focuses on the making of scenes and stories as the fundamental building blocks in biography. It pursues this theme through close readings of two famous dinner parties: Boswell's account of Dr Johnson's meeting with John Wilkes, and Virginia Woolf's description of Mrs Ramsay's dinner party in *To The Lighthouse*. The analyses of the theatrical scenes of the one and the painterly scenes of the other highlight the similarities and differences in scene-making in biography and fiction.

The final chapter gives a brief summary of the main themes of earlier chapters and speculates about future directions in literary biography. However literary biography is represented in the dualisms of history and fiction, craft and art, the life and the works, its hybrid nature asserts itself. This generic 'looseness' suggests that, despite its inbred conservatism, twenty-first-century biography may develop in new ways in which, as in Jonathan Coe's 'story of B. S. Johnson', the 'Life' is not represented in a smooth narrative but reflects, in its style and form, something of the jaggedness of the subject's own life and work. Or, as exemplified by Nicholl on Shakespeare, Bodenheimer on Dickens and Wroe on Shelley, the conventional chronology of the life narrative is set aside as these biographers employ different means to probe beneath the continuity of its events.

The question of the difference between non-fiction narrative and fiction remains the central one. 'All good biographers struggle with a particular tension between the scholarly drive to assemble facts as dispassionately as possible and the novelistic urge to find shape and meaning within the apparently random circumstances of a life. We make sense of life by establishing "significant" facts, and by telling "revealing" stories' (Holmes, in France & St Clair, 2002: 16–17). As the examples discussed in this book amply demonstrate, the biographer's task is more complex than that of the novelist. If we allow that biography is an 'art', we must also recognise that the creative impulse expresses itself in a different way from that of the novelist. To develop a point made by David Cecil, the novelist's creativity shows itself mainly in *invention*, in the power to create characters, to put them in scenes, and to tell stories about them; the biographer's creativity shows itself in *interpretation*, in a capacity to discover in the scenes and anecdotes and the mass of other raw material the dominant, thematic life story to be fashioned into a work of art. Cecil continues: 'Like the maker of pictures in mosaic, his [the biographer's] art is one of arrangement; he cannot alter the shape of his material, his task is to invent a design into which the hard little stones of fact can be fitted as they are' (Cecil, in Clifford, 1962: 153). The analogy is apt: no-one would deny that a mosaic is a work of art; equally, no-one can ignore the amount of sheer craft that goes into its composition.

1

Literary Biography Now and Then

The Cinderella of Literary Studies

There are no prizes for guessing who are the two ugly sisters: criticism, the elder one, dominated literary studies for the first half of the twentieth century; theory, her younger sister, flounced to the fore in the second half. One scorned Cinderella's very existence as 'the biographical fallacy'; the other attempted her assassination by announcing the 'death of the author'. Meanwhile, 'Cinders', who had been doing the chores for centuries, was magically transformed, decked out in new clothes by Michael Holroyd, Richard Holmes, Claire Tomalin, Hermione Lee, Peter Ackroyd et al. and, as the millennium approached, celebrated and admired on all sides. Two decades ago, as Malcolm Bradbury (1988) pointed out, we seemed to live in two ages at once: the age of the Literary Life and the age of the Death of the Author. Nowadays, at the start of the new century, it transpires that reports of the death were greatly exaggerated. Literary biography remains in vogue. The bibliography that carries it forward is rolling and there is no sign of it turning into a pumpkin. Why is Cinderella so popular?

One obvious if superficial answer might be that literary biography is where literary people go who find the contemporary preoccupation with theory to be personally undernourishing and critically unenlightening; they would rather stay with the literary works themselves and with the lives, the minds and the times that produced them. Yet it is not only literary biography that is thriving; life-writing in general is a staple of mainstream publishing for which the appetite of the reading public seems insatiable. This commercial high profile is responding to an evident, if unfocused, need to look at other lives and understand them. Individual reasons for the popularity of biography range from prurient interest and hero worship to a, perhaps unrecognised, search for coherence and purpose in an age that is often disinclined either to accept institutional values or to respect traditional authority.

The motives for this search usually include the desire for recognisable success, to which end the invention of a convincing identity is essential. Biographies offer models of how others live, face challenges and cope with change; they offer prime sites for studying ourselves. Curiously, this justification for biography as providing a model for living was felt most strongly when this literary genre first emerged in its recognisably modern form in the eighteenth century. The difference nowadays is that the model has changed: biography as a moral *exemplum* based upon Christian principles has been replaced in today's celebrity culture by the demand for models of success provided by public personalities. Nonetheless, whatever the range of satisfactions readers seek in biography, life-writing offers detailed pictures of widely different ways of living and, amidst these perhaps, some clues to how an individual sense of identity might be shaped.

Literary biographies, as distinct from the past 'Lives' of politicians and military men, or the part 'Lives' of present-day footballers and pop idols, constitute a significant and, in several respects, a unique sub-genre. Literary biography often deals with subjects who stand apart from society's norms and whose intertwined lives and writings offer a critique of the world the rest of us inhabit. Whether as an outsider like Shelley or as an insider like Dickens, the literary biographer's subject tends to adopt an individualistic, critical view of the principles and practices of society which, on particular issues, may develop into outright opposition. The writer as rebel, the writer as exile, are familiar figures, particularly in the past two centuries.

Literary biography is unique, too, in that its subjects offer the prospect of access, however limited or illusory it may turn out to be, to the workings of the creative imagination. This prospect of gaining some insight into the mysteries of the artistic process is a seductive invitation to readers, one greatly enhanced by the intimacy between the biographer's and the subject's shared medium of words, their common interest in literary forms, and the particular closeness of fictional and historical narrative. When as often happens, an artistic affinity between biographer and biographee is inscribed in their relationship, the mystery of imaginative writing seems even closer. Novelists writing the 'Lives' of novelists (Mrs Gaskell on Charlotte Brontë; Peter Ackroyd on Dickens); poets writing the 'Lives' of poets (Andrew Motion on Philip Larkin; Elaine Feinstein on Ted Hughes); autobiographical writing in the form of poetry (Wordsworth) or fiction (Joyce) – all suggest specialist insights afforded by practitioners of the arts.

Literary biography also has an implicit appeal to readers as would-be authors, to the wish-fulfilment of being able to write poetry or fiction ourselves. Whether the writer's life is seemingly mundane and ordinary, hemmed in by convention or prejudice, dogged by frustration and disappointment, or cut short by tragedy, we tend – despite the facts – to accept it as the essential condition of the creative being, romanticising the quality of the life into an inevitable pattern that reflects the works and which, because it does so, becomes a pattern at some level to be envied. If life could be lived vicariously, the writer's life is the one we would choose; as biography, it offers a secondary life to share and enjoy alongside the secondary worlds created in the writer's works.

Yet, despite the evident attractions of biography, it has become a truism to declare that biography has failed to establish any theoretical foundations upon which to build. In a period given to literary theory, Ellis (2000: 3) speaks of 'the comparative dearth of analytic enquiry into biography'. Backscheider (1999: 2) quotes Ira Nadel's remark on the absence of 'a sustained theoretical discussion of biography incorporating some of the more probing and original speculations about language, structure, and discourse that have dominated post-structuralist thought'. She goes on to lament the poverty of criticism, the absence of a cultivated readership, the failure to engage even with the practical questions of selection, organisation or presentation, and indicates that readers of biography are too easily contented with reading for the life story. The implication is that biography is easy reading for lazy readers. D. J. Taylor, author of the biography *Orwell: The Life*, writing in *The Guardian* (8 November 2002), points to the unstable basis of the genre with a different emphasis: 'Although several universities have recently established centres of biographical research,' he says, 'there is hardly such a thing as a theory of biography, merely an acknowledgement that each age tends to explore the form in a manner consistent with its preoccupations.' This is uncontroversial if one compares pre- and post-Stracheyean biography, but it does not explain why, during the 1990s, there were four biographies of Jane Austen and three each of George Eliot and the Brontës – about all of whom we already know a great deal – let alone a dozen biographies this century of Shakespeare about whom we know next to nothing; or why, in a longer perspective, there have been over 200 'Lives' of Lord Byron (Holmes, 1995: 18). This insistent rewriting of writers' lives stems from more than commercial pressure. It indicates a genre where the life narrative can be explored from many different angles; where the revaluation and interpretation of existing and newly discovered evidence are fundamental to its history; and where biographers constantly respond to the challenge to represent the life in new artistic forms. Literary biography lies between history and fiction and has often been seen as the poor relation of both. As such it has attracted little theoretical interest from either side. Recent writing, however, has increasingly introduced elements of metabiography into studies of the genre

(Miller, 2001; Sisman, 2001); and biographers have reflected in print upon the nature and principles of their work (Holmes, 1985; Holroyd, 2002; Lee, 2005). The issues they raise will constantly recur in the chapters which follow; and the origins of most of them are to be found in the mid-eighteenth century.

The Rise and Rise of Literary Biography

The modern history of literary biography has seen three phases of exceptional development. It was invented in the mid-eighteenth century by Samuel Johnson and James Boswell, reinvented by Lytton Strachey and Virginia Woolf at the start of the twentieth century, and today we are living in a period when the genre is showing a greater variety of formal innovations than ever before. Johnson and Boswell had their predecessors, notably Isaak Walton, who wrote the lives of John Donne (1640) and George Herbert (1670); and that most notorious of seventeenth-century life-writers, John Aubrey, whose *Brief Lives* (1667–1697) aimed to show that 'the best of men are but men at best'. In his accounts of scholars and writers in a wide range of fields, he avoided general comments and empty praise in favour of specific, intimate and sometimes scandalous details. But Aubrey's *Brief Lives* were just that – Milton is given eight pages, Shakespeare one and a half – and their contents are quirky, humorous, solemn and salacious by turns.

In the next two centuries, by contrast, biographies were to become long, substantial books devoted to a single subject; they aimed to incorporate the intimate details of a person's life; and in doing so they ran up against fundamental issues such as verifiable facts versus likelihoods, personal privacy versus public knowledge, the biographer's role in giving interpretations, opinions and judgements – all of which still exercise present-day biographers. No-one was more aware of these genre issues than Dr Johnson. Expressing his impatience with contemporary biographers who were content merely to log the chronology of their subject's achievements, Johnson famously declared: 'more knowledge may be gained of a man's character, by a short conversation with one of his servants, than from a formal and studied narrative, begun with his pedigree, and ended with his funeral' (Johnson, 'On Biography', *The Rambler*, No. 60). Johnson's essay was published in the same year, 1750, as Fielding's *The History of Tom Jones, A Foundling*. From the outset, the line between biography and fiction was a blurred one, as indicated by Fielding's title, or by Sterne's *The Life and Opinions of Tristram Shandy* (1760–1767). And so it continued with *Jane Eyre* (1847), subtitled 'An Autobiography'. Conversely, reading the opening chapter of Mrs Gaskell's *The Life of Charlotte Brontë* (1857) is like reading the start of one of her novels. The concurrent rise of the novel and biography meant that fictions incorporated quasi-documentary items like letters and diary entries more commonly found in biographies, whereas biographies presented scenes and people with the creative eye of the novelist. It is little wonder that boundary disputes should break out, or that biofictions like *According to Queeney* and *Author, Author* should develop the popularity they enjoy today. Nor is it surprising, given the aura that surrounds many writers, to find that recent literary biography often struggles to extricate itself not only from fiction but also from myth. The posthumous mythologizing of Sylvia Plath since her suicide in 1963, and Lucasta Miller's demythologising in *The Brontë Myth* (2001), are two modern examples taken up in Chapter 4.

Fact, fiction or myth? Literary biography has long been a mixture of all three from its beginnings in Dr Johnson's *An Account of the Life of Mr. Richard Savage, Son of the Earl Rivers* (1744), whose extended title attempts to mask by its assertiveness the uncertain status of its subject. Together with his *Lives of the English Poets* (1779–1781), in which the *Life of Savage* reappeared as an outsize component, Johnson is usually seen as the father of modern literary biography. The 'son', his successor and protégé in the next generation, was, of course, his own biographer James Boswell. Their approaches to biography were sharply different. Johnson's style was to assimilate what information he could find about his subjects, to order it, interpret it, and weigh its significance and to produce a series of 'Lives' of generally modest proportions. (His *Pope* and *Savage*, the one through his eminence, the other for friendship, are longer exceptions to this rule.) Boswell's view of biography was to let his subject speak for himself by quoting *verbatim* letters, conversations, stories and words of wit and wisdom, thus creating a 'baggy', loosely formed 'Life' of elephantine size. The contrast between the summary qualities of the 'distilled life' and the inclusiveness of the 'comprehensive life' punctuates the history of biography in various guises in succeeding centuries: in Strachey's scornful rejection of 'those two fat volumes' that characterise Victorian biography and, nowadays, in the difference between, say, Carol Shields's brief, personal life of *Jane Austen* (2001) and Park Honan's fully documented *Jane Austen: Her Life* (rev. edn, 1997), which, its author claims in his Preface, 'is acknowledged to be the most complete, realistic life' of its subject.

Nineteenth-century biography generally favoured the Boswellian fullness without emulating his frankness. It reflected the decorous proprieties of its age and, as in the most celebrated and seminal literary biography of the period – Mrs Gaskell's *The Life of Charlotte Brontë* (1857) – eschewed 'coarseness' and tended to sanitise its subject with the fresh bloom of respectability. As Victorian certainties began to buckle, biography began to change, albeit slowly. In science, in Darwin's account of natural selection; in society, in Marx's analysis of cultural materialism; and in psychoanalysis, in Freud's theory of the unconscious, there developed three powerful forces that subverted the conventional religious, societal and psychological views of the nature of man and the very concept of human identity. Biography, like poetry and fiction, underwent its modernist revolution, even if its Bloomsbury character made it less convincing and pervasive than its counterparts in the other arts. Nevertheless, Lytton Strachey's *Eminent Victorians* (1918) and Virginia Woolf's preoccupation with biography in all her writings during the 1920s and 1930s together form the basis for what is usually called 'the new biography', a reappraisal of life-writing which, in its way, has been as influential as the works of its eighteenth-century originators.

Eminent Victorians made a great impact on its publication in May 1918. In a world disillusioned by war and distrustful of its leaders' soundbites, Strachey's wit and irony directed at four high-profile figures in Victorian society (Cardinal Manning, Florence Nightingale, Dr Arnold and General Gordon) hit the right sceptical and 'slightly cynical' note. His Preface has become a manifesto for later biographers both for its commitment to the value of individual lives and for its stylistic brevity and editorial selectivity. The first is seen in his remark that, 'Human beings are too important to be treated as mere symptoms of the past. They have a value which is independent of any temporal processes – which is eternal and must be felt for its own sake' (Strachey, 1986: 10). Unremarkable as such sentiments may now seem, to the immediate post-war generation they represented a necessary reaffirmation of individual worth. Stylistically, too, Strachey was radical. He argued that the biographer has to 'adopt a subtler strategy' than that of 'scrupulous narration'. He has to be selective, coming at his subject obliquely, revealing character in unexpected ways, illuminating personality in a new light. 'He will row out over that great ocean of material, and lower down into it, here and there, a little bucket, which will bring up to the light of day some characteristic specimen, from those far depths, to be examined with a careful curiosity' (Strachey, 1986: 9). Strachey's style of 'short condensed biography' returned life-writing to the Johnsonian form in that it avoided both the dead weight of heavy documentation and the light weight of facile, conventional panegyric. But Strachey's subjects, unlike Johnson's, were set up as targets, representative of false, misleading or hypocritical values of the Victorian age, not held up to us as individuals whose lives should be a lesson to us all.

Virginia Woolf's contribution to 'The New Biography' (the title of her first essay on the subject in 1927) was of a quite different nature. Biography permeates her work, obliquely and profoundly in her novels, especially *To The Lighthouse*, humorously in *Orlando* and *Flush*, directly in her essays and in her *Life of Roger Fry*, incidentally in her letters and diaries, and movingly in her autobiographical writings collected under the title *Moments of Being*, which Hermione Lee describes as 'an evolving narrative about the process of "life-writing"' (Lee, 2002: xiii). The issues that preoccupy Woolf are fundamental to biography: the relationships between fiction and non-fiction, art and craft, documentary and invention, truth in fact and truth in art. The issues remain 'live', not only, as noted above, in current thinking about biography, but also in the innovations in the form that have appeared in the past two decades. For example, the seven controversial Interludes in Peter Ackroyd's *Dickens* (1999), which challenge the generic boundary between fact and fiction; the ten Interchapters in D. J. Taylor's *Orwell: The Life* (2004), where the biographer steps out of the time-frame and takes a sideways glance at his subject; and, most radical of all (see below in Chapter 12), in Jonathan Coe's biography of B. S. Johnson, *Like a Fiery Elephant* (2004), which, mirroring his subject's work, is fragmentary in structure and confessional in tone, 'more a dossier than a conventional literary biography', as he warns us in his Introduction. Biography is not only thriving but is thoughtfully interrogating itself; and, during its long history, two figures stand out as maintaining a continuing relevance: Dr Johnson and Virginia Woolf.

Dr Johnson: Biographer, Theorist and Subject

The strange case of Richard Savage is an unlikely subject for the first literary biography. Savage was a minor poet, a convicted murderer who received a royal pardon, a vagrant who wandered the streets of London at night, whose life began with uncertain parentage and ended in Newgate Gaol in Bristol. The relationship between Richard Savage and Samuel Johnson which resulted in the latter's *Life of Savage* has puzzled people since its first publication in 1744. The identity of the subject and the role of the biographer lie at the heart of the story. The mystery that encompasses them unites biography then with biography now in Richard Holmes's modern masterpiece, *Dr. Johnson and Mr. Savage*, a title whose Stevensonian echo captures the unusual intimacy of the biographer and his subject.

Literary biography thus got off to a controversial start. Questions abounded:

- What relationship lay behind the *Life of Savage* in the time between Samuel Johnson's arrival in London in 1737 and Richard Savage's death in 1743?
- Why would a morally scrupulous man like Johnson become a close friend and biographer of an apparently unstable, feckless character such as Savage?
- What are we to believe about the selection and interpretation of the 'facts' of Savage's life in Johnson's biography?
- What does the account reveal about the biographer as well as his subject? About his judgements? About his qualities as a writer?

The first two questions concern the biographer/biographee relationship and, in particular, the benefits and disadvantages of friendship between the two, a subject on which Johnson was characteristically blunt: 'If the biographer writes from personal knowledge … there is a danger lest his interest, his fear, his gratitude, or his tenderness, overpower his fidelity and tempt him to conceal, if not to invent' (*The Rambler*, No. 60). The second two questions concern Johnson's skill as a biographer, his handling of his materials and his strategies in turning them into a 'Life'. Three substantive issues arise in reading his *Life of Savage*, each one a particular puzzle and each having a bearing upon these wider questions.

First, who was Johnson's subject? Was he a nobleman or an imposter? His mother should know – but was she his mother and was she honest? Richard Savage claimed throughout his life that he was the illegitimate son of Lady Macclesfield and Earl Rivers, born in Holborn on 10 January 1698, but his 'mother' never acknowledged his claim to be her son and regarded him as a blackmailing imposter or a deluded crank. Johnson, as he makes clear in his full title and in his advocacy throughout the 'Life', supported Savage's claim. Whether he entertained any doubts about its truth remains open to question. Secondly, how does Johnson deal with the central incident in Savage's history – his conviction for the fatal stabbing of one James Sinclair in a coffee-house brawl on 20 November 1727? Was it murder or self-defence? In a forensic analysis of Johnson's account, Richard Holmes lays bare the ways in which Johnson defends Savage by 'bending his own rules of biographical realism' in the biased presentation of the courtroom drama, in the fictional projection of Savage's voice, and in the caricaturing of the presiding Judge Page (Holmes, 1994: 100–132). Here, too, the 'truth' hangs in suspension between fact and fiction, between the incomplete documentary evidence and the 'adversarial skill' Johnson shows in mounting a defence of his friend. Thirdly, what conclusions does Johnson draw in his final set-piece where, if he is to be true to his own principles, his aim is for fair and balanced judgement? Certainly, Johnson catalogues eloquently both his subject's vices and shortcomings and his virtues and abilities. The balance is evident and reflected in his carefully modulated sentences; but so seductive are their disarming tone and urbane style that Savage's faults seem merely the endearing weaknesses of a mercurial character for whom we instinctively make allowances. Johnson's precarious balance is also there in the psychological 'twist in the tail' at the very end of his biography. Richard Holmes argues that this 'Life' has, in effect, two alternative endings, the final paragraph being 'Added', the word Johnson wrote against it when preparing the second edition. This later ending condemns Savage's life as showing that 'nothing will supply the want of prudence, and that negligence and irregularity, long continued, will make knowledge useless, wit ridiculous, and genius contemptible.' By contrast, the original ending which now forms the penultimate paragraph advocates empathy rather than condemnation: 'nor will any wise man presume to say, "Had I been in Savage's condition, I should have lived or written better than Savage"'. Holmes sees this as Johnson's real conclusion, and the later ending as a 'placatory afterthought; a conciliatory gesture to the forces of social opinion' (Holmes, 1994: 226–227).

The ambivalence of the ending is symptomatic of the unstable life upon which the whole biography is built. In Johnson's conduct of the case for the defence, we are simultaneously aware that, however brilliantly it is advocated, his is a tendentious account, a narrative in which the search for truth, the whole truth, and nothing but the truth is compromised through a combination of personal loyalty and rhetorical skill. Desmond McCarthy's much-quoted description of the biographer as 'an artist on oath' may be admirable in aspiration but, as Johnson's *Savage* shows, it papers over the cracks between the truth of art and the truth of fact.

Yet, Johnson believed, in theory, in telling the whole truth, as the ending of his essay 'On Biography' (*The Rambler*, No. 60) shows. In practice, however, Boswell detected some contradiction, or what he tactfully calls Johnson's 'varying from himself in talk'. On one occasion, Johnson argued that mention of Addison's and Parnell's excessive drinking should be censored since it would encourage others to do the same; on another, he argued that such an example would act as an 'instructive caution' (Boswell, 1791/1949, II: 115). There is ambivalence, too, in Johnson's view, quoted above, of the effects of friendship and 'personal knowledge' in the biographer/biographee relationship, both in writing the 'Life' of his friend Savage and in encouraging the writing of his own 'Life' by his friend Boswell. The essay in *The Rambler*, No. 60 is, nevertheless, Johnson's principal statement. Its essential premise is the democratisation of biography: 'I have often thought that there is rarely passed a life of which a judicious and faithful narrative would not be useful'. The motive is educational: 'no species of writing seems more worthy of cultivation than biography, since none can be more delightful or more useful ... or more widely diffuse instruction'. The means should be to 'display the minute details of daily life' which 'lead the thoughts into domestic privacies', rather than dwelling on incidents that 'produce vulgar greatness'. Johnson's educative principle is that people learn from other people's experiences, from particulars not from generalities, from life histories in which everyone can imaginatively recognise shared hopes and problems, not from 'histories of the downfall of kingdoms and revolutions of empires'. Johnson's two later essays in *The Idler*, Nos. 84 and 102 provide a gloss upon these principles. The first stresses the usefulness of biography as a pragmatic guide in daily life and raises the issues of accuracy and belief in autobiography. The second promotes the idea of authors, rather than soldiers or statesmen, as biographical subjects, and ends with a typical Johnsonian side-swipe at his favourite target, the patron. Johnson was able to put this idea of literary biography into practice in his *Lives of the English Poets* in which, in the more substantial accounts of major writers such as Pope, Dryden, Swift and Milton (as well as in the recycled Savage), he shows how, for the first time, biography can explore the relationships between the writer, his works and the times. In the essays, in the 'Lives', and especially in his *Life of Savage*, Johnson did more than anyone to establish biography as a literary genre. He rescued it from the fate of 'tedious panegyric'; he demonstrated that life-writing is based upon narrative skill, on the deployment of data and evidence, and on the (re)creation of historical scenes; and, despite his all-too-human struggle to reconcile theory and practice, Johnson's belief in the ethical basis of biography, grounded in human sympathy and backed by moral principles, is never in doubt.

* * *

Boswell's Johnson is a quite different figure from the implied image of the author of the *Life of Savage*. Young Sam Johnson, newly arrived from the provinces, shows a puzzling if consistent loyalty, a sense of justice that verges on outrage, and a degree of credulity and romanticism over Savage's misfortunes. His attitude has often provoked the question of how much he saw his own early struggles mirrored in the life of his friend. Did Johnson, the biographer, unwittingly write something of his own autobiography? By contrast, the Johnson whom Boswell knew, and the one we have all inherited from his biography, is a mature, successful man in his mid-fifties; the revered Tory of the clubs and dinner tables, the sententious sage, confident in argument and universally respected as poet, essayist, lexicographer – the great man of letters of his age. How did Boswell create this portrait?

There are many ways in which Boswell, while firmly anchored in his time, remains our contemporary as a biographer. His procedure in compiling *The Life of Dr. Johnson* was new to the art of biography, and four of his techniques, with modifications, remain part of the biographer's armoury today. The summaries which follow draw upon Adam Sisman's invaluable and entertaining book, *Boswell's Presumptuous Task* (2001).

First, Boswell kept a journal as an *aide-mémoire* (of which Johnson approved) and which became the source for whole episodes in the 'Life'. Sisman (pp. 149–150) comments: 'A note in Boswell's journal for 25th October 1764 provides an insight into the way he worked: "My method is to make a memorandum every night of what I have seen during the day. By this means I have my materials always secured ..." He called these condensed notes "portable soup": they were a kind of stock cube from which he could cook up a broth, when the time came to feed. Boswell had a remarkable memory; often only a brief note would be sufficient to prompt his recall of a long conversation.'

Secondly, Boswell wanted to portray both the strong physical presence of Johnson and his supreme abilities in conversation. The best way to achieve these ends was, whenever possible, to present Johnson's life 'in scenes'. His readers would then feel that they were watching a series of mini-dramas, with Johnson at the centre of the action. They were meant to feel 'like fellow-guests at the dinner-table. Johnson's remarks, and those of his companions, would be reported, as if in full; and rather than being given in indirect speech, the most dramatic exchanges would be cued to the speaker's name like an actor's lines, sometimes with stage-directions to indicate manner or inflexion' (Sisman, p. 169). The most elaborate example, the celebrated dinner party with John Wilkes, is examined in detail in Chapter 11.

Thirdly, Boswell amassed an enormous amount of material both by and about Johnson and he decided to incorporate as much of it as possible in the 'Life'. Extracts from letters, documents, obituaries, essays and many other sources, together with Johnson's own observations, personal and public utterances, jokes and serious arguments, fill his 'Life'. Instead of 'melting down my materials into one mass, and constantly speaking in my own person', Boswell planned to let Johnson speak for himself (Sisman, p. 171).

Fourthly, so concerned was Boswell to justify his claim that Johnson 'will be seen in this work more completely than any man who has ever lived' (Boswell, 1791/1949, I: 8) that gap-filling became essential. Though Boswell got to know his subject better than most biographers, he did not know the first fifty-four years of Johnson's life first hand; and he was in his company for about 400 days over the remaining twenty-one years. He used much undated memorabilia from many sources (especially from Mr Bennet Langton and the Reverend William Mitchell) to plug gaps in his record for the years 1770 and 1780 when he had been unable to come to London to see Johnson. Boswell placed these anecdotes and data where they seemed to fit best chronologically, or where they illustrated a point he was making. But, as Sisman (p. 214) notes, 'Boswell admitted in his *Life of Johnson* that he had rewritten some of these sayings of Johnson's into what he considered the authentic Johnsonian style'. What Boswell's 'Life' tells us is that, far from being a record of the plain, unvarnished truth, biography is a construct where accuracy may be sacrificed to effect, where the demands of narrative continuity may override the balanced, sequential presentation of events in time, and where the living facts of recorded situations are at the mercy of imperfect memory.

Virginia Woolf: Time, Memory and Identity

Time and memory are also two central and related factors in Virginia Woolf's writings. They are ones she returns to repeatedly in her explorations into the nature of selfhood. Both her fiction and non-fiction works constantly ask the question, 'What is identity?' They answer it by discursive argument in her essays, by autobiographical reflection in her 'Sketch of the Past'; and they represent it by creating fictional characters that demonstrate their multiple selves filtered through fragmented, non-sequential or irregularly patterned narratives. Time, memory and identity are concepts that hover along the boundary between life-writing and fiction-writing in Woolf's works.

Hermione Lee's first paragraphs of her celebrated biography of Virginia Woolf are a *cri de coeur* concerning these problems. Her opening words quote her subject: '"My God, how does one write a Biography?" Virginia Woolf's question haunts her own biographers. How do they begin?' (Lee, 1997: 3). Then follows a first chapter, entitled 'Biography', in which Lee reviews not only the many possible approaches open to the biographer, but also shows how, in Virginia Woolf, 'fiction is often her version of biography' (p. 8). Lying behind Woolf's view of both genres is the conviction that we can never assimilate the multiple perspectives we have of another person into a single, unified vision. From this standpoint, writing 'Lives' has a built-in failure factor. Biography is rendered an impossibility; the written 'Life' will always be elusive, at best an approximation. Yet, this very awareness makes it all the more tantalising to try to capture it in words. Nowadays, the would-be life-writer is even more biographically challenged: 'since we live in an age when a thousand cameras are pointed, by newspapers, letters, and diaries, at every character from every angle, he [the biographer] must be prepared to admit contradictory versions of the same face'. But, this is not – as might be thought – a twenty-first-century media commentator; it is Virginia Woolf in 1939, facing up to the issues in modern biography which were as true then as now. She looks forward to a future when 'Biography will enlarge its scope by hanging up looking-glasses at odd corners ... [and] from all this diversity' create 'a richer unity' (Woolf, 1967: 226). Yet, to pursue this unity was a demanding 'grind', as she called it, when writing her *Life of Roger Fry*, and finding herself shackled to facts, denied her freedom as a novelist, all bearing out her judgement that the biographer 'is a craftsman, not an artist' (p. 227). But, she concedes, through the selection and shaping of facts, the biographer is employing artistic means when creating a 'Life' in words. 'He can give us', Woolf says, 'the creative fact; the fertile fact; the fact that suggests and engenders' (p. 228).

Woolf's thinking about biography is frequently cast in this binary mode. The combination, implied in these phrases, of an artistic imagination operating upon a documentary record is reflected, too, in her best-known figure for biography: the granite and the rainbow. Her earlier essay, 'The New Biography' (1927), describes the biographer's aim as welding together the 'granite-like solidity' of truth with the 'rainbow-like intangibility' of personality into a 'seamless whole'. Truth, she claims, citing Sidney Lee's 'Life of Shakespeare', may consist of dull, dead facts; in order to make the subject come alive, facts need to be presented so as to illuminate personality by the subtle use of chiaroscuro – 'some must be brightened; others shaded; yet in the process, they must never lose their integrity' (Woolf, 1967: 229). The imagery changes but the dualism is essentially the same when, in 'Sketch of the Past', Woolf distinguishes between the routine business of daily living ('the cotton wool of daily life', she calls it) and the significant, exceptional moments which stay in the memory and which supply the invisible, silent 'scaffolding' to an individual life. Woolf is speaking personally but sees her experience as part of a general pattern. Again, in these autobiographical reflections, the binary relationship is evident: 'These separate moments of being were however embedded in many more moments of non-being' (Woolf, 2002: 83–86). In *Orlando*, as discussed below, this distinction is cast in terms of the 'extraordinary discrepancy between time on the clock and time in the mind' (Woolf, *Orlando*, 1998: 95). The implication of all these discriminations is that, as we live with a consciousness of both dimensions, so biography should honour this dualism. Virginia Woolf's criticism of most past biographies is that they deal only with the granite of fact, the orderly procession of events in clock-time, the mass of unmemorable moments of non-being – and fail to explore the changing, elusive, inner life of the subject which holds the key to personality.

'My God, how does one write a Biography?' *Orlando* is a playful *tour de force* in which Woolf has fun toying with the implications of, if not the answers to, her own question. *Orlando* the text and Orlando the character both defy definition. Based on the life of her friend, Vita Sackville-West, openly dedicated to her, originally published with photographs of her and her family, and given the academic embalming of a phoney Preface with acknowledgements and an equally phoney Index of Names, *Orlando* has been variously called a spoof biography, a Shandyean joke, a satire on the conventions of biographical writing. Leon Edel describes it as 'a fantasy in the form of a biography', saying that it is 'neither a literary joke nor entirely a novel: it belongs to another *genre*. It is a fable – a fable for biographers' (Edel, 1984: 192). Hermione Lee (1997: 523) describes it as 'a biography which makes a mockery of the very idea of writing biography'. Rachel Bowlby, faced with the task of editing and introducing the book, begins by echoing Woolf's plaintive question: 'What is *Orlando*'s editor to do?' for the role seems to dictate self-parody. She settles for saying what it is not: '*Orlando* is not exactly a fake biography, of a purely fictitious subject; but nor is it much like a biographical *roman-à-clef*, in which the subject would secretly stand for some real-life personage' (Bowlby, 1998: xix).

The protagonist is equally elusive. Orlando is Vita, whose very name signifies 'life', and whose multiple roles in her actual life provided Woolf with an ideal subject for the dramatisation of the plural nature of identity. 'As writer, traveller, aristocrat, lesbian, mother, diplomat's wife (to name some), she was seen by Woolf as someone who shifted between far more roles than she did herself' (Bowlby, 1998: xix). So, Orlando lives out the picaresque adventures of an engaging English aristocrat. He begins life as a youth in the Elizabethan age; he falls in love with Sasha, a Muscovite princess visiting the English court. They go skating on the Thames during the Great Frost when elaborate ceremonies and pageants are set up on the ice. Sasha proves fickle and sails away; Orlando comforts his broken heart with literature and, perhaps inspired by fleeting glimpses of Shakespeare, begins to write his poem 'The Oak Tree', which will keep him busy periodically for the rest of the book. He becomes ambassador to Turkey where, waking from a dream, he finds he has undergone a sex change: Orlando is now a woman. She lives for a time among gypsies and eventually returns to England in the eighteenth century. There is a law suit to resolve her property rights over the estates of her former male self. She entertains Addison, Pope and Swift to tea and sees the shadows of Dr Johnson and Boswell outlined on a window-blind as she passes by. The great black cloud of the Victorian age descends: Orlando, responsive to the times, becomes domesticated, marries, has a son, and enters the twentieth century travelling in trains and driving a car. Woolf ends Orlando's fantasy life at midnight on 11 October 1928 – the year of the book's publication.

In *Orlando*, Virginia Woolf is letting her hair down. It is a *jeu d'esprit* – 'a joke', 'a writer's holiday' as she called it; but, as the bare bones of the outrageous plot suggest, she pokes light-hearted fun at some targets and serious humour merging into satire at others: romantic love, the concept of historical periods, literary patriarchy, class divisions, diplomatic life, gender roles and, encompassing all, the idea of biography. Biographers, as might be expected, come in for the most persistent criticism. They ignore what is disagreeable (p. 15); their 'first duty … is to plod, without looking to right or left' (p. 63); on occasions, they even have 'to use the imagination' (p. 115)! No doubt with Strachey in mind, Woolf invokes 'Truth, Candour and Honesty, the austere Gods who keep watch and ward by the inkpot of the biographer' and demand 'The Truth and nothing but the Truth!' (p. 129), while a little later she acknowledges, in an archly self-reflexive comment on the present story, that 'only those who have little need of the truth, and no respect for it – the poets and novelists – can be trusted' with it (p. 184). Literary biographers, in particular, need our sympathy, she implies with gentle mockery, since their subjects, like Orlando in role as the aspiring poet, will insist on 'sitting in a chair and thinking'; life goes on inside the writer's head, hidden from view. 'If only subjects … had more consideration for their biographers!' (pp. 254–257). And, at the end, the fundamental puzzle of how to represent the subject – even whether it is possible at all – remains: '*Orlando* is finished!' Virginia Woolf writes to Vita Sackville-West, 'I've lived in you all these months – coming out, what are you really like? Do you exist? Have I made you up?' (Nicolson, quoted in Lee, 1997: 514).

Time, memory and a sense of identity are interwoven in *Orlando* and are the basic concepts in Virginia Woolf's modernist view of biography. In respect of time, she even engages in a paragraph of self-parody of the 'Time Passes' section in her most autobiographical novel, *To The Lighthouse* (*Orlando*, p. 94), and follows it by calling up the figure of the biographer again as one who can merely record, not elucidate, the differential experiences of the subject's double life: 'An hour, once it lodges in the queer element of the human spirit, may be stretched to fifty or a hundred times its clock length; on the other hand, an hour may be accurately represented on the timepiece of the mind by one second' (pp. 94–95). Activities in clock-time in the world we all share may be logged but they are experienced by the subject in a foreshortened time-scale inaccessible to the biographer; mental activities unique to the individual are also beyond the biographer's reach since the variable geometry of thoughts stretches the experience of time in many directions and fills it, Woolf says, with all kinds of 'odds and ends' of unpredictable duration.

What holds together this 'perfect rag-bag of odds and ends within us', providing the individual with a sense of self that biography cannot fathom, is memory. 'Nature', Woolf writes, 'who has played so many queer tricks upon us, making us so unequally of clay and diamonds, of rainbow and granite, … nature who has so much to answer for' has also found a way of stitching together each person's unique history. 'Memory is the seamstress, and a capricious one at that. Memory runs her needle in and out, up and down, hither and thither' (p. 75). If, in acts of self-creation, memory is acknowledged as a capricious, unreliable narrator, the biographer's chances of representing a life in ways that do justice to both granite and rainbow look slim.

At the end Time and Memory coalesce. Orlando muses to herself: '"Time has passed over me", she thought … Nothing is any longer one thing' (pp. 290–291) for, as Orlando steps into her car in Oxford Street, the striking clock punctuates the sequence of memories running through her mind. An attack of road rage propels her out of London at high speed, her fast driving resembling 'the chopping up small of identity', until she pulls herself together and her mind regains 'the illusion of holding things within itself' (p. 293). This experience of potential dissolution, of her sense of self falling apart, provokes the notion of the variety of selves within Orlando and of the biographer's impossible task of trying to accommodate them: 'a biography is considered complete if it merely accounts for six or seven selves, whereas a person may well have as many thousand' (p. 295). It has taken literary theory over half a century to catch up with Virginia Woolf: in a summary of Derrida's notion of 'différance' in relation to biographical narratives, Denzin (1989: 46–47) points out that Derrida's 'deconstruction project' means that 'no reading or writing of a life is ever complete or final. *We must prevent words like autobiography, biography, and biographical method from assuming a force which gives a presence to a centred-life that it cannot have* … there can only be multiple versions of a biography or autobiography.' *Orlando* is the prophet of deconstruction. In expressing his/her multiple selves, while living a variety of lives, in a succession of historical periods, Orlando somehow maintains a recognisable identity, diverse in make up, changeable in outward appearances, yet coherent as a personality – a character who stands for both the lure and the impossibility of biography.

2

Life [Hi]Stories: Telling Tales

Biographies are, after all, plots shaping and structuring the idea of a life; and literary biographies are the plots of the lives of plotters, who are likely to leave some trace in the biography of their own professional sense of plot's strange ambiguities.

(Bradbury, 'The Telling Life: Some Thoughts on Literary Biography', 1988: 139)

The 'shaping and structuring' occurring in literary biography to which Malcolm Bradbury refers follow from its main generic feature: the combination of its concern to document facts driven by a strong narrative impulse. His remarks suggest an exploration of literary biography that ranges its historical necessities against its narrative characteristics and invite discussion of the notion of biographical 'truth'. First, however, it is important to be clear about the nature of narrative and to distinguish between its deployment for historical and fictional purposes.

Aspects of Narrative

Narrative, according to Prince (1982: 4), is 'the representation of at least two real or fictive events or situations in a time sequence, neither of which presupposes or entails the other'. Narrative, in other words, is a discourse that may be generated in history or fiction – even in the blending of the two genres – in which the crucial element is time. The representation of a temporal succession of connected events is its fundamental feature. But, narrative operates differently in relation to historical and fictional texts. Scholes makes the distinction:

> The producer of a historical text affirms that the events entextualised did indeed occur prior to the entextualisation. Thus it is quite proper to bring

> extratextual information to bear on those events when interpreting and evaluating a historical narrative.... It is certainly otherwise with fiction, for in fiction the events may be said to be created by and with the text. They have no prior temporal existence, even though they are presented *as if* they did. (Scholes 1981: 207)

The writers of biographical narratives, therefore, in which the events that comprise their subjects' life [hi]stories are, by definition, incomplete and open to the vagaries of interpretation, are in an ambivalent position. They are charged with the responsibility to present and account for the spectrum of the life from cradle to grave, yet equally expected to give point, significance and interest to that life through narrative modes of representation which are often more readily associated with fiction and which, in the biographer's interpolations and gap-filling, are constantly edging in that direction. In the writing process, the literary biographer is continuously moving between a conception of events that have occurred 'prior to entextualisation' and their representation as 'created by and with the text'. (Reading biography involves a corresponding generic dualism, as outlined in Chapter 3.) Biographers, then, are required to produce narrative continuity and, because they are bound by the chronological imperative, are subject to the demand to tell a coherent story which, like any other conventional tale, must show a beginning, middle and end. And, whichever part of the narrative we are reading, the fundamental distinction is between the 'what' and the 'how', between the *histoire*, the chain of events, the people and their settings, and the *récit*, the discourse that gives them expression. Biography's handling of narrative is both like and unlike that of fiction. There are differences in the 'what' – in purpose and content; there are similarities in the 'how' – in the selection, interpretation and technical presentation of the life story. Openings are significant pointers as to how the biographer views the task.

(i) Beginnings: Charlotte Brontë

Here are the openings of three Brontë biographies. First, Mrs Gaskell:

> The Leeds and Bradford railway runs along a deep valley of the Aire; a slow and sluggish stream, compared to the neighbouring river Wharf. (Gaskell, 1857/1975: 53)

Mrs Gaskell, as we know from her own remarks, had trouble finding a biographical voice: 'And I never *did* write a biography, and I don't know exactly how to set about it; you see you have to be accurate and keep to facts; a most difficult thing for a writer of fiction' (Gaskell, in Uglow, 1999: 397).

In the chapter which follows the opening sentence above, Mrs Gaskell's eye pans like a film camera, from long shots of the Aire valley and the town of Keighley, up into the moors towards the village of Haworth, and homes in on the parsonage and the church, finishing with close-ups of the gravestones of the Brontë family. This opening sets the key for the whole biography – a life set in rural isolation with a predominantly sombre tone, everything calculated to sanctify its subject.

Second, Juliet Barker:

> On the first day of October 1802 a twenty-five-year-old Irishman walked through the imposing gateway of St John's College, Cambridge. (Barker, 1995: 1)

Juliet Barker's opening sentence situates us fourteen years before Charlotte was born and, by placing Patrick her father at the start, it signals a wish to reassess his role in the Brontë story. The ensuing chapter is titled 'An Ambitious Man' and, with a brief flashback to cover the years from Patrick Brontë's birth in 1777 to the turn of the century, it documents his education, ordination and early posts as a curate. This is to be a family biography, albeit one in which Charlotte is the principal character.

Third, Lyndall Gordon:

> 'A private governess has no existence,' wrote Charlotte Brontë to her sister, Emily, in the summer of 1839. (Gordon, 1994: 1)

Lyndall Gordon begins nearly forty years later with a quotation from one of Charlotte's letters and an invocation of one of Victorian England's archetypal images – the governess. Her first chapter is called 'The Unseen Space', an indication that her concern is with the imaginative space that Charlotte created for herself amid the restrictiveness of her home, her role and her upbringing. Gordon's interest is with Charlotte's interior landscape.

Three approaches to the same life – for Charlotte is the main figure in the Brontë story – but different treatments, each drawing on common devices used in fiction. Mrs Gaskell begins with scene, a novelistic opening that finds a successor in the topographical description at the start of *Sons and Lovers*; Barker begins with a point in time, a main character walking into history; Gordon begins with an image, instantly creating the picture of an educated Victorian spinster and simultaneously denigrating it. It is evident from these openings that the art of biography involves invention as well as interpretation, that the skills of narrative are essential to quicken the life on the page. Yet the 'how' must illuminate and not distort the 'what'. It follows that the most useful approach to biography will be one that openly recognises the *récit* as a narration grounded in the *histoire*, that accepts the latter as a 'given' (albeit an incomplete and debateable one), and that reflects the tensions that this asymmetry produces.

(ii) Middles: Thomas Hardy

Narrative is not just 'empty form', a container for the objective recording of a series of real events that made up the life. Narrative imposes a shape on real life which, in view of its messy unpredictability, is both necessary and illusory. For biographers, like the rest of us, need narrative in order to make sense of life; and the sense we make is a provisional construct created from a mixture of elements – selection, continuity, coherence and closure – that characterise the artistic form of narrative. Closure is considered presently. How do biographers select their material to develop narrative continuity and coherence in a genre which, unlike fiction, requires the writer to take a distinct line through the mass of data to tell the story? Three main features recur: the biographer is seen to set an agenda for the life story; to highlight significant scenes or episodes in pursuit of this agenda; and to acknowledge the inevitable gaps in the history and, where possible, to fill each with a plausible scenario or explanation.

In discussing the Brontë openings above, the emphasis was upon their fictional styles as much as upon their agenda-setting. A clearer example of how an agenda is not only set but also pursued is Claire Tomalin's biography, *Thomas Hardy: The Time-Torn Man* (2006). Her subtitle indicates her twin themes. The phrase occurs in Hardy's poem, 'A Broken Appointment', one of several poems which allude to his unrequited love for Florence Henniker. It is promoted by Tomalin to suggest the prominence she intends to give both to Hardy's poetry and to his fascination with women in his life and writings, and the prevailing sense in both of individual destinies thwarted by the accidents of time. The significant woman above many others was his first wife, Emma, whose pre-marital description of herself as 'a mine' of material for Hardy's writing is seized upon by Tomalin (2006: 108) as the red thread to follow through the life, one that is complemented ironically by Emma's later disillusioned comment, provoked by her hatred of *Jude the Obscure*, that Hardy 'understands only the women he *invents* – the others not at all' (Millgate, 2006: 326; Tomalin, 2006: 251). Hence, Tomalin begins with Emma, not with the lively, much-loved, young woman of their courtship days in Cornwall, but with the 72-year-old woman from whom he felt estranged. Hence, too, her stark opening sentence: 'In November of 1912 an ageing writer lost his wife.' The cameo scene of Emma's death is followed by an equally arresting sentence at the start of paragraph two: 'This is the moment when Thomas Hardy became a great poet'; and then, as a lead-in to a powerful account of the elegiac 'Poems 1912–1913', Tomalin describes how Hardy had Emma's coffin placed at the foot of his bed for three nights before the funeral and adds: 'He had become a lover in mourning' (Tomalin, 2006: xvii–xviii). The technique is dramatic, engaging and bold and sets the agenda for the whole 'Life'. It is pursued through her accounts of Thomas Hardy's two marriages and his serial infatuations with young women; through the succinct summaries of Hardy's fictional women from the thinly disguised Emma/Elfrida in *A Pair of Blue Eyes* to the women of the mature novels – Tess and Sue Bridehead – whom Emma found so repugnant; and through the elegiac poems written in her memory that Emma never read but which so offended Florence, her successor. In all, the real women supply the substance for the portraits of his imagined women whose images and stories fill his novels and poems. The relationship between the real and the imaginary was one of willed memories, a deliberate seeking out of intense experiences, recollected in tranquillity, and often tinged with a sense of melancholy or loss.

The significant episode which provides all Hardy biographers with a key scene to illustrate this phenomenon is his visit to St Juliot, Cornwall, in March 1913, a few months after Emma's death, and the poems that he composed at this period. Gittings (1975/2001: 566–570), for example, sees Hardy as 'creating a myth of their life and writing out of himself the nagging guilt of reality', and notes that Hardy himself called these poems 'an expiation'. Millgate (2006: 449–451) speaks of this episode as an example of painful experiences providing fuel for Hardy's art and of his ability to induce this state 'almost as if by contemplative discipline'. It is Tomalin, however, who elevates these poems to the key item on the agenda. She begins her biography with them and, when she returns to them in Chapter 21, she finds in their mixture of 'fact and dream' that 'the outline of an autobiography is there. At the centre of the story of his past was always Emma in her many different incarnations' (Tomalin, 2006: 322).

In pursuing biographical narrative, time and place are crucial, and especially so with Hardy. Time is significant because 'intense autobiographical recovery is central to almost all his [Hardy's] best work, in verse and prose alike' (Millgate, 2006: 475), and because his writing life has a well-known mid-career turning-point when, after *Jude* (1895), he all but abandons prose fiction to concentrate on poetry for the next thirty years. Place is central, too, in his creation of Wessex, the scene in which his own life, in reality and through literature, is played out. Just as biographers create his personal history as a mental landscape of factual memories, imagined relationships and unfulfilled dreams, so Wessex becomes the backcloth, a dream landscape composed of the real and the invented, its most obvious manifestation being in the real names for the natural features of the region, and invented names for towns and villages, all of which lends itself to visually seductive presentation in map form. Tomalin's line on Hardy allows her to bring out this mingling of fact and dream in both the life and the works, not least in her startling reading of *The Return of the Native* as a complement to *A Midsummer Night's Dream*.

> It is the dream of a winter's night, with witches instead of fairies, fateful journeys through difficult terrain, marriage plans which falter, and lovers who exchange their partners for no sensible reason. There is a moonlit love scene, there are fierce quarrels, and there are rustics who put on a dramatic entertainment. In good Shakespearean tradition there is also a young woman who disguises herself as boy.... All this is drawn out of an imagination inspired and nourished by memories of his native heath, where he took his first steps with his once all-powerful mother, and by other dreams and fantasies of boyhood. (Tomalin, 2006: 165–166)

Yet, while she is good on the minutiae of Hardy's descriptions of the natural world, her biography gives little sense of the broad panorama of Wessex, the secondary world in which the novels and poems are set. The only map is in the prelims showing the 'Area around Higher Bockhampton and Max Gate', yet Hardy was alert to both the imaginative and commercial advantages of establishing the region of Wessex in readers' minds, demanding the use of the term by his publishers and promoting the concept by his own map of his 'fictional Wessex'. (Millgate reproduces Hardy's map and includes two modern maps of 'Thomas Hardy's Dorset' and 'The World of Hardy's boyhood and youth'.)

If the broad acres of Wessex are not fully realised, Tomalin's skill at dramatising sharply observed micro-scenes is one of her strengths. Two examples from Max Gate show her imaginative engagement with very different episodes. In one, she enters into the emotional triangle that existed between Hardy and his two wives: 'For two-and-a-half years, from the summer of 1910 until November 1912, the three played out a bizarre triangular game.' She characterises Hardy's day-to-day life at this period as the scene of 'a black farce', with Emma the estranged 70-year-old wife he no longer loved but still needed, and Florence, the soon-to-be second wife who was young enough to be his granddaughter and who showed him, not love, but the fondness and respect typical of such a relationship. She quotes Florence in a letter as saying that 'The "Max Gate ménage" always does wear an aspect of comedy to me' (Tomalin, 2006: 303), brought about, not least, because she enjoyed the growing affection of both Hardys and felt the pathos of their situation. If this scene has an in-built theatrical element waiting to be exploited, the second example – Hardy's purchasing, ground clearance, designing and planting of the Max Gate plot – certainly does not. Given such unpromising material, Tomalin brings it alive by weaving into the narrative Virginia Woolf's description of the site, Giles's and Marty's tree-planting from *The Woodlanders* just two years after his own, and the discovery of three skeletons from the Roman occupation in the preliminary work of digging a well. She adds, with a certain relish: 'Later the workmen making the drive to the house found they had decapitated five more skeletons.' Hardy, apparently, wondered if this was an omen (Tomalin, 2006: 201–203). It is not only continuity that is maintained by such 'snapshots'; it is the emotional colouring and vivid recreation that they bring which lifts the life off the page and into the reader's imagination.

If continuity is sustained by the biographer's creation of scenes, it is subverted by the inevitable gaps in the *histoire*. These are not the Iserian 'indeterminacy gaps' (Iser, 1978: 170–179) contrived by fiction-writers to draw in the reader, but 'information gaps' in the documented record researched by the biographer. An unmediated narration would leave the gaps unfilled; biographical narrative demands selection from a range of possibilities to lend continuity to the life story. This is as true for subjects about whom little is known as it is for ones with whom the biographer is on intimate terms (Boswell on Johnson, Chapter 1). So, with no data about Shakespeare from the birth of his twins in Stratford in 1585 to Robert Greene's reference to him as 'an upstart crow' in London's theatre-land in 1592, biographers have filled this seven-year gap with a variety of stories about Shakespeare's so-called 'lost years' (see Chapter 5). And, even in Wordsworth's well-documented life, gaps such as his 'lost months' in the autumn of 1793 invite biographers to speculative in-filling (see Chapter 8). The gaps in Hardy's life [hi]story are interestingly different – the result of the self-protective actions of an intensely private man. Hardy was both destroyer and creator of the historical record.

> He destroyed many letters, notebooks, and other documents during his lifetime, mandated the destruction of others immediately following his death, and did everything he could to establish and protect the unique authority of the third-person narrative of his own life, written for posthumous publication over his wife's name... (Millgate, 2006: 3)

The unique authority of third-person narrative is, of course, the authority we associate with the 'as if' of fiction, and it is its ambiguous presence in the Hardy life [hi]story that creates interpretative difficulties. Hardy's 'gaps' are, in this instance, closer to the indeterminacy gaps of his own novels than to the information gaps of biography. The ramifications of this ambiguity, in this singularly odd example of hybridism, are taken up presently in the discussion of how biography invents the truth – a further aspect of the genre's complicity in telling tales.

(iii) Endings: Jane Austen

In her essay 'How to End It All', Hermione Lee remarks upon the combined effects of the Christian tradition and of our psychological 'sense of an ending' which together feed our need to create an intelligible meaning to a completed life. She continues:

> We prefer not to read the subject's death, as perhaps it should be read, as without content, merely contingent, just the next fact in a series of facts.... We feel we must stage it and interpret it, or overinterpret it. (Lee, 2005: 104)

How biographers deal with their subject's death, how they relate it to the life, the degree of detail and the tone of voice, all contribute to the narrative closure of a biography. True, there is an 'after-life' which some biographies justly celebrate with accounts of the posthumous success and longevity of their subject's works; but the end of the life [hi]story is preordained in the nature of the genre.

Endings are as diverse as beginnings in their narrative features. Here, in summary form, are the closures of three biographies of Jane Austen.

First, David Cecil:

> Jane Austen's life was so much a family life, she identified herself so much with the feelings and fortunes of her relations that it seems unnatural to say goodbye to her without first taking a look into the future to see what happened to them.

So begins the final section in his last chapter, entitled 'The End' (Cecil, 1978/2000: 182–203). He then proceeds to document the easily predictable futures of the three generations of Austens, commenting, rather in the manner of a school report, that 'The later life of the other Austens was undramatic, generally satisfactory and much as one would expect'. He finishes by quoting the tribute of her nephew, Edward, who associates the novelist with her characters: 'I can indeed bear witness that there was scarcely a charm in her most delightful characters that was not a true reflection of her own sweet temper and loving heart.' And, after further testimony from Edward that his aunt was 'always kind, sympathising, and amusing', he concludes his pen portrait with the confession that: 'While engaged on it, I have come to like her so much that I want my farewell to be one that would have pleased her: and, surely, she would have been pleased by these words of Edward.' This, of course, is the conventional ending of the conventional account of Jane Austen, the one controlled and policed by her family well into the twentieth century. Lee dubs this the "English Heritage" Jane Austen, 'benign, heroine of an idyllic, rural, golden-age England, the saintly and serene maiden aunt making the most of her sheltered uneventful life, her wit and wisdom always on the side of morality, restraint and good sense' (Lee, 2005: 72).

Second, John Halperin:

> From 7 p.m. on 17 July until she died the next morning at 4.30 a.m. in the arms of her sister, Jane Austen, after praying for death, lay apparently insensible. What thoughts, if any, may have raced through the fading light of her mind we of course shall never know. Did she perhaps dream of Chawton ...?

Then follows a series of sentences, 'Did she dream ...?', 'Did she remember ...?', 'Did her thoughts ...?' and so on, which take us back through Jane's life, as if its scenes were flashing before her in the moment of death, until the paragraph finally collapses into Cassandra's lap in an unsightly, overheated heap with

> Cassandra, with whom she had always shared everything; Cassandra, who seemed always to be there, as she was now; Cassandra, in whose arms she lay cradled; Cassandra; Cassandra. (Halperin, 1984/1996: 351–352)

This rhetorical and sentimental ending is all the more surprising because it comes at the close of a biography that set out to subvert the conventional image of 'the "dear Aunt Jane" of Austen family legend – placid, pleasant, and benign', the picture we are given in Henry Austen's *Memoir*. As Halperin makes explicit: 'It was this preposterous image of the novelist I wished in my book to dispute' (Halperin, 1984/1996: ix). Jane Austen seems to cast her spell over her biographers of whatever colour.

Third, Claire Tomalin:

> This is nevertheless an attempt to tell the story of her life, and on this last page I must return to Jane Austen herself. To the child, for whom books were a refuge, offering a world that sometimes made better sense than the one she had to find her way about. To the girl ...

Then, in a series of sentences which unnervingly follow a similar rhetorical pattern to that of Halperin, Tomalin reminds us of nine images of her subject, plotting her development from childhood to death and closing with her 'favourite image of Jane Austen', reading over her notes about what people said of her work, and 'laughing at the opinions of the world'. Her final sentence reads:

> It is lucky she had so much laughter in her; today, the volume of opinions has swelled to something so huge that they could be laughed at for ever. (Tomalin, 2000: 288)

This final portrait is anchored in a preceding history and achieves closure without straining after effect. It leaves us with a summative picture of the life, a modern, more succinct version of the famous Boswellian ending to his *Life of Dr. Johnson*.

The characters of these three endings are sharply distinct, each reflecting different aspects of narrative. David Cecil's is reminiscent of those Victorian novels in which the final chapter is a tidy catalogue which accounts for the fate or fortune of the minor characters of the story. It is as if Cecil's familiarity with such last chapters has spilled over into his decision about how to finish his biography. The tone remains urbane and affectionate to the end with an unmistakeable whiff of sentimentality around the final sentences. Despite his antithetical stance towards the traditional Austen image, Halperin's closure is also sentimental in its inflated, fictionalised picture of Jane on her deathbed expiring in the arms of her sister; so much so that the laboured accumulation of rhetorical questions, culminating in the repetition of Cassandra's name five times in three lines, is enough to make any but the most mawkishly inclined reader burst out laughing. Tomalin's set-piece is also structured as a rhetorical build-up, but without the questions. It creates a cameo portrait that not only functions as a retrospective series of images of the main phases of her subject's life, but also pinpoints the qualities of her personality. The laughter in the last words of this biography gives character to the subject and catches the overall mood of the biography. It is laughter not at but with a biographer who shares with the reader her quiet delight in her subject.

How typical are such endings? A summative image of the subject's life is usually created by one means or another, both to provide narrative closure and to lend an appropriate sense of dignity to the conclusion of a significant life [hi]story. In the past, endings were usually weighted with an explicit or implicit sense of moral judgement. Boswell regards it as part of his 'biographical undertaking' to 'collect into one view the capital and distinguishing features of this extraordinary man' (Boswell, 1791/1949, II: 614) and concludes his biography with a set-piece summary of Johnson's character which acknowledges his weaknesses as well as celebrating his strengths. Mrs Gaskell ends where she had begun – at Haworth church. Her brief final chapter records the mourners at Charlotte's funeral, subtly consigning Charlotte's husband and father to the background and, instead, placing centre stage two humble, nameless village girls, like two Marys at the Crucifixion (one had been seduced, the other was blind), in order to dramatise Charlotte's saintliness. With a letter from Charlotte's friend, Mary Taylor, stressing Charlotte's sense of duty, the apotheosis is complete. It is a closure that is overtly novelistic and, like the opening, a gift to any film director; one can almost hear the Mary Taylor 'voice over' as the camera dwells on the weeping girls. Mrs Gaskell prefers this symbolic scene to Boswell's summative assessment, but both leave us with a sense of moral judgement on the life story. The point here is that in creating their portraits of Dr Johnson and Charlotte Brontë, they are also inevitably creating the moral standpoint from which these portraits are to be viewed. Their narrative closures are just clearer instances of what is true of their whole biographies. They illustrate that narrativity is the necessary means of historical representation and that it carries with it the moral stance of the biographer which is central to the process of interpreting and judging the subject's life story. In modern times when the moral climate is much less certain, endings are more varied as these biographies of Jane Austen show, their moral stances less sure-footed, and their writers content with finding a suitable closure and a tone of voice that reflect their feelings for the subject of the narrative.

The Naked Biographer

So, where does this leave the biographer, caught between the demand to record the life history with a dispassionate account of the facts and the demand to tell the life story as an engaging tale of the subject's literary development? The difference between the *récit* of fiction and that of biography is that the writer of biography has no narrator to play with in order to offer a further dimension to the storytelling, or to provide cover for authorial comments on people's motives and actions. The biographer is naked. But, if there is no narrator *per se*, there is a teller as well as a tale and the biographer becomes part of the finished creation, ostentatiously so in the 'double portrait' of Boswell's *Life of Dr. Johnson*. In some degree or other, all biographies depict the biographer as well as the biographee, but it is only in literary biography that readers carry three images in their heads: one of the biographer and two of the subject. For, as readers of Dickens or Austen or Charlotte Brontë, we come to their biographies with knowledge of each writer's 'second self' – the construct we have formed, however hazily, from the meanings, values and emotional content of their works of art. Inevitably, we range these earlier images of the 'implied authors' alongside their biographical portraits fashioned from quite different data. The juxtaposition may be painful. As Booth indicates, the 'implied author' we infer from fiction is 'an ideal, literary, created version of the real man [*sic*]' (Booth, 1961: 71–75); it may well be at odds with the biographical man. The generous, sympathetic, family-loving Dickens we might infer from his novels may sit uneasily with the Dickens revealed by Peter Ackroyd (1999) and, more obliquely, by Claire Tomalin's biography of Nelly Ternan (Tomalin, 1991: 108–114; 185; 260; see also Chapters 4 and 7). A similar disjuncture lies behind Emma Hardy's comment quoted above to the effect that her husband understood his fictional women but not real ones; and one aspect of the 'Austen wars', as Lee (2005: 72) calls them, is the ambivalence that many modern readers feel about her life and works when trying to weigh up the relationship between the author, her 'second self', and the sanitised image created by her family and sustained by generations of Janeites and the Jane Austen Society.

The *récit* of biography is different from that of fiction in another respect. If there are two images of the biographee, there are also two time-lines: the chronology of a writer's birth, family background, loves, marriages, friends and enemies, and death follows a different line from his or her 'writing life'. The 'life narrative' covers a longer period and flows at a different pace from the 'literary narrative'. Biography may flatten life into a steady procession of dates and events; or it may capture the way time is experienced by the subject and everyone else – that odd mixture of continuity and stillness, anticipation and memory, routine and surprise, a mixture that is likely to be particularly significant in the biography of a poet or novelist. Wordsworth's 'spots of time' and Joyce's 'epiphanies' (see Chapter 8) are autobiographical moments when their literary narratives are represented as giving insight into their life narratives. Less dramatically, literary biographers seek those moments that give the key to their subject's life and works, as we have seen most clearly in Tomalin's beginning with Hardy's 'Poems of 1912–1913'. Towards the end of her Prologue, Tomalin asks: 'Are the poems true?' and comments that Florence Hardy failed 'to understand that poems have their own internal truth to which both fact and dream may contribute' (Tomalin, 2006: xxiii). Biographical truth is composed of similarly unstable elements.

Inventing the Truth

Literary biography is a hybrid form in which a body of facts is cross-bred with the arts of narrative. Lamarque and Olsen (1996: 308–309) distinguish between historical events ('history' in the object sense) and the discourse that mediates them ('history' in the description sense). The biographer has to work with data from the one and create a 'Life' with the other. Narrative theory is responsive to this hybridity. It problematises the old question, 'How much should the biographer tell?' (Altick, 1965/1979: 146) and updates it to 'What sort of truth is there to tell?' by opening up matters of fictional and factual truth that lie in the gaps between documented events and their representations in words. Richard Holmes, in an acutely titled essay, 'Inventing the Truth', shows how fundamental these issues are. They go deeper than the practical problems of mere authenticity, or the ethical questions of the subject's right to privacy. They blur the distinction between 'fact' and 'fiction', implying that authenticity itself is an illusion.

> Biographers base their work on sources which are inherently unreliable. Memory itself is fallible; memoirs are inevitably biased; letters are always slanted towards their recipients; even private diaries and intimate journals have to be recognised as literary forms of self-invention rather than an 'ultimate' truth of private fact or feeling. The biographer has always had to construct or orchestrate a factual pattern out of materials that already have a fictional or reinvented element. (Holmes 1995: 17)

The aesthetic problem of 'fact' versus 'fiction', as Holmes's remarks suggest, is exacerbated by the instability of both terms, hence the inverted commas. For the truth of fact and the truth of fiction are not only different but, as Virginia Woolf claimed, incompatible in biographical writing (Woolf, 1967: 234): the 'as if' of fiction allows it off the hook of having to provide documentary evidence; biography is hamstrung by facts. Moreover, the novelist who transmutes autobiographical experiences into fiction, like James Joyce, is working with materials that are as 'inherently unreliable' as the novelist, like Hardy, who tries to pre-empt future biographers by self-ghosting his own 'Life', or the novelist turned biographer, like Mrs Gaskell who, in attempting to document the facts of Charlotte Brontë's life, finds that many of the materials to hand 'already have a fictional or reinvented element' in her subject's writings. The inherent uncertainties between history and fiction in these three instances stem from different causes. Joyce's self-representation is considered in Chapter 8; Hardy and Mrs Gaskell afford contrasting insights into the problem of biographical truth.

The Life of Thomas Hardy was published in two volumes in 1928 and 1929, under the name of Florence Hardy, the author's second wife, even though Hardy himself had played the central role in its composition. Although the truth of the authorship was known by the 1950s, and though Robert Gittings's biography in the 1970s opened with an account of Hardy's 'deliberate deception' (Gittings, 1975/2001: 15), and despite the appearance of Michael Millgate's edition, *The Life and Work of Thomas Hardy* (1984) establishing itself as the 'standard' text, publishers still continued to peddle the fiction of Florence's authorship (F. E. Hardy, 1994, Studio Editions). Florence's role had been largely secretarial, collaborating with her husband over the compilation of notes, letters and memoranda and typing up the manuscript, while he maintained such strict control over the content that later commentators categorised it as his autobiography (Gittings, 1975/2001: 19; Millgate, 2006: 4). Hardy, an intensely private man, felt, like many other writers, that the world should not pry into his life and personality but concern itself with his writings. Certainly, this feeling pervades the most authoritative account of the actual composition of the 'Life', characterising it as being 'conducted with [a] degree of secrecy', 'written in his study in the strictest privacy' and typed up by Florence in such a way that it would 'contain no visible trace of his participation' (Millgate, 2006: 478).

At one level, it could be argued, no serious deception was practised (Tomalin, 2006: 337): the 'Prefatory Note' to Part 1, initialled FEH, is clear and open about Hardy's extensive contributions. And, according to Gittings, Thomas Hardy confided to Cyril Clemens that 'I intend to write my autobiography through my good wife' to be published posthumously, 'as a biography of myself written by my wife' (Gittings, 1975/2001: 15). Yet, despite such openness, there is the widespread feeling among subsequent commentators that Hardy, by his omissions and evasions if not by deliberate misrepresentation, has been economical with the truth. Gittings takes a tough line describing 'the feeling that the "Life" is, in some sense, a fake' and, though the origins of the project 'seem to have been relatively innocent', the systematic way in which Hardy developed it caused suspicion on several counts: his destruction of original data; his upgrading of his family's social background; and what Gittings regards as Hardy's blatant omissions about his relationships with women in his youth – despite Hardy's teasing list of 'youthful recollections of four village beauties' (F. E. Hardy, 1994: 270). Gittings puts Hardy's motives down to a mixture of ingrained snobbery, his battle against 'the massive social stratification of the Victorian age' and a 'thin-skinned nature' with an acute sense of personal privacy (Gittings, 1975/2001: 16–20). Hardy's most recent biographer, Claire Tomalin, shows little interest in the topic other than to point out that the second Mrs Hardy as quasi-biographer had a similar lack of interest in expanding on Hardy's best years with the first Mrs Hardy (Tomalin, 2006: 158, 337–338). Perhaps she feels that the issue has been resolved by Millgate who concludes that his reconstructed version of the 'Life', *The Life and Work of Thomas Hardy*, based on Florence's undestroyed typescripts and Hardy's final text, supersedes Florence's 'Life', and constitutes 'both an indispensable biographical source and a formidable and sometimes absolute barrier to further and deeper knowledge' (Millgate, 2006: 4). This sounds like the last word on the topic. Yet, in terms of biographical truth, uncertainty remains. How far does Hardy's fictional skill invade his historical purpose in creating the narrative of his own life? Millgate, while less severe in his censure than Gittings, admits the 'widespread suspicion … that he [Hardy] exaggerated his family's social and economic status in order to conceal its actual poverty and obscurity'. He notes, too, about Hardy's accounts of his childhood, youth and early adulthood in Dorset, 'the romantic aura thrown by his memory over the entire place and period' (Millgate, 2006: 5). Both comments suggest that Hardy was massaging the image of his early years beyond the common tendency of those in their seventies and eighties to do so; that, in part, he was fictionalising aspects of his past, *constructing* a tale he wanted to tell and leave for posterity, not *reconstructing* the sequence of events into a full and coherent historical account. It is this distinction that distinguishes fiction from history: 'fiction is construction, history is reconstruction' (Lamarque & Olsen, 1996: 310); and it is unsurprising to find the two confused when a novelist turns biographer. The implicit message of Millgate's reconstruction is to treat the Hardys' account not as a *bona fide* narrative but as a valuable source of information. Modern biography, and Millgate's own research in particular, has made the Hardys' 'Life' into a work of reference, a place where biographical truth may be sought and evaluated, with due scepticism, alongside other sources of evidence.

Mrs Gaskell's struggle with biographical truth was the opposite of Hardy's. Where he wished to pre-empt future biographers, she felt wrong-footed if not pre-empted by her subject's fiction. Her problem became acute when she came to deal with Charlotte Brontë's time at Cowan's Bridge School and its fictionalisation as Lowood School in Chapters 5 to 9 of *Jane Eyre*. It is worth quoting the relevant paragraph in full, since we can listen here to the sophisticated mind of a novelist/biographer wrestling with the problems of factual and fictional truth:

> I now come to a part of my subject which I find great difficulty in treating, because the evidence relating to it on each side is so conflicting that it seems almost impossible to arrive at the truth. Miss Brontë more than once said to

> me, that she should not have written what she did of Lowood in *Jane Eyre*, if she had thought the place would have been so immediately identified with Cowan's Bridge, although there was not a word in her account of the institution but what was true at the time when she knew it; she also said that she had not considered it necessary, in a work of fiction, to state every particular with the impartiality that might be required in a court of justice, nor to seek out motives, and make allowances for human feelings, as she might have done, if dispassionately analysing the conduct of those who had the superintendence of the institution. I believe she herself would have been glad of an opportunity to correct the over-strong impression which was made upon the public mind by her vivid picture, though even she, suffering her whole life long, both in heart and body, from the consequences of what happened there, might have been apt, to the last, to take her deep belief in facts for the facts themselves – her conception of truth for the absolute truth. (Gaskell, 1857/1975: 98)

Mrs Gaskell's dilemma is that she is torn between, on the one hand, being true to Charlotte's stated beliefs that 'her account of the institution' was accurate and that anyway fiction obeys its own rules and, on the other, being true to the concept of Charlotte Brontë that her biography consistently portrays – the dutiful, saintly, long-suffering, respectable young woman. The final sentence is a masterpiece of hesitant, sensitive sophistry. Just how was Charlotte Brontë supposed to 'correct' her novel? As the friend and biographer, Mrs Gaskell would know that Charlotte was rightly resistant to suggested changes in her work. As a novelist herself, Mrs Gaskell would also know that truth in fiction is self-referential; to tamper with it is to be untrue to the novelist's vision. Where does the truth lie? – essentially the question that Mrs Gaskell asks in her first sentence – is more than a punning query. It exposes truth's relativity, a notion that, as her final words show, Mrs Gaskell's own beliefs and those she attributes to Charlotte Brontë, find difficulty in accommodating. So where does the truth lie? A comparison of the relevant passages in the biography and the novel shows that they have different sorts of truth to tell. Compare the 'Life', Volume 1, Chapter 4 and *Jane Eyre*, Chapters 5 to 9, in respect of the following: the site and surroundings of Cowan's Bridge/Lowood; the cook and the pupils' diet; the portrayals of Miss Andrews and Maria Brontë/Miss Scatcherd and Helen Burns; and the portrayal of Mr Carus Wilson/Mr Brocklehurst. Both texts are true to themselves, both are virtual constructs, both are representations of 'reality', both are context-bound by their respective genres. The only untruth would be to claim that one of them has the status of an 'absolute'.

Virginia Woolf offers a useful gloss upon Mrs Gaskell's dilemma. When she says that the 'truth of fact and the truth of fiction are incompatible', she is speaking of the seemingly impossible task for biography of welding together the verifiable evidence of action and events with the more elusive, more speculatively fictitious, yet more insightful probing into personality. The more significant truth lies in the latter: 'it dwells in the personality rather than in the act' (Woolf, 1967: 234). Biography, as Hermione Lee has shown, permeates Virginia Woolf's fiction and non-fiction alike and, if the entry in the latter's notebooks is to be believed, her answer to the problem of the two kinds of truth would be to separate them: 'Let the biographer print fully, completely, accurately, the known facts without comment; Then let him write the life as fiction' (Woolf, in Lee, 1997: 10). The string of adverbs, with their unachievable demands, betrays her frustration. Biography remains unable to unite 'the granite and the rainbow'. Where, for Virginia Woolf, this lack of artistic unity relegated biography to a craft, more recent biographers have accepted its dual, 'operatic' nature as an art form with its own generic coherence, well adapted to explore the interplay of the two kinds of truth. Where Virginia Woolf pleads, 'Let it be fact, one feels, or let it be fiction; the imagination will not serve under two masters simultaneously' (Woolf, 1967: 234), Holmes as we have seen can speak of 'inventing the truth', and Gordon of seeking 'a lasting imaginative truth'. Lucasta Miller calls this dualism 'amphibious':

> Literary biography will continue to raise questions which need to be answered again and again – about the relationship between fact and truth, and between information and interpretation, as well as about the nature of personality and the relationship between writers and their writings. We should not see biography as a failed empirical science striving to produce definitive, objective results but doomed to failure. Nor should we take the extreme post-modernist line which completely collapses the distinction between biography and fiction, regarding both as undifferentiated 'textual constructs'. Instead, we should regard it as an amphibious art form, which ideally has *both* to obey the constraints of evidence *and* to respond creatively to the challenge of making shape, form and meaning. (Miller, 2001: 169)

Narrative theory, as has been argued above, helps to explore the ramifications of this position and to explicate biography's hybrid character. Maintaining the balance of its twofoldness is the fundamental feature of the genre. While it may not measure up to Virginia Woolf's purist requirements for art, biography is nonetheless aptly described in her phrase as 'something betwixt and between' (Woolf, 1967: 227).

3

Reading Biography

Biographer, Biography and the Reader

As we have seen, biography is a hybrid. It is the verifiable facts of history crossed with the conventions of narrative. The biographer has to present the available facts of the life, yet shape their arbitrariness, untidiness and incompleteness into an engaging whole. The readerly appeal lies in the prospect both of gaining documentary information, scrupulously researched and plausibly interpreted, and of experiencing the aesthetic pleasure of reading a well-made work of art with a continuous life story and a satisfying closure. 'In the family of literature,' one of its most respected practitioners asserts, 'biography seems to be the product of a strange coupling between old-fashioned history and the traditional novel' (Holroyd 2003: 20). The invitation of literary biography is thus a dualistic one; the aesthetic experience it offers stems from the twofoldness of its nature and from the stance that this imposes upon the reader. By triangulating the roles of the biographer, the biographee within the biographical text and the reader, we can conceptualise the elements that make up the invitation of the genre.

First, the biographer. Richard Holmes characterises the process he experiences with two key words: it is a 'pursuit' and it is a 'haunting'. They are two sides of the same phenomenon. The pursuit is a 'tracking of the physical trail of someone's path through the past, a following of footsteps', an effort 'to write about the pursuit of that fleeting figure in such a way as to bring it alive in the present' (Holmes, 1995: 27). The haunting occurs when this revivification succeeds and the biographee is brought imaginatively alive. Then the biographer turns from pursuer to pursued. While the subject does not take him over, as it might in some Gothic fantasy, it does exercise the power of the past upon the present and haunt the biographer's imagination. Holmes goes on to explain the two main elements as 'closely entwined strands':

> The first is the gathering of factual materials, the assembling in chronological order of a man's 'journey' through the world – the actions, the words, the recorded thoughts, the places and faces through which he moved: the 'life and letters'. The second is the creation of a fictional or imaginary relationship between the biographer and his subject; not merely a 'point of view' or an 'interpretation', but a continuous living dialogue between the two.... It is fictional, imaginary, because of course the subject cannot really, literally, talk back; but the biographer must come to act and think of his subject as if he can. (Holmes, 1995: 66)

Not every biographer would necessarily subscribe to this particular description but there is ample evidence in the recent spate of books about the genre (Bostridge, 2004; France & St Clair, 2002; Lee, 2005; Parke, 2002) that the biographer's capacity for imaginative empathy is continuously interacting with the verifiable historical data. The present operates upon the past in other ways, too. Earlier biographers who are more or less contemporary with their subjects (e.g. Boswell, Forster, Mrs Gaskell) stand in different relationships with them and the available data about them compared with present-day biographers who may inherit a whole bibliography of 'Lives' laid down in stratified layers on top of the life they are trying to recover. The modern reader, like the modern biographer, has to be a literary archaeologist. Dickens's 'Lives' (see Chapter 7) are constructed on a bedrock of his friend Forster's biography and on the novelist's own writings, neither of which subsequent biographers can afford to ignore. Later 'Lives' have also to be sifted: our inherited Dickens is compounded from a series of accounts from, among a host of others, the Victorian memoirs of his daughter (M. Dickens, 1885/1911) and his reading manager (Dolby, 1885), via Edwardian enthusiasts (Chesterton, 1906/1975) and 1930s revelations of Dickens's private life (Storey, 1939; Wright, 1935), to those of modern academics and writers in our own time (Ackroyd, 1999; Bodenheimer, 2007; Johnson, 1953/1986; Kaplan, 1988; Tomalin, 1991). In such cases, bringing the subject alive means unearthing an identity from the accretions of a literary history that have been deposited on it decade after decade.

Second, the biography. What is true of Dickens's 'Lives' is also true for the 'Lives' of all canonical writers so that, in recent times, biography has been provoked into self-assessment and into finding new forms of expression. There have been a wryly amused and informative history of *Shakespeare's Lives* (Schoenbaum, 1993); an exploration into metabiography in the Brontës (Miller, 2001); and, in the case of Johnson and Boswell, biographies about biography (Holmes, 1994; Sisman, 2001). These studies have been complemented by the increasing willingness of modern biographers to reflect on the genre and experiment stylistically, often doing so as a means of capturing the elusive individual qualities of their subjects. Hermione Lee's *Virginia Woolf* (1997) is bounded by first and final chapters, 'Biography' and 'Biographer', like two bookends, between which the essential identity of her subject emerges – Virginia Woolf as a reader of books and people: 'Reading, quite as much as writing, is her life's pleasure and her life's work' (Lee, 1997: 402). The clearest examples of innovation are Peter Ackroyd's *Dickens*, where biographical continuity is punctuated by fictional interludes, and the structure and style of Jonathan Coe's biography of B. S. Johnson. Different again is Ann Wroe's *Being Shelley: The Poet's Search for Himself*, which abandons the usual chronology in favour of a loosely organised structure fashioned on the four elements, earth, water, air and fire. It is less the conventional life story and more an evocation of Shelley's imaginative universe. And, pushing against the boundaries both of biography as a genre and at the notion of the literary subject, is Andrew Motion's 'experiment', *Wainewright the Poisoner*. His subject, a minor poet and artist, 'lived half his life close to the centre of the Romantic revolution', being good friends with Fuseli and Blake and knowing Clare, Hazlitt and Keats, and 'half in exile and disgrace' as an 'ingenious and unscrupulous criminal' – a fraudster and probably a murderer. As the evidence for the 'Life' is patchy, Motion disarmingly invents what is needed: 'the bulk of it [the biography] is a re-creation of that well-established nineteenth-century form, the Confession', supposedly written by Wainewright at the end of his life (Motion, 2000: xv–xvii).

Biographical texts, then, are of ever-increasing variety. Even when one puts aside memoirs, obituaries, epitaphs, diaries, *Dictionary of National Biography* entries, biofictions and other related writings, biographies themselves still appear highly diverse in their scope and character. It is, therefore, helpful to invoke the notion of the genre's hybrid nature again, and to think of biographical writing as ranging along a continuum whose two poles might be labelled 'documentary biography' and 'aesthetic biography'. Some texts will reflect an emphasis upon documentary information about a life, others upon the narrative shape that gives coherence to a life. Beyond these poles, biography shades off into either history or fiction. Arguably, the most successful biographies are ones which exploit the mobility of the continuum, blending the verifiable information of research with a narrative imagination.

Where does all this leave the reader? The reader is faced with a text that seemingly invites what Rosenblatt termed both an 'efferent' and an 'aesthetic' stance simultaneously (Rosenblatt, 1978: 24–25). In 'efferent' reading the reader's concern is with what will be carried away from the act; the orientation is utilitarian, the focus is directed towards the information that

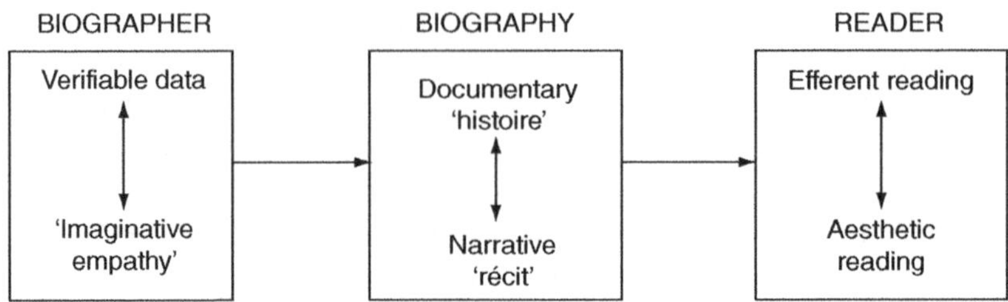

Figure 3.1 Biography: a generic dualism

lies *beyond* the reading event. By contrast, in 'aesthetic' reading the reader's concern is with the feelings and ideas being produced by the act; the orientation is to savour what is being lived through at the time, the focus is on the experience itself *during* the reading event. Acknowledging that to characterise the act of reading in such simplistic, binary terms is facile, Rosenblatt goes on to say that no hard-and-fast line separates the two; and she, too, proposes a continuum between the efferent and aesthetic stances in order to represent the mobility of the reader's attention and changing sense of awareness during the reading process (Rosenblatt, 1978: 35).

These concepts, fundamental to Rosenblatt's transactional theory of the literary work, are helpful in understanding the reading of biography since they reflect its twofoldness. Collating them with what has been said above, the generic dualism that characterises the communication from biographer to reader may be summarised as illustrated in Figure 3.1.

Central to the communication is the biographical text. It has the delimiting necessity of representing a particular life story whose 'histoire' is essentially a given, whatever discoveries may later modify its sequence of events. What changes is the 'récit', the ways of telling, and what these ways reveal about the constantly mobile efferent/aesthetic interaction it invites of its readers. How does this operate in practice?

Imagining Blake

Biographies, like all texts, indicate the ways they wish to be read. The difference between reading a 'documentary biography' and an 'aesthetic biography' can be seen in two modern biographies of William Blake, *The Stranger from Paradise* (Bentley, 2001) and *Blake* (Ackroyd, 1995). The first is by an academic, G. E. Bentley, Jr, who, since the late 1960s, has been painstakingly researching and publishing *Blake Records* (Bentley 1969/1988) and has established himself as the leading authority in the area. The other is by novelist and biographer Peter Ackroyd, who recreates Blake in his eighteenth-century London setting and explores the affinities between his poetry and art. Each defines the reading stance we are tacitly asked to adopt, which, in turn, dictates the pace of our reading, the nature, quality and sustainability of our interest and, ultimately, the construct of the biographee that we create.

The literary historical context against which we read these 'Lives' is significant. Biography saved Blake from obscurity. His rescuer was Alexander Gilchrist, whose book *The Life of William Blake* (Gilchrist, 1863/2005), subtitled *'Pictor Ignotus'* (unknown painter), was published in 1863. At the time of Blake's death thirty-six years earlier, his work as poet and painter was known to only a relatively small coterie of literary people, artists and connoisseurs. His name was virtually unheard of among the wider reading public. Gilchrist's biography remains an excellent, highly readable introduction to Blake and initiated the development of the artist's reputation which, during the past fifty years, has burgeoned into a thriving industry in both the visual and literary arts. Major international exhibitions of his work (notably at the Tate Gallery in 1978 and 2000), the publication of all his Illuminated Books in colour facsimile, hundreds of critical studies and, more recently, expanding Internet traffic connected with his poetry and painting (see especially *The William Blake Archive* at www.blakearchive.org), have all contributed to the global profile that Blake now enjoys. And yet he remains elusive. If biography brought him to life in the nineteenth century, it had difficulty accounting for his life in the twentieth and it is easy to see why. Blake, in the title phrase of Bentley's book, was 'the stranger from Paradise', a visionary who inhabited an imaginative world, whose writings were often obscure and whose thoughts were often clothed in idiosyncratic symbolism. Since he lived 'elsewhere', Blake regarded his earthly life as of little importance. He neither kept diaries nor wrote reminiscences. There were some letters to friends and patrons, and records of his commercial transactions as a professional engraver. But his modest, thinly documented background, his lack of formal education (for which he was later to express his profound gratitude) and the unworldly character of his poetry and painting have made it difficult for biographers to understand the life of William Blake.

How do Bentley and Ackroyd recreate Blake? What reading stance do their texts dictate?

Bentley's documentary knowledge lends his 'Life' both immense authority and cumbersome continuity. His nine chapters are uneven in length and structure: Chapter 5, for example, covers five years in seven sub-sections;

Chapter 6 covers four years in thirty-three sub-sections. Together with copious footnotes throughout (often three or four per page), this fragmentation suggests a biography compiled from working notes, with information spilling outside the narrative frame, rather than a carefully patterned life story. Its title may be poetic but it 'makes no attempt to impose or "discover" a satisfying psychological or aesthetic form to contain the life' (Lindop, 2001: 6). Bentley blends together historical data about Blake's background, his early apprenticeship to Basire, the commercial milieu in which he operated, and a clear, technical account of Blake's relief etching (Bentley, 2001: 100–103, 129ff.), all of which provide a strong, reliable narrative cradle in which Blake's poetry and art are laid. But he offers little interpretation to bring the poems alive in relation to the life; he defines his role as a recorder of raw history rather than as a biographical critic exploring the insights that the life can offer the reader of Blake's poems.

Ackroyd's *Blake*, by contrast, is more fluently written and conventionally organised to tell the life story. Blake's home and family background are handled with a lighter touch and the persona that soon emerges is that of the 'loner' building his own world, a living example of the child as father of the man. Ackroyd's account, while demonstrating its scholarly credentials, is nonetheless vulnerable to correction from Bentley, who barely acknowledges his predecessor, settles for putting him right on details in three footnotes, and offers the double-edged comment that Ackroyd's book is 'a careful and usually accurate biography with few pretensions to originality' (Bentley, 2001: 451). Ackroyd's strengths lie in his linking Blake's art and poetry to his life, in fact suggesting that they *were* his life. For example, in his discussion of the two 'Chimney Sweeper' poems (Ackroyd, 1995: 123–126), he not only situates them in the social context of the time, but also extrapolates from the appalling trade in 'climbing boys' to argue persuasively that through the power of Blake's visionary imagination, 'the plight of the chimney sweep becomes the plight of all humankind trapped in their mortal bodies and longing to be free'. Or again, the pages on the early draft of 'London' (Ackroyd, 1995: 155–158) portray Blake against the background of the French Revolution: 'Blake is to be imagined, then, wandering through the streets in his *bonnet rouge* during those hot spring days,' says Ackroyd, adopting a style that Bentley never employs which infuses poetry and politics with a narrative imagination.

The contrast between these representations of Blake is nowhere more clear than in their corresponding accounts of one of Blake's central ideas, his notion of 'contraries'. In *The Marriage of Heaven and Hell* (1790–1793), he defined this concept as follows: 'Without Contraries there is no progression. Attraction and repulsion, reason and energy, love and hate, are necessary to human existence' (Blake, in Keynes, 1956: 181). His picture, *The Good and Evil Angels Struggling for Possession of the Child* (1795), offers a visual summary as the good angel, standing in the clouds, sweeps a young child beyond the grasp of the evil angel, shackled at the ankle. The image is full of 'contraries': light and dark figures, freedom and bondage, the sun and the flames, the sighted and the blind. The figures incline inwards, challenging each other. The picture is contemporary with his *Songs of Innocence and Experience*, which show, according to the title page, 'two Contrary States of the Human Soul'. Such oppositions are to be seen not as choices between alternatives but as symbolic states – the 'givens' of the human condition – through which Blake represents the nature and limitations of human happiness. What do our two biographers say about this?

Bentley tells us: 'Blake drafted poems and designs for *Songs of Experience* in his Notebook, carefully constructing parallels with the poems of *Innocence*.... The two sets of poems illustrate "the two Contrary States of the Human Soul".' Having given us two pages of summary comment on *Innocence* (Bentley, 2001: 131–133), he contrasts the themes and illustrations of the two sets of poems, commenting on the 'exhuberant, graceful, singing designs of *Innocence*' and the 'sparse, bleak and stark' images of *Experience* (Bentley, 2001: 144). He gives us brief summary comment, too, on 'London', 'The Lamb' and 'The Tyger' and concludes:

> The *Songs of Experience* are the complements to *Songs of Innocence*, not the answers to them. The singers of Innocence feel protected by powerful forces outside themselves, while the singers of Experience feel threatened by powerful forces they cannot control or propitiate. Neither set of singers has yet learned that the power of divinity lies not beyond us but within us. (Bentley, 2001: 148)

Thereafter, Bentley documents the printing history and reception of these works. Though he repeats more than once Blake's phrase, the 'Contrary States of the Human Soul', it is left like a mantra, unexplicated, apparently beyond the biographer's brief.

Compare this with Ackroyd's account. He sees the linking of these two series of poems into a combined volume as significant:

> These are opposites in more than one sense, however, since many of the *Songs of Experience* are etched upon the other side of the copper plates for *Innocence*. Two contrary states could be held, as an object, in the hand.... The technical process is also of extraordinary importance, because Blake was actually writing *backwards* upon the copper on the *back* of the poems he was partly satirising. He was sculpting words as if they were as much images of his ideas

> as the illustrations beside them; he was seeing words as discrete objects, not as transparent signifiers of meaning. They are objects to be looked at, upon which much care has been lavished, and at some point they cease simply to be the medium for lyric expression and become as materially based as any other copper image. But in this process of being formed, they become resistant to conventional interpretation; they do not float off the page in the manner of innumerable poetic volumes, with the words residing somewhere between the poet and the reader, but remain firmly based in the splendid isolation of a unique art-object. 'Two Contrary States of the Human Soul' are fixed upon a few millimetres of copper plate. (Ackroyd, 1995: 141–142)

From the practicalities of printing Ackroyd moves to link the concept of contraries to the technical process of Blake's relief etching. This leads to the daring proposal that Blake saw his words 'as discrete objects', as an aspect of the materiality of his art and, further, that these 'sculpted words' have direct implications for reading since the words 'do not float off the page … residing somewhere between the poet and the reader', but remain as integral elements within a unified art-object. Where in Bentley, contraries are merely an aspect of Blake to be noted and logged, in Ackroyd they are offered as the key to understanding how Blake's unique vision was fashioned.

By deliberately contrasting these two passages, showing one tethered to the documentation of verifiable information while the other moves from technical evidence to interpretative speculation, the generic dualism of biography is stretched to its limits, highlighting difference. The two 'Lives' are pushed towards opposite ends of the continuum when, in fact, the differences are less significant in themselves than as symptoms of the twofoldness that pervades every aspect of the genre. For whether a biography reflects in its form the jagged solidity and unevenness of a subject's life, or smoothes over the hard edges of factual history into a lucid narrative, biographers of whatever colour have to accommodate the twofoldness of their art; to represent, as it were, within a unified whole, its two contrary states.

Problems of a Hybrid Form

To describe biography simply as history cross-bred with narrative glosses over the obvious fact that neither term defines an insulated, autonomous concept. History is conveyed through narrative – indeed, some would argue that the past is irrecoverable and that history is essentially fictional (Lamarque & Olsen, 1996: 310); conversely, fictional narrative is dependent upon history, if not directly then indirectly through its need to create a consistent, believable and recognisable 'secondary world'. This interpenetration of history and narrative destabilises biography in two particular areas: in the plausibility of its deployment of historical data within the time-frame of the subject's life; and in its uncertainty once it shifts from recording the exterior life of actions and events to the inner life of the subject's mind and feelings.

At first sight, the handling of time in biography would seem to be much more straightforward than in fiction; the chronology of the subject's life is, after all, a given. However, the temptation to use, say, knowledge of a writer's mature views to fill gaps in our knowledge about the attitudes and opinions of the writer from years earlier is seductive. Even the meticulous Bentley is tempted to explain Blake's student experiences when attending Sir Joshua Reynolds's lectures at the Royal Academy in 1779–1780, about which little is known, by using Blake's writings from 1801–1809. Bentley dramatises Reynolds's words and Blake's marginalia from this latter period and represents Blake as reacting with all the resentment and vigorous antipathy of an angry student.

> Blake: This Man was Hired to Depress Art
>
> Reynolds: I found myself in the midst of works executed upon principles with which I was unacquainted: I felt my ignorance, and stood abashed.
>
> Blake: A Liar [!] he never was Abashed in his Life & never felt his ignorance.
>
> Reynolds: It is the florid style, which strikes at once, and captivates the eye for a time....
>
> Blake: A Lie [!] The florid style, such as the Venetian & the Flemish, Never Struck Me at Once nor At-All.
>
> Reynolds: [Reynolds] was a great generalizer ... this disposition to abstractions, to generalization and classification, is the great glory of the human mind ...
>
> Blake: To generalize is to be an Idiot....
>
> (Bentley, 2001: 52)

Maybe the 22-year-old student did dislike Reynolds as heartily as when he wrote these remarks as an experienced poet and novelist. But we don't know; there's no evidence and to imply that Blake's views did not change over twenty years is, at the very least, questionable speculation. The biographer's problem is that he is tied to time in a way that the novelist is not. If this were the story of a fictional 'William Blake', the novelist could legitimately attribute remarks to this character in his mid-forties and use them retrospectively to explain the way in which his character's views had, or had not, developed. As readers we could accept this. Fictional characters frequently develop their own histories along these lines. But, in telling the story of the actual Blake, the biographer cannot manipulate time so freely. The chronological imperative is more than just getting events in the right order. While the biographer cannot pretend ignorance of the subject's subsequent life when chronicling his youthful years, he can at least resist attributing views and attitudes expressed in middle age as being equally true of Blake's student days. Otherwise, the slide towards using data from one period of a life to dramatise another is speculation masquerading as reliable evidence. That Bentley is aware of this makes it no more acceptable.

Biography and the novel differ, too, in a second vital aspect: the representation of a person's inner life. Where novelists, as distinct from storytellers, explore beyond mere plot into the psychology and affective life of their creations, confident that these are self-referential, biographers are always looking over their shoulders, checking sources, aware that their referent is an actual life that has been lived and all that they can retrieve is the husk. The kernel of interior life may be fleetingly glimpsed in a writer's diaries or letters, it may be suggested by a writer's poems or novels, but the thoughts and feelings of the poet or novelist who created them will always lie beyond the biographer's reach. Even more frustrating for the biographer is the recognition that the interior life of the writer working at his or her desk – the phenomenon that the literary biographer wants, above all, to capture – will always remain unattainable. So, when we read about Blake's 'The Everlasting Gospel', 'while working on the elaborate and spacious *Jerusalem*, he felt the need to compose these short, sharp lines of radical dissent' (Ackroyd, 1995: 37), scepticism enters our reading. Is there any evidence that Blake 'felt the need' to write differently, or is Ackroyd merely inventing this feeling in order to contrast the styles of the two poems? Or again, in Ackroyd's interpolation of the drafts of 'The Tyger', the subject of much scholarly comment, he has no hesitation in giving us Blake's thought-track. Blake, he tells us, wrote out the first three stanzas in his Notebook. Ackroyd goes on:

> Then he began the fourth verse:
>
> Could fetch it from the furnace deep
> And in the horrid ribs dare steep
> In the well of sanguine woe
>
> He stopped, perhaps not able to find a rhyme for 'woe' or disliking the phrase itself, and tried another couplet:
>
> In what clay & in what mould
> Were thy eyes of fury rolld

> But he was dwelling too long upon the more grotesque attributes of the beast, and he deleted this entire stanza with vertical strokes of ink. He continued with what became the fourth and sixth stanzas, but then turned the page and tried to create a different effect altogether:
>
> Burnt in different deeps or skies
> The cruel fire of thine eyes
> Could heart descend or wings aspire
> What the hand dares seize the fire
>
> It was an attempt to reach the sublime, but it carried on too insistently the cadence and therefore the meaning of the preceding verses. So he crossed out the stanza with three lines and began again.... (Ackroyd, 1995: 144)

Ackroyd's tone of authoritative certainty about something as elusive as the creative process again invites scepticism. His account is plausible, but whether Blake actually followed this precise compositional sequence, or considered that 'he was dwelling too long upon the more grotesque attributes of the beast', or judged the cadence too insistent in particular lines, neither we nor Ackroyd can know. In a passage such as this, excited by the documentary evidence and sensing that he is in hot pursuit of the inner Blake, Ackroyd's imaginative empathy lends a quasi-fictional status to the poet, before settling him back into his historical context with a fascinating discussion of the 'cluster of associations' that the tiger had at this period (Ackroyd, 1995: 145–146).

Reading Lessons

The problems of biography stem directly from its hybrid form, in particular, from the inherent difficulty of maintaining the balance of its twofoldness. We have seen above how 'documentary biography' may yield to the temptation to misuse time-specific data, and how the temptation of 'aesthetic biography' is to shift into novelistic mode. Yet we have noted benefits, too, in approaching biography from the different angles of biographer, textual construct and reader. A genre that entails a 'pursuit' and a 'haunting', that combines verifiable data and imaginative reconstruction, is also one that through its binary nature offers its readers an experience that is both efferently and aesthetically satisfying. Readers are used to reading for the facts of history; they are also used to reading for the pleasures of the literary text. Biographies, from those of Samuel Johnson to B. S. Johnson, offer both together. For readers alert to the biographer's difficulties in fashioning selected, authentic information into a coherent life story, the act of reading offers a source of aesthetic pleasure as they respond to the writer's art in combining the demands of history with the needs of narrative. For, with a biography, the reader becomes aware not only of the past that is retrieved but also of how the present plays upon it, of how a particular piece of history is selected and imaginatively created. Reading for information is just half the story; the other half is the aesthetic impulse which breathes life into it. In its twofoldness, literary biography holds important reading lessons.

4

Literary Biomythography

What are the Gospels but a series of varying attempts at the art of biography?

(A. S. Byatt, *Possession*, 1991: 384)

Several of Addison's Spectator papers were of the first importance in the growth of Bardolatry ... Dr Johnson's 1765 edition of the Works of Shakespeare and David Garrick's Shakespeare Jubilee four years later were long-prepared milestones in the history of the Bard's reputation.

(Jonathan Bate, *The Genius of Shakespeare*, 1997: 169)

Samuel Johnson was the most fortunate event in English literary biography. In three major roles, as the first important theorist and an able practitioner of the art and then as the subject of the greatest biography, he is the giant who bestrides our story.

(R. D. Altick, *Lives and Letters: A History of Literary Biography in England and America*, 1965: 46)

Biomythography

Behind the latter-day literary myths, from the Brontë sisters to Sylvia Plath, stand three superordinate biographical myths of Olympian stature, each casting a particular light through the historical mist. My epigraphs identify the subjects. The life histories of Jesus Christ in the four Gospels emit a sense of biographical sanctity down the centuries whose diffused light infiltrates later hagiographies, shines brightly in the nineteenth century (especially haloing the head of Charlotte Brontë), and can be detected even after Strachey. Shakespeare, the invisible man, whose biographical absence makes his artistic presence even more dramatic, occupies the throne of literary idolatry. Dr Johnson, whose biographical presence in Boswell looms massively over succeeding centuries, is biography's first national celebrity author. All subsequent biographies are touched in one way or another by these enduring presences. Since literary biographies have a special concern for the life of the imagination, mythologising plays a bigger role in this sub-genre than with other subjects. In fact, saintliness, idolatry and celebrity appear so frequently in literary biography that 'biomythography' is a more apposite term since it recognises the role of these aspects of myth-making. It encompasses the necessary invention of self and identity by the writer, and the virtual representation of the subject by the biographer. In doing so, it alters our perceptions of the genre by acknowledging that the biographer is dealing both with historical data and with the self-projections of the author in his or her life and literature. It expresses the elevated status of canonical writers, the sense of their remoteness from the ordinary, that whiff of otherness that implies access to magic and the supernatural; yet it reminds us also of the fact that the painstaking, historical documentation of life-writing is, by its nature, incomplete and can never hope to capture the elusive 'life' without the aid of narrative imagination (Denzin, 1989: 25; Runyan, 1984: 77). It will be apparent by now that I am not using the term 'myth' in its classical sense, nor even in its most prominent sense in literary analysis where Frye (1957) and others have seen the genres and plot patterns of many works of literature as representations of basic mythic paradigms. I use 'myth' in the colloquial sense to mean notions which either lack a factual basis or have evolved and left it behind. The questions I want to ask in this chapter are:

- How are 'biomyths' formed within our literary culture in a genre where facts are supposed to be preeminent?
- What roles do saintliness, idolatry and celebrity play in their creation?
- In its efforts to deconstruct literary myths, is modern biography free from perpetuating them?

Presently, I take Byron, Dickens and Sylvia Plath as examples of celebrity, idolatry and saintliness, but first I need to consider what are the phases of biographical myth-making with which modern biographers are faced. Recent biographies of the Brontës (Barker, 1994; Gordon, 1994; Miller, 2001) illuminate this issue and suggest the paradigm for the process of myth-making.

Myth-Making: The Brontë Paradigm

Five overlapping phases can be distinguished in the biomythography of the Brontës.

(i) *Facts: Selection and 'Spin'*

Mrs Gaskell, like any biographer, had her own agenda. Her concern was to select and edit her data to present Charlotte as both a martyr to duty and a writer blessed with extraordinary talents. She elides the two cleverly, seeing Charlotte as one who 'must not hide her gift in a napkin; it was meant for the use and service of others' (Gaskell, 1857/1975: 334). Literary genius, domestic duty and Christian principles are all blended in this phrasing; it catches in miniature the 'spin' that Mrs Gaskell gives throughout the 'Life', one which enables her to offset any criticism of her subject's supposed 'coarseness' (that very unsaintly term used by Victorian critics to describe anything they considered unfeminine and improper) (e.g. Gaskell, 1857/1975: 335, 495–496) with a compensating image of the dutiful vicar's daughter. Exhibiting the skills of any present-day spin doctor, she has the cunning both to overstate and understate her case as required. Hence, in protecting the respectability of Charlotte and her sisters, she is prepared to all but deny them their imaginative capacities. 'Thoughtless critics … who have objected to the representation of coarseness', she argues, 'should learn that, not from the imagination – not from internal conception – but from the hard, cruel facts, pressed down, by external life, upon their very senses, for long months and years together, did they write out what they saw, obeying the stern dictates of their consciences' (Gaskell, 1857/1975: 335). This has the doubly curious effect of belittling the Brontës' imaginative powers and stressing the confessional nature of their fictions, as if the autobiographical explanation would deflate rather than exacerbate criticism – an oddly overplayed defence for a fellow novelist to mount. Conversely, she underplays the central and contentious issue in the Brontë story of Charlotte's relationship with Constantin Heger. Charlotte's strong affection for Monsieur Heger and her fictional portrayals of him and his wife in *Villette* and *The Professor* were a source of embarrassment to Mrs Gaskell, not least when she visited Brussels and Madame Heger refused to see her. Her technique is to understate the coolness that developed between Charlotte and Madame Heger and to explain the 'silent estrangement' between the two women in terms of religious differences (Gaskell, 1857/1975: 263–264). Not only does the biographical process begin from inherently unreliable sources – partial evidence, uncertain memories, letters slanted towards their recipients – but the facts are soon spinning in the imagination of the biographer with her own agenda. Well might Mrs Gaskell say, as we noted in Chapter 2: 'And I never *did* write a biography, and I don't know exactly how to set about it; you see you have to be accurate and keep to facts; a most difficult thing for a writer of fiction' (Gaskell, in Uglow, 1999: 397).

(ii) Fact into Fiction

The fictionalising of the Brontës' lives took a variety of forms, three in particular: factual sisters promoted themselves as fictional brothers in the pseudonyms they adopted in an effort to protect themselves from the male chauvinist prejudices of publishers and reviewers; the use of their own lives as the imaginative source for their novels; and the images that two novelists, Charlotte and Mrs Gaskell, ostensibly writing biographically, created of the three sisters. The gender issue came to a head with the famous incident, recounted by Mrs Gaskell and subsequent biographers, of Charlotte and Anne setting out in a thunderstorm, travelling to London overnight, and revealing their true identities to Charlotte's publisher, George Smith. Charlotte gave her own account in a letter to Mary Taylor on 4 September 1848; George Smith gave his over fifty years later in his Memoir of 1902. Biography soon set to work, fictionalising the incident in different ways. It had been interpolated by Mrs Gaskell (Gaskell, 1857/1975: 345–347) and, among many others, has been depicted and evaluated (Barker, 1994: 557–560), and imaginatively dramatised (Gordon, 1994: 167–168). The Brontës' seven major novels also make their contribution by showing heroines in adversity, none more so than Charlotte's last and most autobiographical work, *Villette*, 'the last ... of the writer's fictional attempts to come to terms with her own loveless existence' (Gilbert & Gubar, 1979: 399–400). Lucy Snowe is but one of the many representations of the educated single woman in the restricted and emotionally deprived role of governess/teacher that recur in the Brontës' works. And, of course, both Charlotte and Mrs Gaskell had the motive and the talent to fictionalise when writing biography: Charlotte in her 'Biographical Notice of Ellis and Acton Bell' and 'Preface' to Emily's novel, creating images of unworldly, isolated young women living intimately amidst both the rough vulgarities and romantic beauties of Nature; and Mrs Gaskell portraying Charlotte the lonely suffering woman rather than Currer Bell the successful novelist.

(iii) Fiction into Myth

The transition from fiction into myth is characterised by two particular features: the romanticising of Haworth, the parsonage and the surrounding moors as an isolated, lonely setting against which these three mythic figures could enact their solitary tragedy with the stoicism of Greek drama; and the tendency to use the characters in the seven novels to bolster the stereotypical images of the three sisters.

Haworth and the parsonage are presented as a setting from a singularly gloomy fairy tale in Mrs Gaskell's 'Life'. The latter is 'a dreary, dreary place literally *paved* with rain-blackened tombstones' and occupied by an old man 'brooding like a Ghoul over the graves' who 'hardly looked human'. Charlotte is placed in this setting: 'Miss Brontë put me so in mind of her own "Jane Eyre" ... there was something touching in the sight of that little creature entombed in such a place, and moving about herself like a spirit' (Gaskell, 1857/1975: 429–431). Charlotte is here depicted as moving from fact to fiction to being 'like a spirit' from myth all within one brief paragraph.

Beyond the vicarage and the village lies the wider mythic landscape of *Wuthering Heights*, created by Emily and deliberately mythologised by Charlotte in her 'Preface', which concludes with a paragraph of poetic prose that invests Emily's story with the qualities of classical myth. *Wuthering Heights* is seen as a stone book, coming into being through an irresistible creative power that hews a gigantic statue from the granite rocks on the moors around Haworth (Currer Bell, 'Preface', 1850/1965: 41).

And what of the characters of the 'three weird sisters', in Ted Hughes's unkind phrase, who are situated on the 'blasted heath' above Haworth? It is ironic that, though the Brontë sisters created complex characters in their stories, they themselves became fixed into stereotypes in their own life story: Charlotte as the long-suffering victim of duty; Emily as the wild child of genius; Anne as the quiet, conventional one who conforms to the demands of society and religion (Barker, 1994: xvii). So strong has the imagery of this landscape with figures become that the combination of biographical documentation and literary power has produced myths that seem endlessly adaptable. They can be shaped into our preferred likeness. Hence, to the respectable, the Brontës are decent, well-behaved, properly brought-up, conventional young women; to the religious, they are icons of piety; to romantics, tragic heroines in a wild landscape; to realists, spinsters of modest means and limited opportunities, reliant upon their own resources; to feminists, symbols of Everywoman struggling for freedom against the restrictions of a patriarchal society.

The malleability of myths is the key to their essential nature: they evolve with the character of a living organism, and they adapt to the sub-cultures which they inhabit. What might seem like a sequence of discrete phases turn out to be loosely linked, unpredictable developments that spread like a cultural virus. The next phase accelerates this process.

(iv) Myth into 'Faction'

'Factions' in the world of journalism and television are stories with a basis in fact but embellished with invented elements. The Brontë myth has been repeatedly appropriated in this way in our culture. Charlotte has become the iconic figurehead, Haworth the shrine (Miller, 2001: 106). Factions in different media have proliferated: ballets, plays, romantic fictions, Hollywood blockbusters, TV films ... All this serves to detach the Brontës from factual biography and to give them new lives as fictional characters. The job of the modern biographer is to demythologise this process, knowing, even as the attempt is made, that it is in the nature of the organism to reconstitute itself.

(v) Demythologising the Brontës

Virginia Woolf, as we have seen in Chapter 1, described the aim of biography as the effort to unite the 'granite-like' solidity of verifiable evidence with the 'rainbow-like' intangibility of personality (Woolf, 1967: 229). Barker's monumental biography, *The Brontës* (1994), certainly provides solid evidence, emphasises context and historicity, and counters the myth with exhaustive data on the family and the wider community. Gordon (1994) probes the interior emotional life of her subject, representing Charlotte as driven by a passion for words – for exploring in the language of her fictions the nature and role of women. She leaves the granite to Barker and seeks the rainbow, conscious no doubt that the search for such an end is illusory. Miller (2001) situates the Brontës' works and family history in the larger context of cultural myth-making. She is alert to her own potential vulnerability, admitting that her background as a literary critic may be perceived as giving a distorting slant to her study.

All three confront the myth that Mrs Gaskell released. Barker is blunt:

> The portrayal of Charlotte as the martyred heroine of a tragic life, driven by duty and stoically enduring her fate, served its purpose at the time. Charlotte's wicked sense of humour, her sarcasm, her childhood *joie de vivre* which enlivens the juvenalia, are completely ignored. So, too, are her prejudices, her unpleasant habit of always seeing the worst in people, her bossiness against which her sisters rebelled, her flirtations with William Weightman and George Smith and her traumatic love for Monsieur Heger. What remains may be a more perfect human being, but it was not Charlotte Brontë. (Barker, 1994: 829)

Gordon is succinct: 'Mrs Gaskell tells a coherent story ... a lasting imaginative truth based on a selection of facts' (Gordon, 1994: 329), a description that simultaneously both hints at Gaskell's particular mythologising and offers a general definition of biography. Miller (2001: 169) is subtle. She acknowledges the advances in modern scholarship but reminds us that every biography remains a provisional statement, a child of its time. Each generation reconceives the Brontës in its own terms, tells 'their story from a new perspective'. Neither heavy data nor imaginative insight will abolish myth-making; indeed, their combined power ensures its continuance.

Three distinctive approaches reflecting three preoccupations of current literary biography: the fashion for no-stone-unturned research and biographies with massive documentation; the wish to identify the springs of the creative impulse and their workings in art; and the impetus towards metabiography – the search for transferable principles in the studies of particular authors. The paradox of this whole process through its various phases is that the very effort of demythologising can also lead to further mutations of the myths it attempts to explode.

The five overlapping phases of the paradigm can thus be summarised as follows:

(i) the first biographer is commissioned, selects and establishes a factual history, giving the 'facts' a particular 'spin';
(ii) the facts become fictionalised, typically through the writings of the subject as well as those of the biographer;
(iii) the fiction, in turn, becomes mythologised as its characters and landscape become symbols;
(iv) the myth is transmuted into a variety of 'factions' in different media – stories accepted as based on fact but embellished with invented elements; and
(v) modern biographers attempt to demythologise this process by returning to primary sources.

Variations on the Theme

How plausible is it to generalise from the Brontë paradigm and apply it to Byron or Dickens or Sylvia Plath? Clearly, in the biomythographies of these subjects the emphases will necessarily differ from author to author: celebrity reaches new heights with Byron; it metamorphoses into idolatry with Dickens; and, given the late twentieth-century post-Christian culture, saintliness is replaced by secular martyrdom in the case of Sylvia Plath. Biography, of course, is not solely responsible for such developments but, in describing and accounting for them, it both shows a willing complicity in the processes and appears to conform to the phased pattern of biomythography discussed above. The variations which follow exemplify the three dominant themes with which I began: in each instance, the *initial* thrust towards celebrity, idolatry or martyrdom owes much to the energy and behaviour of the biographee. I introduce each with a contemporary 'snapshot'.

(i) Byron

Here is Byron, as described by Lady Blessington:

> Byron had so unquenchable a thirst for celebrity, that no means were left untried that might attain it: this frequently led to his expressing opinions totally at variance with his actions and real sentiments … there was no sort of celebrity he did not, at some period or other, condescend to seek, and he was not over nice in the means, provided he obtained the end. (Quoted in MacCarthy, 2003: x)

How did biography react to such a personality? From first to last, biographers have conspired, deliberately or indirectly, in the making of the Byronic myth.

The phases follow the Brontë paradigm. Byron's friend and fellow poet, Thomas Moore, wrote the first authentic 'Life' in 1830, being both helped and hindered by Byron's surviving family, friends and acquaintances (as Mrs Gaskell was in researching Charlotte Brontë). His facts were also subject to selection and 'spin': he does not – indeed, dare not at the time – deal with Byron's homosexual experiences. The fictionalisation of Byron's life was self-generated, initiated in the persona of the moody, passionate, lonely wanderer who crossed Western Europe thinly disguised as Childe Harold and carried forward in the more explicitly autobiographical *Don Juan*. From these poems, *Manfred, The Corsair* and others arose the Romantic figure of myth – the Byronic Hero, a figure described by Macaulay as 'a man proud, moody, cynical, with defiance on his brow, and misery in his heart, a scorner of his kind, implacable in revenge, yet capable of deep and strong affection' (quoted in Christiansen, 1989: 201). As Christiansen notes, the Byronic myth mutated rapidly. It was soon compounded with over thirty biographies, memoirs and critiques published within five years of Byron's death; and, as noted in Chapter 1, the biographical tally alone now stands at over 200 (Holmes, 1995: 18)! The shift from myth to 'faction' is described by another recent biographer who comments on 'the monster known as Byronism … the mythologised Byron that virtually rose from his corpse at Missolonghi':

> From Byron's lifetime to the present day, competing voices have invoked the poet as an idol in their own image: hero and martyr of revolutionary struggle, aristocratic aesthete and dandy, transgressive rebel of polymorphous sexuality fuelled by forbidden substances and with sulfurous whiffs of the Prince of Darkness swirling about him. These last mutations were recharged by rock culture's canonisation of self-destructive artists hallowed by early death: Elvis

> and James Dean, while "His Satanic Majesty" Mick Jagger still pays tribute to the sneering, demonic Byron of Victorian nightmare. (Eisler, 2000: 752)

Byron's 'posthumous life', like that of the Brontës, has been littered with relics, paintings, literary imitations, operas and musical compositions, ballets, plays, films and, of course, the inevitable 'legacy of kitsch' (Eisler, 2000: 758). There are few more formidable myths anywhere for the modern biographer to demythologise, as the exhibition 'Mad, Bad and Dangerous: The Cult of Lord Byron' (National Portrait Gallery, 2003) demonstrated. Eisler and MacCarthy are free from the constraints imposed upon Leslie Marchand, who produced the first thoroughly researched modern biography in 1957. MacCarthy comments: 'Marchand, writing at a time when homosexuality was still a criminal offence under British law, was compelled to temper his account not only of Byron's incestuous relations with his half-sister Augusta but also, more crucially, of his recurring loves for adolescent boys' (MacCarthy, 2003: xii). Both these recent biographers have enjoyed a more open climate and had access to the John Murray archive so that a much fuller account of their subject emerges. Yet the myth continues to mutate. MacCarthy faces it squarely in her title and in her part headings: 'The Making of a Legend', 'Celebrity in Exile' and 'The Byron Cult'. The effort to demythologise is explicit. Yet, at the end, even she cannot resist a dramatic finale, recalling the Gothic scene in 1938, which she paints with a novelist's relish, when the Byron family vault beneath the parish church of Hucknall Torkard was reopened. Officially, this was for archaeological reasons; unofficially, it was because the vicar wanted to see if Byron was still in his coffin! It was nearly midnight before the embalmed corpse was finally revealed, still intact and recognisable as when it was placed there 114 years earlier (MacCarthy, 2003: 571–574). On such stories myths continue to thrive.

(ii) Dickens

The snapshot of Dickens is from his first American visit in 1842, taken by Edgar Johnson, following Forster's account:

> ... his lionization began to swell to embarrassing proportions; [Dickens was mobbed], women clinging to him while they furtively snipped bits of fur from his coat to treasure as souvenirs, and filling the passage with a soprano clamour of adulation. (Johnson, 1953/1986: 202–203)

Like Byron, Dickens was a celebrity at the age of 24 – Pickwick did for the novelist what Childe Harold had done for the poet (Kaplan, 1988: 82). Unlike Byron, whose fame turned into notoriety and ensured his exile in

Europe, Dickens was idolised at home and fêted in America. Unlike Byron, too, whose celebrity was primarily focused in the upper classes with knowledge of his life and works, Dickens spoke to and for a mass audience. Chesterton was not alone in elevating Dickens into a god: 'He approached the people like a deity and poured out his riches and his blood' (Chesterton, 1906/1975: 77). Johnson makes the specific link with Bardolatry and concludes that Dickens alone among English novelists can stand with Shakespeare (Johnson, 1953/1986: 570).

The pattern of Dickens's biomythography is the familiar one, but there are some significant variations. Both Dickens and Forster knew from an early stage that the latter would be his biographer. Forster as Dickens's closest friend had unparalleled access to data and personal knowledge of his subject over a period of thirty-three years. But the 'spin' here, while different in substance from Mrs Gaskell's on Charlotte Brontë, is typically Victorian. Forster gives a minimalist account of Dickens's separation from his wife, omits Mrs Dickens and Nelly Ternan from the biography altogether, and elects not to draw upon his own unrivalled store of personal reminiscences but upon public documents which he then destroyed. There is no conspiracy here but there are elements of collusion which censor the facts and then 'spin' them to create the image of a life that is suitable for public veneration (see Chapter 7).

The fictionalization of the facts of his life was Dickens's own. Dickens called *David Copperfield* his 'favourite child' (Preface to 1867 edition). This is the novel where Dickens shows his skill in blending truth and fiction (Kaplan, 1988: 245). This 'interweaving', as he called it, occurs most powerfully in his two first-person *Bildungsromane* (the other being *Great Expectations*) and is also reflected in the rich variety of his characters, many of whom are based upon real people.

The shift from fiction to myth is easily effected from this basis that Dickens himself created; and biography is implicated. Kaplan, more than any other modern biographer, interprets Dickens's life and works in mythic terms, seeing *David Copperfield* as Dickens's transformation of 'his private memories and his emotional life into a public myth about himself' (Kaplan, 1988: 249). Dickens not only transforms himself and others; he also initiates a topographical myth which biographers right down to Peter Ackroyd have helped to develop: Dickens's London vies with Hardy's Wessex and Wordsworth's Lake District as one of the prime sites in the literary biomythography of Britain. The starkest evidence of myth detaching itself from fiction is the small, half-timbered house in Portsmouth Street, off Kingsway, which still claims to be The Old Curiosity Shop, even though Dickens made it clear that his shop no longer existed.

This building has been photographed countless times, appeared in TV documentaries and is a seemingly permanent symbol of the factions that have been derived from Dickens's life and works. Plays and films are endlessly recycled and versions of the novels are reworked every decade, testimony not only to the power of the Dickensian myth within our culture but also to the singular affinity that both his life and works have with theatre.

There was much for the biographers of the late twentieth century to demythologise. Two examples will serve to show how biographers have, in fact, remythologised Dickens's story. The first is Dickens's relationship with Nelly Ternan. The modern biographer's task is to establish its nature with hard evidence; but, when the evidence is merely circumstantial, there is ample scope for further myths to flourish. Was Nelly Ternan Dickens's mistress? Edgar Johnson (1953/1986: 500) judges it as 'not unlikely'; Kaplan (1988: 410) says it is 'likely'; Ackroyd (1999: 967) disagrees and says that 'it seems inconceivable that theirs was in any sense a "consummated" affair', and he suggests that their relationship was an acting out of one of Dickens's most enduring fictional fantasies, 'That of sexless marriage with a young idealised virgin'. So much for Dickens's biographers; what of Nelly Ternan's? Claire Tomalin suggests two narratives for the years 1861–1865, one which accounts for Nelly's time in France by the need for secrecy over her pregnancy with Dickens's child, the other which sees this foreign travel as just part of the education that Dickens had supported for her and her family for some years (Tomalin, 1991: 147–149). In her final chapter, 'Myths and Morals', she comes off the fence and suggests, on balance, that it seems most likely that Nelly was Dickens's lover and mistress (Tomalin, 1991: 261). Yet, even then, there is a postscript. Tomalin adds a final few pages on 'The Death of Dickens' with fascinating fresh evidence that she received only in 1990/1991 that Dickens's death at Gads Hill, to which Georgina and Forster testified, was not the whole story, for he may well have collapsed hours earlier at the house he rented for Nelly in Peckham some 25 miles away. With the same sense of fictional freedom that MacCarthy shows in her description of the opening of Byron's tomb, Tomalin constructs a dramatic three-hour journey for Nelly and her dying lover in a closed carriage drawn by two horses in order to get him home for a decent, respectable death in his own dining-room (Tomalin, 1991: 277–279). New evidence or new myth? Biomythography feeds on doubt.

The second example is Ackroyd's *Dickens* (1999). It is long (1,200 pages), exhaustively researched, and innovative. Written by a novelist on a novelist, its one-word title signals its focus on the complexities of character, with all the contradictions that Dickens's restless energy entailed. It also interprets the art of literary biography afresh, ignoring some common biographical conventions in its desire to capture the continuous flow of its subject's life (see Chapter 7). Nor is his Dickens allowed the comfort of historical distance. In the fifth of the seven imaginative interludes scattered through the book, Ackroyd takes part in a dramatised conversation with the novelist in the Geffrye Museum (Ackroyd, 1999: 793–796) which turns on the issue of biography and fiction as means of understanding the self. In the course of some polite fencing between the biographer and his subject, the fictional Dickens bursts out with, 'Oh, biographers! Biographers are simply novelists without imagination!'. After a few more probes at his subject's identity which Dickens counters with the remark: 'Are you saying that I live in a world of my own devising?', Ackroyd throws in the towel and replies: 'Actually, I don't know. I'm making all this up'. This interlude figures as a *mise en abyme* for the whole biography, a biography which deliberately blurs the boundaries between history and fiction. In doing so, Ackroyd in effect remythologises the figure of Dickens as a man who, as he says in another interlude, '*saw* reality as a reflection of his own fiction' (Ackroyd, 1999: 994).

(iii) Sylvia Plath

The snapshot of Sylvia Plath is a self-portrait:

> I have done it again.
> One year in every ten
> I manage it –
>
> A sort of walking miracle, my skin
> Bright as a Nazi lampshade ...

She possesses – is possessed by – a unique skill:

> Dying
> Is an art, like everything else.
> I do it exceptionally well.
>
> I do it so it feels like hell.
> I do it so it feels real.
> I guess you could say I've a call.
> (From 'Lady Lazarus', *Ariel*, 1965: 16–17)

Sylvia Plath's suicide on 11 February 1963 has provoked a 'posthumous life' of over forty years, a decade longer than her actual life, during which time she has achieved remarkable fame. Google her name on the Internet and tens of thousands of references are recorded. Why this extraordinary interest in someone who published just one novel and one slim volume of poems during her own lifetime? Clearly, the reasons are more than literary. Here are four:

- (i) The suicide at the age of 30 of a woman whose writing was uniquely personal – writing which anatomised her own identity as daughter, wife and mother.
- (ii) Fascination at her marriage to an even more famous poet, Ted Hughes; their often troubled relationship and separation in 1962; and Ted Hughes's admission that one volume of Plath's journals 'disappeared' and that he burnt her last journal in his desire to protect their children (Hughes, 1994: 177–190; Wagner, 2001: 12).
- (iii) The rigorous control that the Plath Estate, in which Ted's older sister Olwyn played a significant part, exercised over the poetry, novel, letters and journals, making any publication both legally difficult and highly protracted.
- (iv) Her death at a time when the 'second-wave' feminist movement was getting underway in the 1960s for which she quickly became an iconic figure.

In all, a potent mix for both myth-making and martyrdom. Biographers continue to be fascinated (Malcolm, 1995: 66) and to have a hard time making sense of it. What is pertinent here is the opportunity to observe the process of mythologising while the pattern is mutating. Currently, we are in phase three and edging into the next, the phase of commercial and media exploitation.

The facts have been subject to distortion and 'spin' from the start. The three main sources are:

- (i) the censorship of information by the Plath Estate – not even Aurelia Plath could quote from her own daughter's letters home without official approval;
- (ii) the 'spin' that the first biographers put on her life where Anne Stevenson (1989) was seen as unduly influenced by Olwyn's view of Sylvia as sick, violent and self-destructive; where Paul Alexander (2003) seemed to express the fawning admiration of a Plath devotee; and where Linda Wagner-Martin (1987) could be regarded as an opportunist intent on creating a feminist icon;
- (iii) the perception of Sylvia's life that emerges from her novel, poetry, journals and letters, as well as from Hughes's writings (1994: 177–190), of her two 'warring selves': her external image, notably in her *Letters*

> *Home*, of 'Sivvy', the happy-go-lucky success; and her private, tortured self beneath this surface which emerges in her journals and in *Ariel* (Stevenson, 1989: 22–23, 163–165, 262). Given that her autobiographical motivation is a pervasive, deliberate search for self-knowledge and its literary representation, biographers cannot ignore its data.

The facts of her life and her descent into suicide have been fictionalised both by the two poets and by the writers of memoirs and biographies, all spinning their stories in a sophisticated version of Chinese whispers. The posthumous life was aptly described by Alvarez as 'the myth of the poet as a sacrificial victim' (Alvarez, 1974: 55); and his memoir became 'the foundation text of the Plath legend' (Malcolm, 1995: 20). The focal period is, inevitably, the end-game – the six or seven months from July 1962 to her death the following February when much of *Ariel* was written and *The Bell Jar* was published. Both interrogate her own identity – fictionalising it, symbolising it, attacking it, celebrating it, and finally destroying it. Has there ever been such a self-lacerating analysis by a writer? Identity is the subject for both the writer and the biographer. Plath's self-representation is expressed differently in the novel and the poems. Esther Greenwood's story falls into two distinct halves before and after a suicide attempt similar to the one Sylvia Plath made in 1953. It is a novel that falls somewhere between autobiographical fiction and self-administered psychotherapy (see the American publishers' comments quoted in Stevenson, 1989: 285). Biographers have responded uneasily to the challenge this poses, showing varying degrees of willingness to read the life through the fiction (Hayman, 2003: 152; Stevenson, 1989: 152; Wagner-Martin, 2003: 34).

With Sylvia Plath, self-representation is more than just fictionalising her own experiences; she mythologises both her life and her death. Having mythologised her mother in *The Bell Jar*, she did likewise with her father and husband in her most famous poem, 'Daddy', written like an incantation, an angry nursery rhyme chant to dispel Otto's ghost with which, in the last four stanzas, Ted Hughes becomes associated. The poem interpolates her earlier dicing with death as trying to get back to her father:

> But they pulled me out of the sack,
> And they stuck me together with glue.
> And then I knew what to do.
> I made a model of you,
> A man in black with a Meinkampf look

And a love of the rack and the screw.
And I said I do, I do.
So daddy, I'm finally through.
(From 'Daddy', *Ariel*, 1965: 56)

Plath's own bleak comments explain the self-mythologising.

> The poem is spoken by a girl with an Electra complex. Her father died while she thought he was God. Her case is complicated by the fact that her father was also a Nazi and her mother very possibly part Jewish. In the daughter the two strains marry and paralyse each other – she has to act out the awful little allegory once over before she is free of it. (Quoted by A. Alvarez, in Newman, 1971: 65)

The vampire and Nazi imagery that pervade the poem are ways of heightening the victim–oppressor relationships she projects with her father and husband. This mythic Sylvia, engendered by the equally mythic male and female figures symbolised by Otto/Ted and Aurelia, is at the core of all her writing and most powerfully in these *Ariel* poems.

But, if the foundations of the cult and the legend were self-laid in 1963 (Hayman, 2003: 198), it took the biographers to develop the actual myth. The battle-lines were sharply drawn from the start and the Plath Estate was a major combatant. Olwyn Hughes's intervention in Anne Stevenson's biography resulted in a highly unusual 'Author's Note' which (despite the singular position of the apostrophe) described the book as 'almost a work of dual authorship'; and Olwyn complained that Wagner-Martin (1987) (who according to her 'Preface' had clearly found negotiations frustrating) 'hadn't been writing a biography, but a feminist thesis on "Plath-as-the-libbers-wish-to-iconise-her"' (Hayman, 2003: 207). However, Olwyn's judgement is lent some credence in the light of Wagner-Martin's diatribe sixteen years later against Ted Hughes's *Birthday Letters* – eighty-eight poems, all but two of which are addressed to Sylvia Plath, written over a twenty-five-year period. They give us, according to Andrew Motion, 'his [Hughes's] account of her psychic history inside a portrait of their domestic history' (*The Times*, 17 January 1998). Hughes's last act in these quasi-biographical poems, coming as they did only months before his own death from cancer, polarised opinion. Elaine Feinstein, Hughes's biographer, argues that 'These poems should be read not as self-exculpation but as a form of self-discovery ... This whole book resonates with loss and love' (Feinstein, 2002: 265). In contrast, Wagner-Martin's account shows feminist biomythography at its most virulent and ill-considered.

Before I justify that judgement, it is worth recording that, for thirty years, Ted Hughes was abused and heckled at poetry readings; reviled on arrival in Australia with placards accusing him of being a wife murderer; tormented by the repeated desecration of Plath's grave in Yorkshire – the letters HUGHES hacked off her name on the headstone; and vilified by feminists in print, one of whom (Robin Morgan, later the editor of *Ms* magazine) published a poem, 'Arraignment', which accused Hughes of Plath's murder and threatened his dismemberment (Alexander, 2003: 357–358; Wagner, 2001: 10–11). (Some myth-makers, it seems, cannot bear too much reality: it does not do to defrock a saint.) Wagner-Martin's vocabulary is less violent than Morgan's yet is as unworthy as it is misguided: *Birthday Letters*, she says, is 'a secret missile'; it is 'conceived to infuriate Plath readers'; it is 'an affront' which 'argued with' and set about 'the task of correcting her story'. It is 'a betrayal'; Hughes's poems 'usurp the authority of Plath's narrative; they nearly erased her voice'. The poems are mostly 'skewed'; the book is Hughes's final 'insult'; feminists (the inclusive "we" of her last paragraph) are 'angered'. Propelled by all this fury, Wagner-Martin's critical judgement spins out of control. She states:

> There are several dozen poems in which Hughes begins with a poem that readers of Plath would recognise, and then rewrites her text so that nothing sensible remains of her original work. (Wagner-Martin, 2003: 150)

Apart from the distortion that Ted Hughes often begins with a Plath *poem* rather than with experiences they shared, the idea of his rewriting her text and obliterating hers in the process is bizarre. Both remain available – the more valuable through their complementary nature. Alvarez (1974: 30) understood this and prefigured it. Germaine Greer has given a more measured assessment: 'Ted Hughes existed to be punished. We'd lost a heroine, and we needed to blame someone' (quoted in Wagner, 2001: 11).

So, this is where we are in the myth-making. Hughes and Plath have associated their own myth with that of the Brontës, weaving the supposed setting for *Wuthering Heights* into their poetry, becoming the Cathy and Heathcliff of their generation (Miller, 2001: 250). The 'factions' have begun: there was a film of *The Bell Jar* in 1979, and another, *Sylvia*, went on general release in 2004. Emma Tennant has published *Burnt Diaries* (1999) and *The Ballad of Sylvia and Ted* (2001). Paul Alexander, capitalising on his work as a biographer, has written a one-woman stage show, *Edge* (2004), set on the last day of Sylvia Plath's life which 'unashamedly mythologises Plath as victim and confessional genius' (*Times Literary*

Supplement, 22 February 2004). The publication of *Ariel* in 2004 with the poems in Plath's original manuscript order instead of that of Ted Hughes's edited version (1965) provoked renewed controversy. In this third unfinished case, what biomyths have yet to come? The key to their future is, literally, secure: they will feed not on a corpse in the crypt, not on a covert death at a mistress's cottage, but on a locked chest. It was deposited four years ago along with two and a half tons of papers collected in the Plath Archive at Emory University, Atlanta. It is not to be opened for 100 years and (who knows?) may contain the last journals of Plath, not burnt or lost by Hughes after all (Hugo Williams, *Times Literary Supplement*, 12 March 2004).

Conclusions

My conclusions take the form of ten brief reflections on the notion of biomythography.

(1) Biomythography is a term that subverts any concept of life-writing based on a simplistic account of supposed 'facts'. It acknowledges the importance of context and historicity; but, more than that, it reflects the ways in which what we take as facts are subject to narrative representation and cultural mutability (Denzin, 1989: 81). Lucasta Miller's *The Brontë Myth* (2001: x) is the most explicit example, but instances of the metabiographical interest she demonstrates are evident too in several biographical studies mentioned earlier. For example: the opening and closing chapters, entitled 'Biography' and 'Biographer', that frame Hermione Lee's *Virginia Woolf* (1997); Jonathan Bate's description of his book, *The Genius of Shakespeare* (1997: x), as 'a kind of biography', one which covers not only the life of the man but the living body of his 'words and stage images'; and Adam Sisman's account of Boswell the biographer, rather than Boswell the man, and his 'presumptuous task' in writing his *Life of Dr Johnson* (Sisman, 2001). In such books, literary biography has begun to interrogate itself. Reflexiveness is their common quality, one shared with Ackroyd's *Dickens*. They recognise in different ways that literary biography deals not only with life stories but also with biomyths.

(2) Biomythography dissolves the distinction between the 'actual life' and the 'posthumous life', between the period of the biographee's existence and the period of biographical interpretation that succeeds it. Successive biographies ineluctably take account of their antecedents and perceive the

subject's life through a historical lens that, tantalisingly, both clarifies and obscures. It offers a sharper focus on facts, yet becomes more opaque as the myths mutate over time and become absorbed into the biographer's vision.

(3) Virginia Woolf was right – biography is an impossibility (Woolf, 1967: 234). Fact, fiction and myth (not to mention forgery, lies and innocent error) are so interwoven in our perceptions of human lives that 'life-writings' must not assume to tell the truth. Holmes's description of biography as 'inventing the truth' (Holmes, 1995: 18) reminds us that the genre is a construct of historical narrative. Biomythography is a way of expressing this and of indicating the sort of truths that myths tell: not literal truths but symbolic ones. We must resist the pressure for a single, legalistic 'truth' (Rose, 1992: 104–105); at best, it is a mere convenience, an attempt at fairness or balance. Biography must embrace the more difficult concept of multiple 'truths', versions of the self as expressed in different contexts, driven by different motives, for a variety of purposes (Denzin, 1989: 81). Cultural myths, as indicated earlier, are malleable; so are the 'truths' they carry.

(4) Biomythography signals that there is no such thing as 'the definitive biography' – a phrase that still occurs frequently and indicates our psychological need for certainty more than anything else.

(5) Biomythography acknowledges our 'unconscious hunger for explanatory myths'. The phrase is again Richard Holmes's, writing about the Shelley myth (Holmes, 2004). 'We like our "lives"', he goes on, 'to conform to archetypes, or fables, or even fairy tales … myths are easily formed but difficult to change.' As I have argued, we need our heroes and heroines, celebrities and idols, saints and martyrs – they are the leading characters in these explanatory myths.

(6) Biomythography is as susceptible to a gendered concept of characters and roles as traditional myths and fairy tales are. (The latter, particularly, have been reconceived in recent decades with books like the aptly titled *The Practical Princess and Other Liberating Fairy Tales* (Williams, 1980).) It will not have escaped the reader's notice that, of my four writers, the men are portrayed as heroes, the women as martyrs. Feminists have seen both women as martyred on the patriarchal cross. In Charlotte Brontë's case, she is the martyred saint to Christian duty and Victorian respectability – both things controlled by being the daughter of a vicar and, latterly, the wife of another one – and subject to all the constraints of male-dominated, nineteenth-century provincial England. Sylvia Plath has become a secular martyr in our post-Christian society, her life dominated by the spectral love affair with her father, and her death seen as directly attributable to her

husband's infidelity. While feminism has a good deal more to offer (Rose, 1992; Malcolm, 1995) than the vandalism and abuse of its extremists in explicating the gender roles inherent in biomythography, it is surprising to find that a standard account of psychobiography, published at a time when the Plath story was at its height, ignores her case completely, citing instead the safer instances of Emily Dickinson and Virginia Woolf (Runyan, 1984).

(7) The fictionalising of personal experience in *Jane Eyre*, *Villette*, *Childe Harold* and *David Copperfield* moves into a new dimension with *The Bell Jar* and *Ariel*. With Sylvia Plath, we have a myth within a myth. The autobiographical compass swings 180 degrees with these fictions: whereas Charlotte Brontë, Byron and Dickens drew upon their own lives and externalised their experiences in their art, Plath uses her art to interrogate her life, constantly internalising and reliving, dramatising and analysing her experiences in her effort to exorcise her past and understand it. Hughes describes her poems as 'chapters in a mythology' (Hughes, in Newman, 1971: 187). The personal myth she created lies inside the cultural myth that has grown up since her death. Richard Murphy, the Irish poet whom Sylvia Plath visited in 1962, speaks of her then as sowing the 'seeds of the future myth of her martyrdom' (Stevenson, 1989: 245, 352). Literary biography is uniquely susceptible to the biomyths created by its subjects' writings.

(8) Biomythography needs a good death. Often it will act as the prologue to a 'Life', as it does in Ackroyd's *Dickens*; sometimes its importance is enshrined in a title, as in Hayman's *The Death and Life of Sylvia Plath*. If it is premature, youthful, violent, in a good cause – so much the better. Of my main examples, Dickens is the only one to outlive the 'thirty-somethings'. And even then we find Claire Tomalin promoting a new version of his final hours. Death defines the 'Life' with its mythic shadow as well as its chronological full stop.

(9) Biomythography is a process of gathering and organising the scattered fragments of the past to meet the needs of the present. Actual living is experienced as an unpredictable mixture of the known and the unforeseen, of planning and serendipity. Yet its biographical representation into holistic narrative patterns is more than the mere ordering of events; for biomythography acknowledges a sense of fate in this narrativising, recognising that the 'Lives' of those we mythologise assume a predetermined character as we look back retrospectively for the 'red thread' linking beginnings, middles and ends. This urge to create a unidirectional, teleological reading of a literary life reflects our profound human needs both to define a consistent sense of identity and to give shape and coherent meaning to the pattern of events that make up an individual's life.

(10) For biomythography is all we have. Poets and novelists, writers and readers of biography, all have to live with 'epistemological insecurity' (Malcolm, 1995: 154). Faced with the fumbling uncertainties of self-knowledge and the limitations of knowing another's life, we mask our instability and partial ignorance with myths. Suspending our disbelief is not an option with biography. This is not the 'as if' of fiction; it is real life and we want to know about it. Life-writing cannot sustain the anxiety of uncertainty: so its writers and readers keep it at bay by perpetuating the necessary myths – which is why, in this chapter, I have urged the insertion of 'myth' into our concept of 'biography'.

5

Inferential Biography: Shakespeare the Invisible Man

And almost thence my nature is subdued
To what it works in, like the dyer's hand.
(Sonnet 111)

Shakespeare eludes his would-be biographers. Some glimpse him in his sonnets, in the implied author of his plays, in the roles he might have acted, or as a figure in the society of Elizabethan Warwickshire and London. In the end, all have to admit defeat. Yet the biographies keep coming, powered by the twin engines of inference and imagination. With such an elusive subject, the dangers of both are as evident as the benefits. These inferred Shakespeares, created from official records, historical extrapolations and traces found in unstable play texts, are little more than ghosts. Biography, along with portraiture (as illustrated in the exhibition *Searching for Shakespeare*, National Portrait Gallery, 2006; see Chapter 6, vi), constantly strives to materialise the ghost and, in doing so, demonstrates the rules which govern the biographer's imagination and the virtual nature of the Shakespeares it creates. Biography can tell us a great deal about the social, cultural and political world Shakespeare lived in and can deduce from such history what Shakespeare *might* have experienced. But no amount of inference and imagination can produce the 'Life'. Nor can his writings reveal the man. What, then, can biography do with an all but invisible subject?

The answer would seem to entail a shift from the man to the ideas and thinking that are represented in the plays and poems; not Shakespeare's actual beliefs, opinions and prejudices, but Shakespeare's thought as represented in his works. The range, depth and variety of thinking are such that, when reading his works, we feel we are being given access to the 'biography of a mind'; and, when imaginatively engaged in the theatre, to the intricate play of this mind in dramatic form. For the quality of thought we encounter in Shakespeare is that which Keats recognised as 'Negative Capability, that is when man is capable of being in uncertainties, mysteries, doubts, without any irritable reaching after fact and reason' (Keats, 1817/ 2002: 41–42). This is not thought as a line of argument, conducted as a logical sequence of steps towards a rational and plausible conclusion, with the aim of convincing its auditors. This is thought as the representation of intellectual issues, embodied in characters and events, where the dramatic conflict also constitutes a dialectical conflict with the aim of allowing opposing notions to develop together, thus engaging the imaginations of the audience with ideas as well as narrative. This 'play of contraries' is, for Shakespeare, 'the natural condition of being a dramatist' (Ackroyd, 2005: 182) and, as we shall see, one which manifests itself whatever issues are the subject of his drama.

This alternative biographical agenda still remains problematic both through the profusion and complexity of Shakespeare's works and through the vast bibliography of Shakespeare studies. The aims of this chapter are necessarily modest. An introductory section summarises the known facts and the main sources of inference which contextualise them. The body of the chapter discusses what a range of recent biographers have inferred about the thinking of the implied author in the sonnets, and then focuses on the insights offered by four recent biographers on four key plays. The final section attempts to draw some conclusions about the legitimacy, plausibility and appropriateness of inferential biography.

Virtual Shakespeares

Biography, like nature, abhors a vacuum. Ranged around the absent Shakespeare are a host of virtual Shakespeares invented, in varying degrees, from six main sources: from the scraps of documentary evidence, from the cultural context of contemporary playwriting, from the social context of contemporary politics and religion, from four centuries of myth-making, from four centuries of canon formation, and from the implied author of the works. I separate them out merely for convenience; the last of these is the approach adopted presently. Of the others, in the sketches that follow, I exemplify them from studies that have appeared within the past two decades.

(i) The Facts

All biographers acknowledge the paucity of the documentary record: 'during his lifetime William Shakespeare is only mentioned by name in seventy-nine hand-written documents'. Of these, thirty-one are in the Shakespeare

Birthplace Trust, thirty-five in the Public Record Office in London (Bearman, 1994: vii–viii). The conventional markers of Shakespeare's existence in the Stratford Parish Records, of his birth, marriage, the christenings of his children and his burial, can be numbered on the fingers of one hand. To these can be added documentary evidence which gives glimpses of his life in Stratford – the only surviving letter written to him by Thomas Quiney asking Shakespeare for a loan of £30 (Bearman, 1994: 33–35); and documents connected with the purchase of New Place and with various land deals. His will, entries in the Stationers' Register that record the publication of his plays without naming him, and documents associated with the family's application for a coat of arms, these and other sketchy details are like the disconnected remnants of an ancient mural. We have to try to imagine the richness of the complete image from these fragments. By themselves, they reveal little of Shakespeare the man or the writer: property deals and financial transactions are their business. An abridged version of Schoenbaum's survey of the biographical facts (*A Compact Documentary Life*, 1987) is given in Part One of his *Shakespeare's Lives* (1993: 1–37). It adds a little anecdotal colour to such glimpses with documented references to Robert Greene's jealous description of Shakespeare as this 'upstart Crow' (1592), Frances Mere's list of eleven plays, some poems and 'sugared sonnets' (1598), and the First Folio edition of Shakespeare's plays (1623) compiled by two of his former colleagues, Heminges and Condell. This factual basis is sufficiently strong to allow biographers to interpret the details in their contemporary cultural and social contexts, and sufficiently weak to encourage the Anti-Stratfordians and others in denial to invent alternative authors for Shakespeare's writings (the Earl of Oxford, Sir Henry Neville and Francis Bacon are the current favourites: Anderson, 2005; James & Rubinstein, 2005; Jackson, 2005). The instability of the biographical structures erected on these flimsy foundations is often betrayed by their stylistic awkwardness in such repeated provisos as '"perhaps", "maybe", "it's most likely", "probably", or the most desperate of them all, "surely"' (Shapiro, 2005: xxiii). There is no clearer indicator of inferential biography than the biographer's vocabulary of frustrated speculation.

(ii) The Theatrical Context

What virtual Shakespeare is to be found in the accounts of Elizabethan theatre? There are two main figures, each containing a double image of Shakespeare depending on the angle from which it is viewed. Shakespeare the practical man of the theatre is seen both as a collaborator and a competitor with other dramatists; and Shakespeare the writer at his desk is seen as consciously exploring and exploiting the tension between literary and theatrical values. Inferences drawn from the first lead to suggestions about Shakespeare's artistic development; inferences from the second are taken as evidence that Shakespeare was aware of the need to write for a comprehensive audience, for the groundlings as well as for the court.

The context from which this virtual Shakespeare emerged was established by E. K. Chambers (1923/1951) and refined by Andrew Gurr (1970). The ghost is given a human face in Peter Thomson's account of what he calls, pragmatically, 'Shakespeare's job' (Thomson, 1999). The job, as he expounds it in his central Chapter 4, demanded a sensitive awareness of the relationships between 'three distinct but closely related groups – playwrights, actors and audiences' (Thomson, 1999: 82). Yet despite the impressive volume of scholarly information about the theatrical context unearthed here and elsewhere in recent times, biographers are still left with an insubstantial Shakespeare. In his early career, he is usually presented as actor, freelance playwright and published poet; as a collaborator with others, possibly Nashe and Peele (Greenblatt, 2004: 195, 207), and as a competitor of Marlowe (Greenblatt, 2004: 256–257; Honan, 1999: 199; Wood, 2003: 166). His dramatic development (in both senses) is attributed to the stability afforded by his role as resident playwright of the Chamberlain's Men from 1594/5, and focused on his *annus mirabilis* five years later in which, during a twelve-month period, he became a shareholder in the new Globe Theatre and wrote or drafted four of his most famous plays – *Henry V, Julius Caesar, As You Like It* and *Hamlet* (Wood, 2003: 238). Shapiro's biography of this crucial year in Shakespeare's life, *1599: A Year in the Life of William Shakespeare* (2005), is complemented by Kermode, who identifies the same period as the time when 'personation', involving the fuller representation of characters' thoughts than mere 'playacting', developed in the theatre (Kermode, 2000: 6). His book argues that something remarkable happened to Shakespeare's language around the turn of the century: 'There were great changes in both dramatist and audience. Shakespeare became, between 1594 and 1608, a different sort of poet' (Kermode, 2000: 13). These changes evoke the second figure of Shakespeare, the writer at his desk, the poet whose instincts and genius led him to represent on stage the interior life of his characters' thoughts and feelings through the media of their external actions and their reflective speech. At its crudest, this has fuelled the old argument between those who treat the plays as acting scripts and those who read them as extended poems. Wells sees this as creative tension rather than a cause for argument: 'there may well have existed a tension in Shakespeare's mind between theatrical and literary values.

It was a fruitful tension: the theatrical Shakespeare was dependent on the literary, and vice versa' (Wells, 1995: 37). At its most sublime, this produced the extraordinary variety in tone, speech and action that we find in *Hamlet*, a compelling theatrical experience in the revenge idiom yet sustained by equally compelling poetry that helps to lengthen the play to 4,000 words which, at roughly 1,000 words per hour, extends it way beyond the norm for an afternoon performance at The Globe. (The only uncut production I have seen was directed by Peter Brook and Trevor Nunn at The Round House in 1971. It lasted 4 1/4 hours.) In this, his longest play, as in *Macbeth*, one of the shortest, Shakespeare's blend of visually dramatic elements – from ghosts and witches, gravediggers and drunken porters, to hallucinations and on-stage murders – with the quieter but no less intense, internal struggles of his protagonist's mind not only marks the single most significant development in Shakespeare's writing, it also has a calculated inclusiveness to engage the imaginations of all sorts and conditions of men and women who attended his plays.

(iii) The Social Context

The Shakespeare who inhabits the biographies which situate him as a man of his times is fashioned from two further double images, one set against the other: the countryman working in the city; and the figure set against the backdrop of post-Reformation religion and the machinations of Tudor politics. All biographies start in Stratford and move to London. This shift has Shakespeare vanishing into the biographical black hole of the 'lost years': the boy from the provincial market town, eldest son of a glove-maker and local alderman, who probably attended the local grammar school, and who married and became a father by the age of 19, is swallowed up in the mid-1580s, no-one knows where, only to emerge in London as an actor-playwright and poet some seven years later. Theories of his disappearance abound, the most popular, if no more plausible than others, identifying the youthful Shakespeare as one William Shakeshaft who was tutor in the Hoghton household in Lancashire for two years, and who moved on to employment with Sir Thomas Hesketh who, in turn, eased his passage into one of his visiting groups of actors, probably the Earl of Derby's Players, later those of his son, Lord Strange's Men (Holden, 1999; Honigman, 1985/1998). (Others argue for The Queen's Men but, as Wood notes, none of the theories of the 'lost years' is mutually exclusive (Duncan-Jones, 2001: 31; Wood, 2003: 112–119).) The links in this chain are acknowledged as self-evidently tenuous yet also attractive since they offer a framework for how a teenager from a modest background in a country town could gain knowledge of aristocratic life-styles and access to one of the touring troupes of actors all of whose paths eventually led to London.

Another aspect of this virtual Shakespeare draws upon particular circumstantial evidence from Stratford and Lancashire: that is, the persistence of the old religion in post-Reformation England. Shakespeare's parents appear to have been Catholics and raised their son in a town where Catholic practices and loyalties remained strong in civic life, in families and in the school which Shakespeare attended (Honan, 1999: 60–71). And if, as many are persuaded, Shakespeare's last schoolmaster, John Cottam, was a Catholic and had connections with the Catholic Hoghtons in Lancashire in a period when political pressure was increasing on recusants, then it is possible that the teenage Shakespeare spent some time in the north-west. Everything depends upon identifying young Shakespeare with young Shakeshaft. On this, as on so many other matters, the jury is still out (Wood, 2003: 86–87).

Whatever his actual identity, the broad picture of society in which this virtual Shakespeare lived and worked can be more confidently drawn. A recent study singles out religion and politics as the underlying elements that shaped people's lives. Susan Brigden (2001) shows how the Protestant Reformation, achieved in England at great cost, together with the steady shifting of political power from the old landed aristocracy to the new nobility centred on the court and owing loyalty and advancement to the crown, were inseparably entwined features of Tudor England. That Shakespeare was deeply aware of this history is clear from the dominance of history plays in his work, nowhere more so than in *Richard II*, the play that could easily have ruined the Chamberlain's Men. The performance of *Richard II* that the company gave at the request of the Earl of Essex's conspirators just a day before their abortive coup on the monarchy in 1601 was a rash move. Richard lacked a direct heir, was surrounded by favourites and enemies, and was deposed. Queen Elizabeth was aware of the parallel: '"I am Richard II, know ye not that?" she said' (Honan, 1999: 216–217). The theatre could be a dangerous arena in which to work. Essex lost his head; Shakespeare could have lost his career. This incident, especially, indicates the importance of setting Shakespeare's virtual life within the social and political context of the period: the norms of growing up in a rural market town, the pressure of the religious and political nexus on daily life – these formative influences are perhaps the hardest for modern biography to imagine.

(iv) The Shakespeare Mythos

Fictions, 'factions', fantasy, forgery – frustration fuels all forms of myth-making whether the aim is fictive truths or factual lies. From Anthony Burgess's

Nothing Like the Sun (1964) to Marc Norman and Tom Stoppard's film *Shakespeare in Love* (1998), the creators of fictionalised Shakespeares would willingly anchor their stories in a bit more fact were it available. Gary O'Connor's book is an example of a 'faction' in that it mixes well-researched data with the views of present-day 'witnesses', mostly from the theatre (O'Connor, 1992: 14), to provide a racy image of the Bard's life. Nor is there any shortage of anecdotal fantasies: the willingness to plug the gaps in the record with speculative guesswork started early. Some anecdotes may be innocently misleading (Aubrey thought Shakespeare's father was a butcher); others are simply unproven hearsay (Rowe's account of Shakespeare's deer-stealing). The stories range from the wittily salacious, like Manningham's diary anecdote from 1601 in which Shakespeare outwits Burbage for the favours of a female fan (Schoenbaum, 1993: 17), to the implausibly romantic, like Richard Ryan's tale about Shakespeare picking up Queen Elizabeth's glove on stage and improvising a couple of lines of blank verse as he returned it to the monarch. Schoenbaum comments drily: 'While not enhancing the biographical record, it contributes to the Shakespeare-Mythos' (Schoenbaum, 1993: 225–226). But while these various ways of fictionalising Shakespeare may be harmless fun, and even occasionally claim some imaginative truth, forgery, by contrast, subverts biography with its imaginative falsehoods. The two most notorious forgers were William Henry Ireland and John Payne Collier. Ireland's inventions were seemingly created in part to impress his credulous father. In his twenties, he faked the Blackfriars mortgage deed, a promissory note supposedly from Shakespeare to John Heminges, an exchange of letters between Shakespeare and the Earl of Southampton, a love letter to Anne Hathaway and a lock of Shakespeare's hair, a manuscript of *King Lear* ... all contributing to the infamous *Shakespeare Papers*, an exhibition of which was thrown open to the public in February 1795. Ireland's fraud was later exposed by Edmond Malone. Collier seems less naïve and, therefore, less excusable – an 'excellent scholar' who made genuine contributions to Shakespeare studies who nonetheless faked aspects of his data. Schoenbaum (1993: 245) comments that 'his case confronts us with a strange manifestation of the criminal mind'. The virtual Shakespeare that derives from all such myth-making can be fashioned to suit all tastes. Conceived positively, it represents our desire for a romanticised, full-colour image of the Bard; conceived negatively, as with the forgers, it represents nothing more than an obsessive desire for academic fame.

(v) The Shakespeare Canon

Schoenbaum (1993) is the best guide to the 'canon' of Shakespeare biography. I use the term deliberately to indicate the salient feature of his book as one that discriminates between those valuable works in the biographical tradition – ones that combine significant historical research from primary sources with interpretative insights – and those that form the mass of derivative 'secondary lives' that have accumulated around them. Taken together with Honan's essay at the end of his book (Honan, 1999: 415–424), a canon can be identified which makes a faltering start with Aubrey (*c.*1661) and Rowe (1709) before establishing itself in serious scholarly fashion with Edmond Malone, whose edition of the *Works* (1790) set new standards in editing authentic texts of the plays. Malone's incomplete *Life of Shakespeare* was published posthumously in 1821 by James Boswell's son. The line then continues with Halliwell-Phillipps (1848; 1881–1887), Edward Dowden (1875), Sidney Lee (1898) and E. K. Chambers (1930), before diversifying into a bewildering variety of Shakespeare studies in the second half of the twentieth century. Schoenbaum concludes on a note of despair that a conventional biography combining documentary detail and narrative flair can ever be written. He points out: 'It is after all a melancholy truth that the three greatest of all contributions to the biographical tradition – Malone's posthumous biography, Halliwell-Phillipps's *Outlines*, Chambers's study of facts and problems – abandon continuous narrative' (Schoenbaum, 1993: 568). Honan (1999: 424) offers some solace, suggesting that 'Shakespeare biography might be seen as a flawed, co-operative project'. Who was Shakespeare? No-one knows the answer. Shakespeare's very invisibility makes the biographical enterprise a combined effort in which inference plays a major role. Honan adds: 'Our collective picture of the poet's life is surely best when many people test it, doubt it, or contribute to it, and when we are not under the illusion that it is to be finished.'

The Implied Author: Inferential Biography

Does the life of the mind we infer from the works correspond to the characteristic mode of thinking of an implied author? Wayne Booth defined the implied author as the writer's 'second self' which the reader deduces from the works, 'the literary, created version of the real man' (Booth 1961: 73–75); whereas the inferential biographee is a version of the author that the biographer makes available to the reader, created primarily from the texts. Despite the asymmetry in the apposition, this aspect of Wayne Booth's rhetoric of fiction remains helpful. Granted, we experience the voices of fiction differently from those of plays: novels are embalmed voices and it is the reader's role to breathe life into them; plays are given voices for the actors to bring to life. Yet, when reading a play, the difference in the inner ventriloquism that carries us forward is one of degree, not of kind. The auditory imagination of the reader is stimulated more readily into 'hearing' the voices of the characters whose vividness and immediacy tend to mask the single voice that creates and controls them all. When seeing a play, the live dialogue and physical action screen out its creator even more effectively. Shakespeare, as Borges's story 'Everything and Nothing' says, is everywhere and nowhere (Borges, 1992). The inferences we can draw, therefore, will be general rather than specific, impersonal ideas, not a personal credo, patterns of thinking, not solutions to issues or problems. 'If you read and re-read Shakespeare endlessly, you may not get to know either his character or his personality but you will certainly learn to recognise his temperament, his sensibility and his cognition' (Bloom, 1995: 52–53). In the following discussion of selected writings, aspects of Shakespeare's temperament and sensibility may incidentally be inferred, but it is the evidence of his cognition which describes the clearest recurrent patterns and offers the most fertile area for inferential biography. I explore these patterns in five representative works, each reflecting aspects of Shakespeare's thinking; representative, that is, of his poems and of the 'tragical-comical-historical-pastoral' range of his plays; and reflecting that 'play of contraries' which is his characteristic mode of thinking.

(i) The Art of Love: The Sonnets

The representation of love in all its guises permeates Shakespeare's works; and the variations on this theme play upon the contrasts of 'real' and 'seeming' love, of true and feigned affections, and upon the extremes of passion, jealousy, betrayal and self-deception. All are subject to the contraries of physical desire and rhetorical language. As Auden comments: 'What makes it difficult for a poet not to tell lies is that, in poetry, all facts and all beliefs cease to be true or false and become interesting possibilities' (Auden, 1963/1975: 19). This meta-ethical stance sorts well with the view of *The Sonnets* that finds their central theme in 'a division between eye and heart, between what a lover wants to believe and what he knows is true', a hiatus that culminates in 'the emergence in the sequence of a form of subjectivity founded on perpetual alienation between the poet and the object of love' (Shakespeare, ed. Burrow, 2002: 132–133).

Along with Burrow, recent editors have generally resisted the temptation to connect *The Sonnets* directly with Shakespeare's life and personality (Shakespeare, ed. Duncan-Jones, 1997: 82): 'a form of subjectivity' is as far as they will go. Recent biographers have been divided. The historians like Rowse (1973) and Wood (2003) have committed themselves to an autobiographical reading, voting for the Earl of Southampton and the Earl of Pembroke respectively as the 'young man' to whom Sonnets 1–126 are addressed and agreeing that the 'dark lady' of sonnets 127–154 is Emilia Lanier. The literary biographers have been more circumspect. Schoenbaum (1993: 33–34) and Wells (1995: 15–17) vacillate, the latter finding it hard to escape an autobiographical reading while conceding, when he thinks about the varieties of love in the plays, 'Well, perhaps after all they are dramatic sketches, fragments of an imagined psycho-drama inhabited only by invented personae, not products of a real-life drama' (Wells, 1995: 17). Duncan-Jones, as biographer rather than editor, adjusts her emphasis, noting that the title page, 'Shakespeare's Sonnets', 'both proclaims the genuine authorship of the poems and suggests Shakespeare's "presence" in them' (Duncan-Jones, 2001: 215). The rest, with one teasing exception, remain firmly agnostic. Ackroyd (2005: 288) rejects any parallels with Shakespeare's private life; Greenblatt (2004: 254) infers from the sequence a lack within Shakespeare's marriage and finds in the young man and dark lady not identifiable people but compensatory images of 'ecstatic idealization' and a 'capacity for desire'. Honan (1999: 185) considers 'the sonnets are too paradoxical and mixed to be labelled as either "fictions" and "literary exercises", or as straightforward "biographical revelations"'; and, along with Burrow (Shakespeare, 2002: 131), points out that 'the myth that Shakespeare's nameless Young Man and Dark Lady had exact counterparts in his life only began in the late eighteenth century' (Honan, 1999: 180). Nonetheless, Honan argues that 'the poems take us inside Shakespeare's mind.... In this theatre of the mind it is rehearsal time, as he tries out this and that, tests his style, moods and perceptions, brings some lyrics to the highest levels of his art, or leaves others as simpler experiments' (Honan, 1999: 185).

The lapsed agnostic is Jonathan Bate (1997). He argues persuasively that 'it is a mistake to make a choice between biographical and anti-biographical readings' (p. 51), that we should 'allow the sonnets to rest in a middle space between experience and imagination' (p. 52), and concludes that 'the sonnets are best thought of as *imaginings of potential situations which might have grown* from the initial Southampton situation' (p. 53, Bate's italics). And then, with self-parodying awareness, he augments his earlier case for the Young Man as a composite of Southampton and Pembroke (p. 47), with his own Dark Lady as the wife of John Florio, Southampton's Italian tutor, in the period 1592–1594. He comments wryly on himself as a biographer who could have stepped out of Oscar Wilde's story, *The Portrait of Mr. W. H.*, as one 'unable to hold fast to my unbelief' (p. 58). By exposing his biographical vulnerability, Bate offers the most subtle insights into how biography can elucidate the theme of love in *The Sonnets* and into the magic they continue to exert over their readers. He locates the heart of *The Sonnets* not in the supposed story of the ups and downs of a triangular relationship, but in the two-way mirror of love itself. Taking his cue from Sonnets 3 and 22, Bate extrapolates the pervasive theme of the sequence in the question: 'Is love a reception within of the "thou", the beloved other perceived by the "eye", or is it a projection outward of the "I", the voracious self?' (p. 51). The rider to the instability of love is the generic instability of the language that expresses it: the voice of *The Sonnets* is self-consciously aware of its own rhetorical art.

(ii) Prejudice, Discrimination and the Law: The Merchant of Venice

What contribution can biography make to our understanding of one of the most controversial areas of Shakespeare's thinking – his representation of how the law deals with the prejudice and discrimination that arise from the competing ideologies that govern societies? For modern western audiences, *The Merchant of Venice* is (along with *The Taming of the Shrew*) the most uncomfortable of Shakespeare's plays. What does the twenty-first-century theatre do with sixteenth-century anti-Semitism? Remain true to its authentic voice? Reject it as an evil anachronism? Dilute its effect by deflecting interest on to the homosexual relationship between Antonio and Bassanio, or by shifting the emphasis so that the Christians become repulsive? Biography can document Shakespeare's sources (the medieval story *Il Pecorone*, The Dunce, printed in Milan in 1558); assess the influence of Marlowe's contemporary play, *The Jew of Malta*; inform us about the number, status and occupations of Jews in Elizabethan London; and give an account of the Portuguese Jew, Ruy Lopez, one of the Queen's physicians, found guilty of trying to poison her and of the public feeling this episode provoked. All of these matters, no doubt, had a bearing on Shakespeare's thinking and Honan (1999: 257–262) is a good guide to their significance (even allowing for his speculative suggestion that Shakespeare's revulsion at his own affluence in the wake of his son's death affected his dramaturgy). But the principal benefit of inferential biography is to help us resolve these awkward questions by interpreting the law in its contemporary historical context and by inferring, from the pattern of arguments and ideas in the play, the balance of thinking that is represented.

The clash of ideologies and cultures between Christianity and Judaism was a 'live' issue in the Elizabethan period (Greenblatt, 2004: 271–281; Gross, 1992: 20–23). Money, Antonio's trading wealth and especially Shylock's usury, is the driving force of the play. Its power resonates curiously in the context of a romantic comedy where the love story of the caskets provides both a fairy-tale framework and an alternative set of values to offset those of mercantile Venice. To many, money-lending in order to exact interest was sinful. Christian teaching was against it and, according to Gross (1992: 35), until the mid-sixteenth century it was also a criminal offence. But times were changing: the theological approach to money-lending was giving way to one defined by economic needs, such that Honan concludes that, in this context, 'it is only too plain that he [Shakespeare] had no personal prejudice against Jews or money-lenders' (Honan, 1999: 259).

The dramatic conflict of *The Merchant of Venice* is that the practice of usury, in the form of Shylock's infamous bond, runs up against the spirit and the letter of the law – and plays ghoulishly on the gap between them. 'At the play's heart is a conflict between Tudor common law and the mitigating equity of the Chancery courts. Shylock's bond stipulating a pound of Antonio's flesh, has the rigidity of statute law at its worst, whereas Portia *at first* represents the fairness of equity' (Honan, 1999: 258, my italics). But this is neither the way the trial ends, nor the only way of looking at its legal niceties. Honan tacitly recognises that Portia later uses the letter of the law against Shylock, with all the rigidity and none of the mercy she had so movingly preached, in order to defeat him legally; while Antonio humiliates him spiritually by demanding as part of his punishment that he renounce his religion (IV.i.83). Shakespeare's thought here about the law cannot be reduced to simplistic oppositions of Old Testament versus New Testament, justice versus mercy, intransigent Jew versus humane Gentile, or even 'the civil law of Portia pitted against the common law of Shylock' (Ackroyd, 2005: 234), though all of these contraries are present. In terms of the law, both sides use whatever weapons and arguments will enable them to win. Each is as ruthless as the other: the Jew demands a physical death; the Christian demands a spiritual death. Interpretation is all. Winning, not religion, is sacrosanct. Shakespeare leaves us balancing the scales of 'justice', wondering what the word means.

Yet, the clash of ideologies and cultures goes deeper than money. It lies beyond the reach of the law, within the very texture of religious belief. The first exchanges between Antonio and Shylock (I.iii) make clear that Shylock's hatred of Antonio is both religious and commercial, and that Antonio's hatred of Shylock is religious. Biography can interpret this history and remind us that, before any deal has been struck, the social context on which Shakespeare draws reflects the mutual loathing of two cultures, based on two religious dogmas, weighed down by their own histories. What Shakespeare exposes, through the way he presents this personal antipathy between Shylock and Antonio, is the spectre of institutional racism ingrained in the very tenets of their religious beliefs (Honan, 1999: 260). Here, too, as with justice, we are left wondering about the meaning of such beliefs, about their potential for evil as well as for good.

The essential contraries of *The Merchant of Venice* reside in the figure of Shylock – a deeply contradictory figure. As the villain in a romantic comedy whose evil plans are thwarted and who loses everything, he is a figure of fun. Yet, as the representative of a persecuted minority constantly the butt of religious and racial abuse, he elicits our sympathy. Shakespeare's portrayal is finely balanced (Wells, 1995: 159), extending even to Shylock's eloquent protest against anti-Semitism:

> I am a Jew. Hath not a Jew eyes? Hath not a Jew hands, organs, dimensions, senses, affections, passions? Fed with the same food, hurt with the same weapons, subject to the same diseases, healed by the same means, warmed and cooled by the same winter and summer as a Christian is? – If you prick us do we not bleed? If you tickle us do we not laugh? If you poison us do we not die? And if you wrong us shall we not revenge? – If we are like you in the rest, we will resemble you in that. (III.i.52–62)

Shylock's rhetorical questions make that most fundamental of all appeals – that to the recognition of our shared humanity; yet, within that easy phrase, as the final sentences show, lie the seeds of man's inhumanity to man. The rhetoric swells our sympathy for Shylock, only for it to fall as he single-mindedly pursues his bond, before it is partially restored with his humiliation at the end of the trial scene. As with the concepts of 'justice' and 'belief', so with the notion of cultural identity, the issue is left in the balance and we remain wondering how far Shylock the villain is also the victim of circumstances.

(iii) War and the Politics of Nationhood: Henry V

Henry V is not so much the story of Agincourt as essentially a debate about war. There is a lot of arguing, justifying, exhorting, praying and reflecting on this issue, from the theological and legal longiloquence of the Archbishop of Canterbury in Act I – which Shapiro relates to Bishop Lancelot Andrews's sermon prior to Essex's Irish campaign (Shapiro, 2005: 88–96) and Duncan-Jones to Shakespeare's preoccupation at the time with his attempts at self-gentrification (Duncan-Jones, 2001: 110) – to the sceptical challenge of Williams, the ordinary soldier, in Act IV whose view of the ethics of war subverts his leader's patriotic militarism (Nuttall, 2007: 159–165). To conduct this dialectic on warfare, Shakespeare both rewrites history and reads the runes of contemporary politics. He creates a theatrical portrait which mirrors the political order of Queen Elizabeth I's England and the tensions which beset it. To do so, he dramatises a period of national politics and battlefield triumph over six years, selectively chronicling events from 180 years earlier, between 1414 and 1420. Thus the play becomes a curiously inverted palimpsest where the present lies beneath a vivid picture of the past. Inferences about Shakespeare's thinking can be drawn from the two seminal images of the play: the monarch and the nation.

Henry V has two unique features which show that Shakespeare was deeply engaged with current political issues. No other play has a Chorus who speaks five prologues and an Epilogue whose main purpose is to promote the image of the monarch; and no other play contains such an explicit, contemporary political allusion as that which occurs in the prologue to Act V where the Queen, Essex and Henry V are deliberately linked. In describing Henry V's triumphant return to London after Agincourt, the Chorus urges the audience to imagine a similar scene:

> Were now the general of our gracious empress,
> As in good time he may, from Ireland coming,
> Bringing rebellion broached on his sword,
> How many would the peaceful city quit
> To welcome him!
>
> (V.i.30–34)

The Globe's audience would immediately have identified 'the general' as Essex and 'our gracious empress' as Queen Elizabeth. It is, as Shapiro notes, 'an extraordinary moment and the only time in his plays that Shakespeare breaks the theatrical illusion and directs playgoers' attention away from the make-believe world of his play to the real world outside the theatre' (Shapiro, 2005: 101). The Chorus acts as a poetic frame for the play's action, with a Prologue in epic tone and an Epilogue in the form of a valedictory sonnet. In between, he is dramatised narrator, continuity man, patriot and eulogist of the monarch, polite apologist for the limitations of the theatre and, especially at the start and before Agincourt, mouthpiece for some of Shakespeare's finest poetry. Shakespeare gives us a 'warlike Harry' who assumes 'the port of Mars' (Prologue); the rigorous and just monarch who deals summarily with corruption and treason (Act II); the determined leader who cannot be bought off (Act III); the 'royal captain' whose rapport with his troops gives them courage for the fight (Act IV); and the conquering hero who avoids triumphalism, 'Being free from vainness and self-glorious pride', and who attributes his victory to God (Act V). It is from these elements that the portrait of 'this star of England' (Epilogue) is created. The balance of qualities speaks out from this depiction: the demands of public leadership are tempered by the common touch; dignity and importance are free from pompousness and egotism; personal achievement is represented as gaining its value from public works on behalf of the nation in the service of God. Yet, Shakespeare balances this inflated choric image of the monarch with a different image of Henry in the play's action. The King's defensiveness and annoyance with Williams, who counters his arguments (IV.i); Henry's war crime in ordering the slaughter of the French prisoners (IV.vi); and his anger and violent retaliation at the French killing of the boys in the unguarded English tents (IV.vii) – all counterpoint the effusions of the Chorus. The inferential biographer may thus deduce: 'Shakespeare resists revelling either in reflexive patriotism or in a critique of nationalistic wars, though the play contains elements of both.... It wasn't a pro-war play or an anti-war play but a going-to-war play' (Shapiro, 2005: 104).

The concept of nationhood is, similarly, weighed in the balance. The spirit of national unity epitomised in Henry's rousing speeches in the face of a common enemy is counterpointed throughout the play by images of actual or potential disunity. As early as the second scene, the King is aware that a foreign war means that he must guard his back 'against the Scot' (I.ii.136–139); and the Archbishop of Canterbury, while urging him to invade France, counsels him to 'Divide your happy England into four', three-quarters of the forces to be left to defend the country. Just as Queen Elizabeth's position was vulnerable to plotters like the Earl of Essex, so was Henry's to traitors like Cambridge, Scroop and Grey (II.ii). Disunity, real or threatened, lies just below the surface of the play: treacherous factions in the aristocracy, disaffected subjects, soldiers who either exploit the war for their own ends intent on survival, or undermine morale by querying the King's motives. Shakespeare weaves all these anti-heroic elements into the texture of the play. The clearest example of the tension between unity and disunity is Shakespeare's inclusion of four officers, one each from the four nations of the British Isles. Captain MacMorris, the stereotypical, hot-blooded Irishman, takes issue with the voluble and affable Welshman, Fluellen, over the matter of nationhood.

> Fluellen: Captain MacMorris, I think, look you, under your correction, there is not many of your nation –
>
> MacMorris: Of my nation? What ish my nation? Ish a villain and a bastard and a knave and a rascal? What ish my nation? Who talks of my nation?
>
> (III.iii.64–68)

Shapiro explains the subtlety of Shakespeare's thought embedded in these exchanges:

> MacMorris's name may provide a clue to his defensiveness. The so-called Old English or Anglo-Norman, who had settled in Ireland centuries earlier, had adjusted to local custom by changing their names' original prefix 'Fitz' to the Gaelic 'Mac'. No wonder, then, the part-English, part-Irish, and part-Norman MacMorris is so touchy about his unfixed national identity: what is his nation? English? Irish? An Anglo-Irish mix? If so, what of his loyalties? (Shapiro, 2005: 109)

Shapiro also points out Shakespeare's 'obsessive interest in the play in dialects and in the connection between nationality and language' (Shapiro, 2005: 110). The violent rhetoric before Harfleur and the patriotic exhortation of the St Crispin's Day speech are offset by Williams's quiet, humane voice of scepticism: 'We few, we happy few' is countered by 'I am afeard there are few die well that die in a battle; for how can they charitably dispose of any thing when blood is their argument?' (IV.i.143–146). Nationhood, no less than the debates about warfare and monarchy, is essentially about language and the ways in which it reflects thinking. *Hamlet* represents this relationship directly.

(iv) Language and Thinking: Hamlet

> *What do you read, my lord?*
> *Words, words, words.*
> (II.ii.192–194)

> *... for there is nothing either good or bad but thinking makes it so.*
> (II.ii.249–250)

It has long been a truism that the centre of *Hamlet* is Hamlet's mind. We gain access to it through his soliloquies and learn that in and around Hamlet's head swirl the memories and demands of his father, the wickedness of his step-father, the anxieties and frailties of his mother, the bewilderment of his lover, the foolish and fatal intrigues of her father, the duplicities of false friends ... His seven soliloquies, those passages of self-communion, are dramatisations of the thoughts of a fevered mind. Yet, they are more than that. For, through his unfolding of Hamlet's particular consciousness, Shakespeare probes not only the dilemmas of an individual caught in a revenge plot, but the dilemmas of human existence – the questions of a sceptical humanity 'crawling between earth and heaven'. Moreover, the manner of these dramatisations creates a unique bonding between Hamlet and the audience. Hazlitt noted it when, writing about Hamlet's 'speeches and sayings', he commented: 'They are as real as our own thoughts. Their reality is in the reader's mind. It is *we* who are Hamlet.' This play is special because it is about thought itself. It dramatises the nature of human consciousness, probing the spaces between language and action, between what is said and what is done. Here, more than anywhere, we might expect some clues about the character of Shakespeare's thinking (Nuttall, 2007: 201–202).

Hamlet's existential questions frequently point beyond their immediate contexts, indeed beyond the play, towards a nihilistic sense of the impermanence of the human condition which most people can recognise, even if they do not directly experience it: 'What a piece of work is a man … and yet to me, what is this quintessence of dust?' 'To be, or not to be, that is the question.' 'Get thee to a nunnery, why woulds't thou be a breeder of sinners?' 'What should such fellows as I do crawling between earth and heaven?' 'What is a man /If his chief good and market of his time/Be but to sleep and feed?' As the Arden editor points out, 'Hamlet himself seems always to be asking questions much bigger and more searching than those we ask of him. When we expect him to be discussing whether and why and how he should revenge, he is liable to be ruminating on the mysteries of our being' (Shakespeare, ed. Jenkins, 1982: 125). Hamlet's questions grow beyond the needs of the revenge plot. They are questions posed by Shakespeare's own intellectual curiosity about the nature of man's lot. The revenge plot is the vehicle to dramatise the dilemma of polarising good and evil into moral absolutes when 'conscience' simultaneously demands and opposes action – the dilemma that Hamlet faces up to in his most famous soliloquy. And 'conscience', as Bate argues, contains a significant double meaning:

> The word 'conscience' in Elizabethan English did not only mean internal acknowledgement of the moral qualities of one's motives and actions. An older usage of the word was still audible: it could also refer to the mere presence of inward knowledge. 'Conscience' was 'consciousness'. It is Hamlet's extreme self-consciousness which sets him apart from the traditional revenger. When alone on stage, reflecting on his own situation, he seems to embody the very nature of human *being*; it is consciousness that forms his sense of self, his 'character' … (Bate, 1997: 257)

In this way, Bate concludes, 'Hamlet has become a universal dramatic character because he is an icon of human consciousness'. Unlike Hamlet's other soliloquies, 'To be, or not to be' (III.i.56–88) is not solely concerned with his personal predicament. It is cast in general terms; it deals with metaphysical matters; it is inclusive in its use of 'we', 'us' and 'all'. Prior to his statement that 'conscience does make cowards of us all', Hamlet poses two questions: one raises the issue of suicide; the other, the burdens of living. A gloomy prospect, yet his conclusion and his answer to the overriding question of 'To be, or not to be' are positive. He is resigned 'to be', 'to suffer' and 'to bear'. 'Conscience', the ethical demand to do what is right, and 'consciousness', the anxious reflections on what is, in practice, the right thing to do, both lead Hamlet to the conclusion that there is no alternative but to submit to the implacable nature of the human condition.

Jonathan Bate locates the tensions between language, thought and action in the two powerful iconic images of the play: the skull and the book. Hamlet, addressing Yorick's skull, is 'a memorable visible representation of mortality'; the complementary image is of Hamlet, 'the slender, melancholy prince, clad in black, holding a book'. The one is an 'icon of the body', the other an 'icon of the intellect' (Bate, 1997: 254). Character becomes icon when it transcends the play in which it appears, becoming detached from it and symbolising some more general human qualities. So here, Shakespeare remains the invisible man, whereas Hamlet, his creation, is visualised so tellingly that, holding Yorick's skull, he becomes the icon of everyman's mortality; and, reading from his book, he becomes the icon of language and thinking.

The inferences we can draw from *Hamlet* about Shakespeare's thinking derive from the nature of a play that exemplifies what it argues. The play's external actions are vehicles for its psychological movements, 'objective correlatives' for the arguments Hamlet conducts with himself, primarily in his soliloquies. Yet, typically covering his tracks, it is in the play-within-the-play that Shakespeare expresses the contraries at the heart of Hamlet's problem:

> Our wills and fates do so contrary run
> That our devices still are overthrown;
> Our thoughts are ours, their ends none of our own.
> (III.ii.206–208)

Bloom (1998: 426) comments: 'Desire and destiny are contraries, and all thought thus must undo itself.' Shakespeare's thinking suggests that we can devise means to our intended ends but we have no control over outcomes. Thinking, and the language in which it is cast, take us to the threshold of action, but they operate in a parochial dimension different from that of fate, which obeys no recognisable rules. Thinking and language, two sides of the same mental coinage, are unique to our humanity yet powerless in the face of unpredictable destiny.

(v) Art and Artifice: The Tempest

Islands, from those of Prospero and Caliban, Gulliver and Crusoe, to the desert islands of Ballantyne, Golding and the modern cartoonist, are favourite allegorical settings; and allegory, by its nature, invites diversity of interpretation. *The Tempest* is no exception. Political, religious and autobiographical readings of the play have all been made and, in recent times, revisionist readings stressing the historical context of Jacobean colonialism have proliferated. Do Shakespeare's self-imposed constraints of time and place in observing the neo-classical unities reflect some special quality in his thinking? Wells hints at such:

> The fact that he [Shakespeare] seems to have made up the story – such as it is – for himself, along with the obviously symbolic nature of the action, may suggest that the play reflects peculiarly personal concerns ... (Wells, 1995: 360)

The Tempest encapsulates the allegorical opposition of Prospero's Art and Caliban's Nature within the artifice of a dream-like pastoral romance. Two aspects of this allegory are especially significant in the present context. First, what does the play indicate about Shakespeare's thinking on the nature/nurture theme? And, by extension, how far will this theme bear interpretation in terms of colonisation? Secondly, how plausible is the claim that *The Tempest* is Shakespeare's farewell to the stage?

The central theme of the play is expressed explicitly in Prospero's assessment of Caliban as 'A devil, a born devil, on whose nature / Nurture can never stick' (IV.i.188–189). Yet neither of these characters represents unmixed evil or good. If Caliban is deformed in nature, unresponsive to the education which should improve him (I.ii.364–366), Shakespeare nonetheless shows that he can do rather more than curse by giving him the play's most poetic description of the island (II.ii.133–141). And if Prospero is ennobled by nurture, a scholarly and cultivated man endowed with supernatural powers, Shakespeare also shows that his most 'potent Art' is the instrument with which he not only controls the elements but also enslaves the life of Caliban. Nature and nurture both host contraries within themselves as well as being mutually opposed. Who is worse, Shakespeare invites us to ask, natural man like Caliban who knows no better than brutish behaviour, or the nobleman Antonio who usurps his own brother? And is not Prospero's usurpation of Caliban's island (I.ii.333–334) also morally indefensible?

The sharp focus on these issues is achieved through the narrowed lens of the unities of time and place. The colonising of the island began twelve years before the play opens. The full narrative of *The Tempest* needs to distinguish its *histoire* (the chronological sequence of events) which can be deduced from its *récit* (the text's representation of events). The whole play – itself the denouement of a long history – thus contains several issues and confrontations. The play's storm and magic are devices to bring these matters before us. The play's action is to resolve the political story and reconcile the brothers. The play's main theme is to explore the clash between 'indigenous man' whose birthright is the land he lives on and 'civilised man' who has the power and knowledge to take it over. Wells acknowledges that the issue of colonisation is embedded in the play: contemporary pamphlets on voyaging, generally accepted as having influenced its composition, and Caliban's justified complaint against Prospero's enslavement of him, both indicate that this issue was present in Shakespeare's consciousness. But to admit its relevance is not to endorse it as an exclusive interpretation. 'Prospero is, after all, a coloniser only upon compulsion' (Wells, 1995: 365–366). Wells's caution here (echoed, too, by Kermode, 2000: 300) is no doubt in reaction to the 1980s emphasis in both Britain and America upon *The Tempest* as a colonialist text. Post-colonial readings jostle with the conventional aesthetic interpretation of the play (Bate, 1997: 240). What is remarkable here, as in the other plays we have discussed, is that the quality and nature of Shakespeare's thinking render it uniquely open in its implications and suggestiveness while remaining uniquely balanced and coherent in its dramatic realisation.

But where does this leave the notion of *The Tempest* as a personal allegory? The nineteenth-century Romantic tradition stressed the intimacy between writers and their works. The most influential biography reflecting this emphasis was Dowden's *Shakespeare: His Mind and Art* (1875), published when it was customary to see *The Tempest* as Shakespeare's farewell to the stage and Prospero's Art as a symbol of the poet's genius. Subsequently, commentators have been more sceptical, but the play retains its power as a personal allegory (Nuttall, 2007: 376). One recent biographer comments: '*The Tempest* has seemed to many readers and audiences inescapably personal and valedictory ... a one-man show, with its central controlling consciousness a transparent image of that artist-magician William Shakespeare' (Duncan-Jones, 2001: 224). The famous lines after the masque, 'Our revels now are ended' (IV.i.148–158), are followed in the next scene by Prospero's assertion that his magical powers which have controlled the action are to be laid aside, for 'this rough magic/I here abjure' (V.i.50–51). The analogy with the playwright/director who manipulates the plot and characters for his own ends is inescapable and leads Duncan-Jones to describe *The Tempest* as 'the most revealingly personal of all Shakespeare's plays – the one in which his lifelong craft is most deeply woven into the text ... [his] last and most self-revealing work' (Duncan-Jones, 2001: 236). The Epilogue, the twenty lines of octosyllabic verse at the end of the play, compounds the issue. Is this last speech of Shakespeare's last, solely authored play a conventional appeal to the audience as Prospero steps out of his mage's role? Is it Shakespeare's farewell to the theatre? Or both? Wells comments on the dualism of Prospero's role:

> Prospero functions in the play as a ruler, a magician, a father, a teacher, a moralist, but also as an artist, the controller of the action of a play, the conjuror up of a vision that derives from the traditions of literature, a figure who, at whatever stage of the dramatist's career the play had been written, would inevitably have borne some relationship to the author himself. (Wells, 1995: 370)

And just twelve years after the composition of *The Tempest* and a mere seven years after Shakespeare's death, two of his colleagues chose to open their edition of the posthumous collected works with this play. Here, in the First Folio, Shakespeare is already the invisible artist: implied, revered, teasingly suggested in his Art, but never seen.

The Limits of Imagination

Henry James claimed that the author makes 'his reader very much as he makes his characters' (James, 1866: 485). One of the side effects of Shakespeare's invisibility is that he creates his biographers who, like characters in search of their author, assume a range of artistic forms through which to express themselves. The diversity in biographical studies of Shakespeare is a direct result of their subject's absence. Discounting the more popular 'Lives' which, while well informed, rely for their continuous narratives either upon secondary sources (Ackroyd, 2005; Bryson, 2008), or upon plugging the many gaps with tendentious theories (Holden, 1999; O'Connor, 1992), there are seven modern biographers in search of Shakespeare whose distinctive portraits we have drawn upon earlier to represent the range of inferential biography. They show the use and abuse of imagination, from Honan's 'Life' grounded in the 'Tudor social milieux' to Greenblatt's flights of fancy where evidence is repeatedly used to take off into speculation. Honan (1999: x) uses documentary evidence of Shakespeare's life 'in conjunction with other facts in the continuum of its own time'; Wells's *Shakespeare: A Life in Drama* (1995) treats Shakespeare as a man of the theatre; Duncan-Jones (2001: x) offers 'scenes from Shakespeare's life, not a comprehensive survey', adopting a method that is 'more thematic than narrative', with each chapter comprising 'a collection of short related essays' that often read like extended footnotes of the Arden editions of the plays to which they are kin; Bate (1997: x) expands the life beyond its chronological boundaries to include 'the pre-life' and 'the after-life' of Shakespeare's art – its origins and its effects that lie outside the years 1564–1616; Shapiro (2005) does the opposite, writing a micro-life of the crucial 'annus mirabilis' of 1599, the pivotal year upon which Shakespeare biography turns; Wood (2003: 382) 'argues that the key to Shakespeare's thought world is the traditional society of Warwickshire and the conflicts engendered in it by the Tudor Reformation'; and Greenblatt (2004: 14) attempts to understand 'how Shakespeare became Shakespeare' by following 'the verbal traces he left behind back into the life he lived and into the world to which he was so open'.

Greenblatt's case is helpful in marking the biographical boundaries, for he then adds the questionable comment that 'to understand how Shakespeare uses his imagination to transform his life into his art, it is important to use our own imagination'. Aside from the dubious notion that Shakespeare transformed his life into art, most biographers would acknowledge the danger signals in allowing the imagination to run free. The biographical imagination needs to be anchored in evidence – contemporary documents, the cultural and social conditions of the period, the subject's own writings – as indicated earlier. Inferential biography, in particular, is vulnerable to the seduction of unfettered imagination. Greenblatt's book begins:

> Let us imagine that Shakespeare found himself from boyhood fascinated by language, obsessed with the magic of words. There is overwhelming evidence for this obsession from his earliest writings, so it is a very safe assumption that it began early, perhaps from the first moment his mother whispered a nursery rhyme in his ear … (Greenblatt, 2004: 23)

Greenblatt then quotes two nursery rhyme lines, tells us that Shakespeare had these in mind when writing *King Lear*, and then launches into a romanticised rhapsody of the 'love and pleasure' of language in Elizabethan England. The shifts from 'Let us imagine' to 'a very safe assumption' to the definitive statement of a childhood rhyme recalled in *Lear* are biographical fantasies. Responsible biographers administer a stylistic antidote to such excesses in the hesitancies indicated by Shapiro earlier: 'perhaps', 'maybe', 'probably' and the like; and a more substantive antidote, by situating Shakespeare in the documented context of his times, the achievement of Honan's book, which still remains the standard 'Life'. Greenblatt's biographical method places the needs of narrative above those of historical evidence. How early are the 'earliest writings' mentioned above? Certainly, they are not from boyhood. Or again, on the question of whether Shakespeare left Stratford in the mid-1580s because he was caught deer-poaching (as Rowe, his first biographer, claimed), Greenblatt answers that what matters 'is not the degree of evidence but rather the imaginative life that the incident has' (Greenblatt, 2004: 151). In other words, what matters is to tell a good story. Biographers can make a case for their virtual Shakespeares in a range of ways, some of which inevitably lead to conjecture; but even when one finds conjectures implausible (as I find the speculation that Shakespeare was among the players from Leicester's Men in the Netherlands in 1586 (Duncan-Jones, 2001: 33–34)), the risks in making them are legitimate and worth taking as long as the historical imagination is disciplined by evidence. Six recent biographers contrive to do this, each contributing to the composite picture of Shakespeare; Greenblatt oversteps the limits of imagination, touching up the picture and compromising its authenticity.

So, what do such imaginations, varied as their approaches are, infer from Shakespeare's writings about Shakespeare's thinking? Two patterns stand out in their accounts of the life of the extraordinary mind that created the poems and plays. First, in the pattern of literary development across the two decades of Shakespeare's writing life, which is superficially associated with the changing genres of histories, comedies, tragedies and pastoral romances, there is a marked increased sophistication in language and thinking that occurred around the middle of his career. Secondly, there is the characteristic, dialectical mode of thinking which externalises opposing ideas in the characters and arguments in his plays and by which such contradictions (or 'play of contraries' in the apt phrase we have adopted from Ackroyd) are held in suspension.

The change in Shakespeare's language and thinking is, as we have seen, associated with his shift towards interiority in characterisation. Shapiro (2005: 152) pinpoints this development in 1599, locates its origins in Shakespeare's reading of Plutarch's *Lives*, and exemplifies it from *Julius Caesar*. He quotes Brutus's famous soliloquy as marking 'a significant breakthrough' in Shakespeare's development, 'a sense of inwardness new to the stage' which was to flower a few months later in *Hamlet*. Brutus, contemplating Caesar's murder, dwells in a state of mental limbo, seeking the language that will reconcile his moral scruples with his proposed action.

Between the acting of a dreadful thing
And the first motion, all the interim is
Like a phantasma or a hideous dream.
The genius and the mortal instruments
Are then in council; and the state of man,
Like to a little kingdom, suffers then
The nature of an insurrection.
(II.i.63–69)

The poetry takes us inside the mind of the character. The key words, 'interim' and 'insurrection', direct us inwards. The one lays out the mental space for Brutus's nightmare imaginings; the other, through the familiar image of the body politic, depicts the sense of internal rebellion that he is experiencing. As we eavesdrop on Brutus, or Hamlet, or Macbeth, brooding upon their dilemmas, we are experiencing the ebb and flow of their thought processes as ideas and feelings jostle with imagined actions. As Shapiro suggests, such transformations that occur in the mind between conception and execution are also germane to Shakespeare's own craft. It is as if Shakespeare is putting on stage his own interiority and, through this new form of characterisation, both expressing what his characters are undergoing and simultaneously representing what their creator is experiencing to bring them alive before us.

This preoccupation with the ways in which thinking, language and action are represented in staged narrative is linked to the other pattern in Shakespeare's thought, one that we have noted in all the writings we have discussed – his liking for 'the play of contraries'. Again, his thinking is intrinsically theatrical, imbued with the stage. All of the five themes, in fact, are represented as themes and variations. They invite conflicting notions of their meaning. They can be played in different ways. Shakespeare delights in oppositions, pairings, doublings, parodyings, reversals. Whether they occur within the thought-track of an individual mind, or in the identities of characters, or in the mirroring of plots and sub-plots, Shakespeare's 'contraries' are a constant. The alternative, stable-state agenda – our notions of the constancy of love, of the justice of the law, of the morality of warfare, of the rational nature of thought, of the power of art to represent us to ourselves – is challenged and subverted. Pretensions to truth are bogus, assumptions of moral and social superiority are folly when human beings are seen in perspective on their proper stage, 'crawling between earth and heaven', in the created universe. So Isabel warns Angelo in *Measure for Measure*:

... man, proud man,
Dress'd in a little brief authority,
Most ignorant of what he's most assur'd –

His glassy essence – like an angry ape
Plays such fantastic tricks before high heaven
As makes the angels weep.
(II.ii.118–123)

Man has no more understanding of his role in life's drama than a performing monkey. Yet, the mind that can create such an image can also have his most famous character say:

> What a piece of work is a man, how noble in reason, how infinite in faculties, in form and moving how express and admirable, in action how like an angel, in apprehension how like a god: the beauty of the world, the paragon of animals … (*Hamlet*, II.ii.303–307)

The dramatic oppositions in Shakespeare are essentially in the theatre of his mind. The theatre, both in metaphor and in practice, is the image of this drama. The actors, both as metaphors for mankind and as actual players, express both the absurdities and delights of the human condition. But the theatre image, Shakespeare's favourite figure for the world we inhabit, also implies an audience. In the theatre, the actors are the catalyst, but the mind of the spectator is the medium. So, the ultimate 'play of contraries' lives in the imaginations of the beholders. For the inferential biographer, this gives fresh significance to Shakespeare's closing lines of *The Tempest*. Prospero's Epilogue to the audience is Shakespeare's final comment on the theatre as metaphor: its 'art to enchant' needs the audience's response if its spell is to work and the 'project' not fail. Typically, Shakespeare leaves us wondering whether we have just caught a glimpse of an otherwise invisible man.

Note: *Jonathan Bate's biography* Soul of the Age: The Life, Mind and World of William Shakespeare *(Viking) appeared too late in 2008 to be considered. It should be read alongside his earlier book,* The Genius of Shakespeare *(Picador, 1997).*

6

Literary Biography and Portraiture

[The biographer] walks along a knife-edge. For he is under an equal obligation to art and to life; his book must be equally satisfying as picture and as likeness.

(David Cecil, 1936: xvi. Cited in Clifford, *From Puzzles to Portraits: Problems of a Literary Biographer*, 1962: 153)

At its most abstract, portraiture is a question of the relationship between the self as *art and the self* in *art.*

(Marcia Pointon, *Hanging the Head: Portraiture and Social Formation in Eighteenth-Century England*, 1993: 1)

Sister Arts

In *The Aspern Papers*, the first request that the nameless narrator makes to Miss Tina in his obsessive and devious search for information about Jeffrey Aspern's life is not, in fact, for the papers but for a portrait (James, 1888/1994: 61); and the last action in James's story finds the papers burnt and the hapless literary researcher gazing sadly at the portrait of the poet above his writing-table (p. 137). The visual image is little consolation for the loss of a biographical scoop. James's cautionary tale suggests three things: it indicates the ambivalence, if not hostility, that writers and their close family and friends commonly show towards biographers; it is a sign that literary portraits have a cultural status inferior even to that of literary biography; and it hints at the long historical connection that exists between the two arts.

In appropriating the term 'sister arts' from its common usage comparing poetry and painting and applying it to biography and portraiture, Wendorf (1990: 6, 18) and Pointon (1993: 85) are echoing Hazlitt's description of portrait-painting as 'the biography of the pencil' (i.e. the brush). But how valid is the comparison? Certainly, it had become common in aesthetic theory of the seventeenth and eighteenth centuries (Reynolds, 1770/1975: 50). Yet, as the pen portraits of Aubrey's *Brief Lives* grew into Boswell's 'Flemish picture' of the *Life of Dr. Johnson*, the sheer size and documentary detail made the analogy with visual portraiture less appropriate even as it gained currency. Given that there is some historical validity in the comparison, is sisterhood actually anything more than a loose metaphor? Does portrait-painting arise from the same motives and share the same purposes as biography? Despite the longevity of the analogy, it will become apparent in what follows that the similarities are limited, and that portrait-painting owes more to the conventions and contexts of visual art than it does to biography, to which it bears only a tangential relationship. Nonetheless, their associated histories and overlapping purposes – as well as their material differences – confer a relevance that invites consideration. The caution necessary in any comparative study of these 'sister arts' urged by Hagstrum (1958) and Wendorf (1990) is salutary; 'sister arts' is an easy phrase that obscures the distinctive characters of biography and portraiture behind their outward appearances. Accordingly, this chapter offers a gallery of ten portraits, each with an accompanying commentary designed to link them thematically to aspects of literary biography dealt with in other chapters. The relationship of these sister arts is closer in some respects than others and, like any relationship, it changes over time. Two general issues arising from this gallery are the origins and cultural standing of these verbal and visual portraits and, secondly, their role in respect of the literary canon, both matters that are taken up in the final section.

(i) Biography and Portraiture: Reynolds's Portrait of Dr Johnson

Most portraits are painted of living subjects; most biographies chronicle the dead. Dr Johnson was painted five times by his friend, Sir Joshua Reynolds, over a twenty-five-year period. The image here is the earliest, depicting 'Dictionary Johnson' at the height of his fame within a year of the publication of his monumental work. Boswell, on the other hand, did not meet Johnson until six years later, an occasion famously described in his *Life of Dr. Johnson* (1791) on the basis of his journal entries made shortly after the unexpected encounter in Davies's bookshop on 16 May 1763 (Sisman, 2001: 23, 28–30). On Johnson's death, Reynolds gave the painting to Boswell who had it engraved (with the additions of an inkstand, the Dictionary, and a larger desk), and used it as the frontispiece for his biography. Wendorf (1990: 286–290) suggests that Boswell chose this image with its added writer's 'props', rather than any later one, to cement his position as biographer, to promote the most favourable picture of his subject and, perhaps, to offset the more critical verbal portraits he had drawn in his biography which were themselves much gentler than his original impressions in his journal, where he had described Johnson as 'a man of a most dreadful appearance'. Certainly, Reynolds's portraits of an admittedly older Johnson are not as flattering as this one. Boswell and Reynolds seem to have conspired to show their friend at his optimum.

How does Reynolds's picture create the likeness and character of Dr Johnson? Johnson's physical distinctiveness – his massive frame, large facial features and ungainly bulk – are all suggested by Reynolds. Compare this with the verbal portrait that Boswell records as his impression a few days after he first met Johnson (Boswell, 1791/1949, I: 245). Clearly, Reynolds's portrait is a tidier, cleaner image; Boswell's has more of the authentic likeness that Johnson's friends – including Reynolds – would recognise. Reynolds portrays his subject as the man of letters identified by the tools of his trade, the quill pen, the papers on his writing desk, and captures him in a thoughtful, reflective moment. The self-absorbed gaze, cocked head and clenched fingers of his left hand imply that Johnson is looking inwards, pausing for thought. Johnson's gaze, complicated as we know from Boswell (1791/1949, I: 16) by his partial blindness in his left eye, is the key to the picture, suggesting a man for whom the life of the mind is more important than external appearances. Reynolds leans towards classical hagiography: this is as much a portrait of 'the great man' as of the close friend. It has none of the detail of a Boswellian 'Flemish picture'; the room is clear of domesticity, the background and surroundings bare and shadowy; the light focuses us on the

Figure 6.1 Sir Joshua Reynolds, *Samuel Johnson* (1756–1757). Oil on canvas, 127.6 × 101.6 cms. National Portrait Gallery, London

head. Everything encourages us to see Johnson as the intellectual giant of the age engaged in his prime activity – what Boswell called 'the art of thinking'.

Boswell's biography has numerous word pictures of Johnson to keep his subject continuously before the reader. They range from brief cameo glimpses to more elaborate portraits. Perhaps the best known introduces his celebrated conclusion to his 'Life' (Boswell, 1791/1949, II: 614). It is a portrait which is far from flattering, sketching in Johnson's face, figure, dress and ways of looking and moving – cumbersome and comical by turns – giving the reader enough to create a mental picture and achieving a sense of animation that is denied to visual portraiture. Reynolds rightly said that 'What is done by Painting, must be done at one blow' (Reynolds, 1770/1975: 146). His interpretation of Johnson's character is frozen at a particular time and works through the suggestibility of pose, expression, setting and the inclusion of significant details. Biography lacks the immediacy of impact but can paint a whole gallery of pictures to convey its subject's multiple selves.

(ii) Reading the Image: Cassandra Austen's Sketch of Jane Austen

These two interrelated images of Jane Austen were made sixty years apart. Cassandra, two years older than Jane, inherited the manuscripts and effects on her sister's death in 1817, preserving some, destroying others, and distributing items among family members. If other portraits from life exist, then they have not come to light, although there are contenders, notably the oil painting thought to be by Ozias Humphry, known as the 'Rice Portrait' (1792–1793). However, Cassandra's small pencil sketch, with Jane's face and hair in watercolour, is regarded as the only authentic likeness (Cassandra also did a back view of her sister, seated out of doors). The second image was engraved in steel from a portrait made from Cassandra's sketch by James Andrews, a professional artist commissioned by Jane's nephew, James Edward Austen-Leigh. It formed the frontispiece to Austen-Leigh's *Memoir of Jane Austen* in 1870.

Formally, the different media help to create two quite distinct images: the unsophisticated, seemingly unfinished, pencil sketch offers us little more than an expressive face; the engraving sets Jane in an elegant chair against a dark background showing her in a simple indoor dress and framing her face in the ruffles of her collar and mob-cap. As visual biographies, they portray two different personalities. Cassandra's sketch represents her sister as a sharp-featured, tight-lipped young woman with a determined, intense, maybe censorious, look. The engraving shows her soft-featured, modest, mild, thoughtful – even the curls of her hair are gentler. How far either image accurately represents the original in life is unknown; but it is easier to imagine Cassandra's Jane as the writer, the ironic observer of domestic lives, and to imagine the Victorian Jane as the angel in the house ready to assume her domestic duties.

Biographically, there is a curious mismatch in the 'Jane' we have inherited: Cassandra's picture, endlessly reproduced, is the unflattering visual image of a woman with opinions who knows her own mind; but the character so often promoted as existing behind the image is that of 'St Aunt Jane of Steventon-cum-Chawton Canonicorum' (Sutherland, 2002: xv), the figure who is depicted in Austen-Leigh's hagiographic memoir with its sanitised frontispiece. In this sense, the two pictures stand for the two opposing personalities that have developed over the last two centuries: the 'English Heritage' Jane, and the 'more robust, less sanctified' Jane seen in a social context, riven by class divisions and driven by money, towards which she may be deemed to take either an oppositional or supportive stance (Lee, 2005: 72–74).

Figure 6.2 Cassandra Austen, *Jane Austen* (*c*.1810). Pencil & watercolour, 11.4 × 8.0 cms. National Portrait Gallery, London

Figure 6.3 James Andrews/Lizars, *Jane Austen* (1870). Steel-engraved portrait for Austen-Leigh's *Memoir*. National Portrait Gallery, London

(iii) Visual Myth-Making: Henry Weekes's Shelley Monument

Many writers on portraiture have commented on its dual nature: its commitment to representing a 'likeness', together with its drive to go beyond likeness towards representing a conventional or idealised 'type' (West, 2004: 24). Portraits of literary people offer some clear examples. Jonathan Richardson's portrait of Pope (*c.*1737, National Portrait Gallery), showing him in dignified profile, crowned with a laurel wreath like a writer from classical antiquity, aspires beyond likeness to become a symbol of the Augustan Age. Similarly, our visual image of Tennyson is filtered through cultural and conventional lenses, further complicated by the technology of the camera. Through Watts's portraits (he painted seven portraits of the poet between 1856 and 1890) and Julia Margaret Cameron's series of photographs (taken between 1860 and 1875), Tennyson has become an icon of the Victorian Age. His own preferred image of himself – Cameron's photo which he famously dubbed 'the Dirty Monk' – is both a representation of 'likeness' and a projection of him as a prophet of the times. In the period between Pope and Tennyson, the corresponding image is that of Shelley, especially as caught in Aemelia Curran's painting (1819) showing him almost full-faced, large-eyed and framed by his open-necked white shirt. Despite widespread dissatisfaction at the picture shared by the artist, critics and biographers (Holmes, 1987: 512), Curran's Shelley has become the icon of the Romantic Age.

However, literary subjects seem particularly susceptible to being transformed into something other than the iconic types of their age. Henry Wallis's *Chatterton* (1856) and Henry Weekes's Shelley Monument at the Priory Church, Christchurch, Hampshire (1854) both express the mid-Victorian myth of the youthful Romantic poet, beautiful in death, and invested with a quasi-religious aura. Both have lost contact with their subjects. The artists have substituted mythologised images – Chatterton modelled literally by Wallis's friend, the novelist George Meredith, in what looks like a 'still' from a Victorian melodrama; Shelley, the doomed poet washed ashore into the arms of Mary, his wife, modelled as a *pietà* – 'a curious tribute', as Piper remarks, 'to a notorious atheist' (Piper, 1982: 163)!

The Shelley monuments – for there is another more famous one by Onslow Ford (1894) installed behind bars in a special shrine in University College, Oxford – are potent examples of the visual myth-making that the poet's short life and dramatic drowning in the Gulf of Spezia attracted. During the nineteenth century, pictures (notably Louis Fournier's painting, *The Cremation of Shelley*, 1889), memoirs and poems, as well as monuments, invented an image of Shelley more as an angelic spirit than as a man of flesh

Figure 6.4 Henry Weekes, *Memorial to Percy Bysshe Shelley* (1854). Marble. Priory Church, Christchurch, Hampshire

and blood, what Holmes (1995: 151) calls 'the Ariel syndrome'. It was this received biographical image, summed up in Matthew Arnold's description of Shelley as 'a beautiful and ineffectual angel, beating in the void his luminous wings in vain', that Holmes set out to explode in his celebrated biography of the poet. What makes this image especially resistant, as Holmes says elsewhere, is that 'Shelley's death was used to define an entire life, to frame a complete biography. It produced not hagiography, but thanatography' (Holmes, 2004: 2). The makeovers of Shelley's death in the monuments by Weekes and Onslow Ford, in which 'likeness' and even the iconic 'type' of the Romantic Age have been submerged in favour of myth, suggest a pattern akin to that described in Chapter 4 – a process of visual biomythography.

(iv) Celebrity Image: Thomas Phillips's Portrait of Byron in Albanian Dress

'I awoke one morning and found myself famous.' The exhibition at the National Portrait Gallery in 2003, 'Mad, Bad and Dangerous: The Cult of Lord Byron', quotes Byron's well-known remark on the fervour following the publication of his *Childe Harold's Pilgrimage, Cantos 1 and 2* in March 1812. It describes the poet as 'a superstar'. Byromania, to use his wife's term, took off during the next few years. The 'Byron' we have now is a construct of numerous portraits, eye-witness accounts, memoirs and biographies and, of course, the poet's own thinly disguised self-representation in his works.

Thomas Phillips's portrait of Byron in Albanian dress gives us Byron the performer. The National Portrait Gallery image is a copy by Phillips of his original in the British Embassy in Athens. It shows the poet in the Albanian costume he bought in 1809. It is one of over forty portraits – oils, drawings, miniatures and busts – made during his lifetime, many of which were widely disseminated in engraved versions in books and magazines. Byron was complicit in the process of his visual representation, if not always pleased with the results and sufficiently provoked, in the case of Thorvaldsen's bust, to pillory the sculptor in verse (*Don Juan*, Canto 1, vs. 218). He cultivated and protected his image, dieting to counter his tendency to plumpness, instructing John Murray, his publisher, to destroy any pictures of him of which he did not approve. The dandy in Byron enjoyed dressing up, and it seems clear that he relished this particular commission (MacCarthy, 2003: 216).

Phillips gives us the dazzling Byronic surface – colourful and theatrical, bringing out the dark eyes, white skin and sensual mouth, showing him as the dashing adventurer, cradling a sheathed sword, standing half-turned with a touch of aristocratic hauteur. Criticism has focused on Phillips's superficiality: 'a vapid portrait ... a superficial realisation of the romantic, Byronic hero' (Brilliant, 1997: 101); and for Piper the portrait has 'a very unconvincing whiff of fancy-dress ball, or of Hollywood spectacular, almost Errol Flynn playing Byron' (Piper, 1982: 130). This picture was exhibited at the Royal Academy in 1814 alongside Phillips's second portrait, showing Byron in more poetic pose with a dark cloak and open-necked shirt. Hazlitt was as critical as later commentators, finding the images 'too smooth, [they] seem, as it were, "barber'd ten time o'er"' (quoted in Piper, 1982: 127). But, is it fair to direct these criticisms solely at the painter? Isn't the extroversion of the subject an integral part of his character? Whatever our judgements of Phillips's pictures, there is little doubt that he caught the performer in Byron, the poseur who alienated some and attracted many, making him both romantic hero and diabolic anti-hero, both man of action and brooding,

Figure 6.5 Thomas Phillips, *George Gordon Byron, 6th Baron Byron* (1835). Oil on canvas, 76.5 × 63.9 cms. National Portrait Gallery, London

melancholy poet. In neither portrait are the usual details of the writer's work depicted – no pen, paper, books or desk; such trademarks would be just that – they would demean the aristocrat for whom poetry was to be seen as a pursuit to be fitted into the hectic context of social life. Phillips painted two of Byron's many selves. Byron's tendency to depression, as Fiona MacCarthy has pointed out (MacCarthy, 2002), made him prone to mood swings that still affect celebrities today, dependent on the signs of adulation yet detesting them. And she quotes some lines Byron penned in 1816 which show his sardonic humour at being cast in the role of the heartthrob of his age:

> With false Ambition what
> had I to do?
> Little with love, and least of
> all with Fame!
> And yet they came unsought
> and with me grew,
> And made me all which they
> can make – a Name.

(v) Visual Memoir: Joseph Severn's Portrait of John Keats

The emphasis in a biography is upon the subject's developing self, written either by a contemporary or by a literary historian, sometimes centuries after the subject's death. The focus of a memoir is a personal selection of particular, maybe intimate, reminiscences, commonly written by a family member or close friend.

Joseph Severn (1793–1879), a minor artist, was just such a friend of John Keats, whose portrait he painted on many occasions. Perhaps the best-known pictures are his miniature, which hung in the Royal Academy Exhibition at Somerset House in 1819 – against Keats's friendly advice (Keats's letter to Joseph Severn, 29 March 1819); his *Keats Listening to the Nightingale on Hampstead Heath* (1845), painted almost a quarter of a century after Keats's death; and his *John Keats* (1821), painted shortly after the poet died in February of that year, and which Severn himself has described in terms of a visual memoir:

> After the death of Keats the impression was so painful on my mind, that I made an effort to call up the last pleasant remembrance in this picture which is posthumous. This was at the time he first fell ill and had written the 'Ode to the Nightingale' (1819) on the morn[ing] of my visit to Hampstead. I found him sitting with the two chairs as I have painted him and I was struck with the first real symptom of sadness in Keats so finely expressed in that poem. (Saumarez Smith, 1997: 112)

Severn had sailed with Keats to Italy in September 1820 in the hope that the milder climate would improve Keats's health; he was his constant companion during the poet's final months as he battled vainly against tuberculosis in what he called his 'posthumous existence'. For seven hours on 23 February Keats lay in his friend's arms before he died, seemingly calm and free of pain (Gittings, 1968/2001: 429). The traumatic memory of this experience is fused with the mental image of his visit to Keats two years earlier and with the Ode that Keats had written that day. Perhaps Severn recalled particularly the lines in stanza six:

> Darkling I listen; and, for many a time
>   I have been half in love with easeful Death,
> Call'd him soft names in many a mused rhyme,
>   To take into the air my quiet breath;
> Now more than ever seems it rich to die,
>   To cease upon the midnight with no pain,
>   While thou art pouring forth thy soul abroad

Figure 6.6 Joseph Severn, *John Keats* (1821). Oil on canvas, 56.5 × 41.9 cms. National Portrait Gallery, London

In such an ecstasy!
Still wouldst thou sing, and I have ears in vain –
To thy high requiem become a sod.
(Keats, 'Ode to a Nightingale', lines 51–60)

The studied informality of Severn's portrait with the young poet as an absorbed reader beneath a picture of Shakespeare places Keats in the context of literary history; and the richness of the natural world seen through the open doorway evokes the sensuous language that is the signature of his poetry.

(vi) Bardography: The Chandos Portrait of Shakespeare

Graphic representations of Shakespeare in the past four centuries occur in a wide variety of media and styles (Piper, 1982), yet our knowledge of Shakespeare's appearance remains as sketchy as it is of his documented life. Many of the attempts to visualise this invisible man show traces of the two posthumous portraits, made shortly after his death in 1616, which were commissioned either by Shakespeare's family or by his friends who must have judged them to be acceptable likenesses. The two portraits are the memorial bust by Gheerart Janssen which forms part of the Shakespeare monument erected in Holy Trinity Church, Stratford-upon-Avon (*c*.1620); and the engraving by Martin Droeshout the Younger which appeared on the title page of the First Folio edition of Shakespeare's plays compiled by his fellow actors, John Heminges and Henry Condell, in 1623. Differences in the graphic media and in the apparent age of the subject could account for the dissimilarities – the bust shows a balding, robust man in middle age; the engraving shows a younger man with the same receding hair and domed forehead but with more sensitive features. While neither image is an example of distinguished portraiture, both are authenticated as having been created close to the life of the subject.

In the search for a painted portrait, the exhibition 'Searching for Shakespeare' at the National Portrait Gallery in 2006 presented six contenders. The first four are all thought to originate in the period of Shakespeare's lifetime. They are:

- The Chandos Portrait (*c*.1600–1610), attributed to John Taylor and 'regarded as authentic within the living memory of the playwright' (Cooper, 2006: 52).
- The Grafton Portrait (1588), by an unknown artist, showing a portrait of an unidentified gentleman, aged 24, the same age as Shakespeare.
- The Sanders Portrait (1603), by an unknown artist, purporting to show Shakespeare at the age of 40.
- The Janssen Portrait (*c*.1610), by an unknown artist, now thought to be of Thomas Overbury, and fabricated to look like Shakespeare.

The two later contenders, the Soest Portrait (*c*.1661) and the Flower Portrait (*c*.1820–1840), date from long after Shakespeare's death and cannot claim to be authentic likenesses.

The Chandos Portrait opposite has been accepted as Shakespeare since the mid-seventeenth century. There is much evidence to support this claim but

Figure 6.7 John Taylor (attributed), *William Shakespeare* (*c*.1600–1610). Oil on canvas, 55.2 × 43.8 cms. National Portrait Gallery, London

no conclusive proof of likeness or even of identity (Cooper, 2006: 54–61). The picture shows Shakespeare against a feigned oval background, brown-eyed and fairly dark featured, with a receding hairline, domed forehead, a light beard and moustache, looking straight out at the viewer with just a hint of quiet amusement in his expression. The earring, which looks startlingly modern, was, in fact, a not uncommon fashion accessory for men in the early seventeenth century. The facial features bear comparison with the bust and the engraving; and the dress is typical of the period and appropriate for Shakespeare's status in life. The evidence is circumstantial but, until the unlikely discovery of a stronger contender, this is Shakespeare.

Note: *While this book was going through the press, just such an unlikely discovery was made public. In March 2009, it was announced that the Cobbe Portrait (c.1610) has a strong claim to be an authentic painting of Shakespeare. Opinions, as ever, are divided.*

(vii) The Inner Life: R. W. Buss's Dickens's Dream

Neither the biographer nor the portrait-painter can access that singularly vital area of their literary subject that we most want to know about – the author's inner life that provides the source of the creative impulse. Among the authors themselves, some are more reflective upon the nature of their activity than others; many feel that to enquire too closely would inhibit their creativity. Diaries, notebooks, drafts, the available documentary evidence, are the visible traces of creative work already past. Virginia Woolf is unusual in the degree to which she used her diary to talk to herself about her own process of writing; but even her persistent and penetrating insights into the representation of human identity in both fiction and auto/biography reveal little about the unknown world inside the head.

The portrait-painter has even less chance of exploring this territory and has to settle for suggesting the author pausing for thought, pen in hand (Reynolds's *Dr Johnson*); or lost in a book (Severn's *John Keats*); or, as in Robert William Buss's unfinished, partly coloured painting, *Dickens's Dream* (*c*.1875), showing the author seated in his study chair, his eyes open but seeing nothing but his inward imaginings as he dreams about his characters. As a young artist, Buss had been chosen to illustrate the serialised version of *The Pickwick Papers* but, to his great disappointment, his efforts were judged unsatisfactory. Yet, no artist of his generation could remain immune from Dickens's characters; this was Buss's tribute on the novelist's death (Ackroyd, 1999: 193–194). The figures float around the room: Little Nell with her basket perches on Dickens's knee, gazing at her creator; and, beyond the diminutive Paul Dombey in red, she is shown again all in white on her death-bed. Moving left into the uncoloured area, Little Dorrit approaches the door to the Marshalsea Prison; and Jo the crossing sweeper sits with his broom. Above Jo, there is a cluster of characters from *David Copperfield*: David is shown arriving at the cottage of his formidable and kindly great-aunt, Betsey Trotwood; Steerforth speaks with the tiny figure of Miss Mowcher; Peggotty and his nephew, Ham, stand at the doorway of their home, a converted barge on the beach, while behind them the sea sweeps the wreckage of a boat towards the shore, prefiguring Ham's tragic drowning; and, above them, an older David is seen weeping at the death-bed of his wife, Dora. There are dozens more figures in this ghostly gallery, around the walls, the bookshelves, the windows and the floor, some more finished and more easily identifiable than others, depicting a wide range of Dickens's creations from the haunted Scrooge, top right, to the portly Mr Pickwick holding forth while standing on a chair, top left. The figures serve as souvenirs of the creatures of Dickens's mind and raise questions about the representation and mythologizing of the author and his characters. How did Buss arrive at his portrait of Dickens, given that he painted it after the author's

Figure 6.8 Robert William Buss, *Dickens's Dream* (1875). Watercolour, 70.0 × 90.0 cms. The Charles Dickens Museum, London

death, and at his representations of these recognisably Dickensian characters? Buss's Dickens shows the novelist towards the end of his career, his head similar to that of the albumen print of 1858 by Herbert Watkins (National Portrait Gallery) (Kitton, 1899: 56). The characters are mostly copies of work by other illustrators: David Copperfield's arrival at Betsey Trotwood's cottage derives from the well-known picture by Phiz; while standing on the floor, as it were, to the left of Dickens are two male figures facing each other who derive from Marcus Stone's illustration of Pip 'taking leave of Joe' in *Great Expectations*. *Dickens's Dream* is really Buss's dream, one which combines an imagined Dickens taken from a contemporary photograph with the virtual projections of the novelist's mind reworked from the representations of earlier illustrators. Buss's picture is a visualisation that Ackroyd draws upon to suggest that Dickens lived his inner life through his characters. As was noted in Chapter 4, in the Interlude set in the Geffrye Museum, he has Dickens ask his biographer: 'Are you saying that I live in a world of my own devising?' And he follows this up with Dickens's concern for 'the books that will remain unwritten and the characters who will stay unborn. I have so many of them in my head, you know, I *see* so many of them in front of me' (Ackroyd, 1999: 795).

(viii) Sisters' Arts: Vanessa Bell's Portrait of Virginia Woolf

I cannot remember a time when Virginia did not mean to be a writer and I a painter.

(Vanessa Bell, quoted in Dunn, *Virginia Woolf and Vanessa Bell: A Very Close Conspiracy*, 2000: 126)

The painting of Virginia Woolf seated in an armchair is one of four early portraits of her by her sister executed during 1911–1912. The picture is nearly square, painted on a panel with broad, often rough, brush strokes or dabs of colour. The wing-backed chair is very close to the picture plane with the figure inclined towards the viewer, her left shoulder dropped as she concentrates on her knitting. Her hands, particularly her left one, are crudely delineated but her face and head, though free of physiognomic detail, are remarkably suggestive of her person, caught through three characteristic features: the contours of her elongated face, the hair parted in the middle and the prominent nose. The sense of repose and absorption in the painting is emphasised by the diagonal lines of her body recumbent within the black horizontal and vertical outlines given to the chair and background shapes, and by the dominant warm colouring in orange, flesh tones and pale green. The yellow ground colour is allowed to show through, adding an inner glow to the whole composition.

Picturing a likeness is not the issue here. The face is all but featureless; indeed, the refusal to depict the left eye looks almost like a deliberate piece of overpainting, as if revealing such a telling detail would deflect attention from the personality of her sister to mere surface appearance. As in her portrait of *Virginia Woolf in a Deckchair*, where the facial features are totally blank, Vanessa Bell reflected the aesthetic stance of Bloomsbury which emphasised the formal autonomy of art. The modernist character of the picture is expressed through the Bloomsbury aesthetic in which 'the artist's aim is to discover expressive form in order to reveal the underlying reality that is parallel with or equivalent to the reality of daily life' (Shone, 1999: 13). The absence of detail, the simplified lines and firm contrasts in colours owe much to Bell's awareness of Matisse's paintings, which she was familiar with in connection with the Second Post-Impressionist Exhibition that she helped Roger Fry to hang at the Grafton Galleries in the same year (Gruetzner Robins, 1997: 10). Vanessa Bell's shift away from portraiture's emphasis on significant details parallels her sister's impatience with biography's burden of facts. Here, the difficult shift in going beyond catching a likeness to capturing identity is made more achievable, since her subject is the person about whom she possessed a more intimate knowledge than any other painter or

Figure 6.9 Vanessa Bell, *Virginia Woolf* (1912). Panel, 39.5 × 33.0 cms. National Portrait Gallery, London

biographer. In both this portrait and the Deckchair portrait, commentators now and then suggest that Bell has captured the personality of her sister. Of the latter picture, Shone says what is true of both, that 'the image would have been instantly recognised by those who knew her', and he quotes Leonard Woolf as saying that 'It's more like Virginia in its way than anything else of her' (Shone, 1999: 99). The implication is that by denying herself the easy masks of representational details of her subject's features and any iconic references to her occupation, Vanessa Bell has forced the viewer to contemplate the 'underlying reality' of her subject; to see a personality that is contemplative, self-absorbed, retiring, still, whose vibrant imaginative life is implied in the rich colours and firm composition of the portrait. Her aesthetic principle is what, in painting, her husband called 'significant form' (C. Bell, in Alperson, 1992: 120); it shares an affinity with her sister's aspirations for biography in her well-known desire for life-writing to go beyond the 'granite' of mere facts and seek the 'rainbow' of personality.

(ix) 'To prepare a face ...': Patrick Heron's Portrait of T. S. Eliot

The biographer and the portrait-painter have to contend with the same impossible challenge: how to respond to the multiple perspectives of their subject lodged in the mind. Our sense of another's identity, as Virginia Woolf constantly reminds us, is plural, multi-faceted, elusive; and, to represent this sense, art must work by inference and association, selecting and juxtaposing significant fragments of being in its efforts to catch the flow and texture of life as it is experienced. The contemporary in whose work Virginia Woolf saw this happening was not, as might be expected, James Joyce, but T. S. Eliot (Briggs, 2006a: 251). Given this sense of identity in Eliot, and his awareness, expressed in *Prufrock*, of the impulse 'To prepare a face to meet the faces that you meet', Patrick Heron's empathy with his subject is felt both in the evocation of Eliot's personality and in the semi-Cubist style he adopts to represent him.

The artist himself has described how he came to paint the portrait. It was completed towards the end of 1949 after he had made some drawings and a study in oils from a number of sittings during 1947 and 1949 (Saumarez Smith, 1997: 203). Eliot, as ineluctably as any other sitter, must have prepared a face to meet the scrutiny of the artist. The portrait is built up from fragmentary lines and irregular blocks of colour with the figure only sketchily differentiated from its background. There is little sense of pictorial depth; the shapes surrounding and encroaching on the figure are non-representational, subdued in tone, with occasional suggestive fragments such as the outline of a (practical?) cat to the left of Eliot's head. The focus is on the face. We are given two images of T. S. Eliot: the full face evoking a person of sombre thoughtfulness; the profile offering a more direct, penetrating look. The subtlety is not only in the technique but in its implications. Is the full face overlaid with the profile, or the profile embedded within the full face? The two images are one, implying two of Eliot's multiple selves; implying, too, that as viewers we cannot attend to both at once. We can be aware of the two images, we can remember one while looking at the other, and we can switch rapidly between them, but we cannot actually experience them simultaneously. This is the point with which Gombrich opens and closes his classic work, *Art and Illusion*, choosing as his illustration the trick drawing 'Rabbit or duck?' (Gombrich, 1960: 4–5, 331–332). When applied to portraiture, it reminds us that our perception of another person is not only limited by nature and circumstances, but also tends to become an *idée fixe*. Art, as here in Patrick Heron's picture, can free us from the distortion of the single, unified image. Heron has created the illusion of T. S. Eliot for us in a

Figure 6.10 Patrick Heron, *T. S. Eliot* (1949). Oil on canvas, 76.2 × 62.9 cms. National Portrait Gallery, London.

representation suggesting plurality; but, more than that, he has done so via technical means that themselves reflect Eliot's modernist style. That he was aware of how intimately his style reflected his subject's is apparent in some remarks he made on the art of Juan Gris where he explicitly likens Eliot's poetry to Cubist painting:

> The processes are remarkably similar … it is obvious that Mr Eliot's compressed images, with their invisible interstices of association between image and image, phrase and phrase, are very closely related, as a mode of communication, to the segmented visual statements of Cubist painting. (Patrick Heron, in Gooding, 1998: 35)

(x) Branwell's Ghost: Branwell Brontë's Portrait of his Three Sisters

One of the most instantly recognisable portraits of literary figures, along with the Chandos Portrait of Shakespeare and Reynolds's of Dr Johnson, is Branwell Brontë's picture of his three sisters. It is an undistinguished, clumsily executed portrait in poor condition which owes its fame wholly to the importance of its subjects. After Charlotte's death in 1855, the picture remained with her husband, the Reverend Arthur Nicholls, who so disliked it that it lay for many years folded up and creased on top of his wardrobe where it was discovered after his death in 1906 by his second wife.

The picture shows three teenage sisters, aged 14, 16 and 18, painted by their 17-year-old brother. From left to right are Anne (1820–1849), Emily (1818–1848) and Charlotte (1816–1855). The two younger sisters are physically similar with elongated features and hair in loose curls. Charlotte's face is broader and her hair in ringlets – a plain if open appearance in line with the earliest photograph of her, a daguerreotype profile from *c*.1849, and quite different from the well-known idealised portraits by George Richmond (1850), John Hunter Thompson (1839) and the circular 'Brussels portrait' (*c*.1843) showing her in half-profile. When Mrs Gaskell saw it in 1853 she noted that 'the picture was divided, almost in the middle, by a great pillar' (Gaskell, 1857/1975: 155), hence its popular name, 'the pillar portrait'. Deterioration in the painted surface over the years has revealed the ghost of Branwell steadily emerging from the pillar. His shadowy presence looks disproportionately large, particularly as Emily was, in fact, taller than him. There has been much speculation about the painting out of Branwell's self-image, most of it deriving from his career of self-destruction through drink and opium which led to his sudden, ignominious death at the age of 31. The conservators at the National Portrait Gallery, however, attribute the painting out to Branwell himself and consider it was done at the same time as the rest of the picture was painted (Barker, 1994: 878). In the light of this, the most likely motive would seem to be Branwell's dissatisfaction either with his own image or with the balance of the composition.

There is a measure of biographical justice in this pentimento which sees Branwell 'rejoining' the group in that the picture offers historical evidence of a period in the early, interdependent lives of these four siblings. At this time, Branwell as the only son in a conventional family of a Victorian vicar took the lead in daily life. He was central to the creation of the imaginary lands and characters of Gondal and Angria on which the four of them spent much of their time: 'his sisters prepared themselves to live through him … Branwell set the pace for his sisters' (Gordon, 1994: 30). Charlotte, in particular, was

Figure 6.11 Branwell Brontë, *The Brontë Sisters* (*c*.1834). Oil on canvas, 90.2 × 74.6 cms. National Portrait Gallery, London

influenced by her brother with whom she paired off to create the 'Angria stories' (Barker, 1994: 201–209). Behind this group portrait, then, lies the intense, affectionate rivalry, the mutual support and criticism, that fed the literary efforts of the four Brontës during their formative years and led to the great novels of the 1840s and 1850s.

Art to Order

The most obvious feature shared by these sister arts is that both are generally commissioned and often subject to contract. Unlike the artist, novelist and poet who are free to choose their subjects and the way to treat them, the portraitist and the biographer tie themselves voluntarily to a specific task and a particular way of working. If it's art, then it's art to order. At the very least, this inhibits experimentation. As Marcia Pointon comments, 'Portrait-painting ... is an innately conservative practice, controlled by the strict requirements of a contractual relationship between artist and patron (who is also frequently the subject)' (Pointon, 1993: 79). The commission may be sought or offered; either way, the expectation is that the representation of the subject will be life-like, recognisable, balanced and fair. If it is not – and here is the problem unique to biography and portraiture – the subject (or at least the subject's descendants) can answer back. The law has been invoked in countless cases, from Mrs Gaskell's *Life of Charlotte Brontë* to the restrictions placed on biographers by the Hughes–Plath Estate. The biographer may retract or edit; the portraitist may rework the image. These very processes point to the intractable difficulties of representing the subject for a particular social and cultural milieu. The room for manoeuvre is small. The best portraits and biographies often show signs of straining against the limitations imposed on them: Ackroyd's *Dickens* (1999) with its seven controversial, fictional interludes; or Taylor's *Orwell: The Life* (2004) with its interchapters on 'Orwell's Face', 'Orwell's Voice' and others which step out of the time-frame and take a different, oblique angle on their subject. Or, as we have seen above, Patrick Heron's portrait of T. S. Eliot (1949), which interprets the conventions of portraiture through Cubist lenses; and Vanessa Bell's portraits of her sister, which refuse to depict her subject's facial features but succeed powerfully in expressing her personality.

More commonly, however, the special relationship between the biographer/portraitist and his or her subject generates a power play between art and patronage. Typically, this special relationship relies on a degree of trust that the contract will be fulfilled according to the spirit as well as the letter of the agreement; but the opportunities for disagreement are legion in such a personal undertaking. In extreme cases, deceptions and distortions beyond even those described in *The Aspern Papers* have been practised. In biography, when the relationship is one of contemporary friends or family, the advantages of intimacy can yield to the temptation to influence the nature of the story to be told. As we have seen in Chapter 2, the biographer may be manipulated into being a pseudo-biographer, a front for the subject's own version of his life, as Florence Hardy was for her husband. Conversely, the biographer may be tempted to manipulate the subject, in effect creating episodes in the life so that they can be recorded, as Boswell did when engineering the famous dinner party when Dr Johnson met his arch-enemy, John Wilkes (see Chapter 11). Portraiture, even more than biography, is prone to the most obvious aspect of this special relationship: flattery. In fact, social and artistic conventions may require the portraitist to flatter and idealise the subject, as we have seen in the images of Byron and Shelley, and in the portraits of Charlotte Brontë by official or commissioned artists as distinct from the amateur picture done by her brother.

In all, then, the ramifications of these commissioned arts are far reaching: these sisters are not free spirits. They have been hired, or have voluntarily chosen, to tether their imaginations to the changing requirements of history or the acceptable face of the visible. Their creations are simultaneously works of art and verbal/visual documents. Writing about the portrait in terms that apply equally to biography, Wendy Steiner summarises the effect of this dual allegiance:

> the portrait poses the general artistic problem of the aesthetic versus the referential as an overt conflict: it represents a real person whose actuality it announces through its title and through 'individualising' detail; at the same time it represents itself as a work of art – framed, highly structured, of interest 'in itself'. (Steiner, cited in Pointon, 1993: 8)

In their different ways, the two epigraphs at the head of this chapter imply a similar dualism.

Where does this ambiguous position leave these sister arts in relation to the broader literary and artistic culture? One significant effect of their existence is that they bolster the traditional canon since their motivation springs from a concern to represent writers of distinctive status and achievement. However, the symbiotic relationship between works of literature and their authors that literary biographers and portraitists often take for granted is one that authors themselves have frequently rejected in principle and hindered in practice. Proust's insistence that 'un livre est le produit d'un autre moi que celui que nous manifestons dans nos habitudes, dans la société, dans nos vices' (Proust, *Contre Sainte-Beuve*; cited in Tomalin, 2003: v) has been acted upon by many others who have taken practical measures to thwart biographers and portrait-painters – burning letters and journals, refusing interviews, sittings and photographs – showing indifference if not contempt for those who want to record their lives. Literary biography and portraiture stand in an uneasy relationship with writers and their works. Yet, offsetting the unease that verbal and visual biographers are dependent – some would say parasitical – on their subjects, is the fact that they also promote them in celebrating and helping to form the literary canon. They play their part in deciding which writers' names slip through the sieve of history and which are kept for succeeding generations. Just as most of Dr Johnson's fifty poets have now vanished into oblivion (Johnson, 1779–1781/1906), so Ian Hamilton is sure that many of his twentieth-century list will be forgotten (Hamilton, 2003: xv). But the big names survive: Pope, Swift et al. appear in Johnson's *Lives of the Poets*; Hardy, Yeats, Eliot and Auden are deemed to need no help from Hamilton since 'there are numerous biographies' of them already (Hamilton, 2003: xvi). In this broader historical perspective, there is an element of mutual dependency. Writers need their reading public; and readers demand personal knowledge and visible recognition of the writers as well as experience of their works. The National Portrait Gallery, with its collection of images of poets and novelists, stands as testimony to this need for recognition. The portraits of literary figures, like the subjects of literary biography, are elements in the development of the literary canon.

7

Comparative Biography: Dickens's 'Lives'

It is a truism that each age rewrites the biographies of its favoured authors to suit the changing times. Each new biography reflects the social mores, values and attitudes of its period as well as its literary and historical conventions. Each new biographer defines his or her role and agenda to distinguish them from those of both contemporaries and predecessors. From this mix, each new biographee is born – unique, independent, yet recognisably related to all its other reincarnations; related, too, to the image of the implied author created from the subject's own novels or poetry. Richard Holmes sees this process as opening up 'virtually a new discipline, which might be called comparative biography ... [one which] examines the handling of one subject by a number of different biographers, and over several different historical periods' (Holmes, 2002: 16).

Dickens's 'Lives' offer a rich resource in which to observe this process of reinvention. He is especially interesting as no biographer can ignore the 'Dickens' who is refracted through the personalities of David Copperfield and Pip, nor the countless ways – in scenes, recurring motifs, characters and patterns of feeling – in which the novelist's experiences are transformed into fiction. There are other reasons, too: he was a very self-conscious subject, highly concerned about his public image during his lifetime and about his reputation for posterity; and further, the three-way relationship between the public man of affairs, the private, domestic family man and the creative, literary man at his writing desk offers insights into the way biography explores its most elusive quarry – the nature of its subject's identity.

Dickens's 'Lives' have been many and varied in the 138 years since his death. Pre-Stracheyean memoirs and biographies ranged from the social condescension and academic snobbery of Sir Leslie Stephen to the exuberant eulogising of G. K. Chesterton. The one included in his entry in the *Dictionary of National Biography* the notorious judgement that 'if literary fame could safely be measured by popularity with the half-educated, Dickens must claim the highest position among English novelists' (Stephen, 1888, quoted in Slater, 2004)! The other worshipped at the shrine: 'There is no way of dealing with the ultimate greatness of Dickens, except by offering sacrifice to him as a god' (Chesterton, 1906/1975: 174). Post-Stracheyean biographies all take into account the revelations (suppressed during the nineteenth century) about the relationship between Dickens and Nelly Ternan which had developed at the time of his marriage breakdown in the mid-1850s. From the 1930s, when Thomas Wright (1935) and Gladys Storey (1939) published their accounts of this liaison, up to those of recent biographers of Dickens (Kaplan, 1988; Ackroyd, 1999) and Nelly Ternan (Tomalin, 1991), biographical detective work and speculation have inevitably coloured our views both of Dickens the man and Dickens the author. Moreover, these two biographical personae – the man who, in middle age, expelled his wife from the family home, allowing her custody of just one of their ten children, while cultivating a relationship with an 18-year-old actress; and the author whose novels constantly celebrate 'the Victorian cult of domesticity' (Slater, 1983: xii) – provide an ironic contrast. These biographical constructs affect our reading of Dickens's novels, subtly influencing our aesthetic responses to fictional characters and events. The ghost of Dickens the man hovers behind the implied author whose words we are reading. But Dickens's biographical ghost, like the spirits foretold by Jacob Marley, appears in different guises in the past, in the present and, no doubt, in biographies yet to come. The three upon which I concentrate are representative of their times and diverse in their authorship. The 'Victorian Dickens' is that of John Forster (1872–1874), Dickens's friend, a lawyer by training, a literary man by inclination. The 'Modern Dickens' is that of Edgar Johnson (1953/1986), an American academic, whose biography displays all the characteristics of modern scholarship and presentation, and is still regarded as 'the standard life' (Mengham, 2001: 129). The 'Post-Modern Dickens' is Peter Ackroyd's (1999), a long, 'baggy' and very Dickensian book, exhaustively researched, yet written with a fiction writer's flexibility of style, as might be expected from this novelist-cum-biographer. How do the different emphases in style and content of the friend, the academic and the novelist reflect the social mores and literary conventions of their periods?

The Victorian Dickens

The Victorian Dickens was created by John Forster, born in the same year as the author, a man whose advice was sought by many other writers, from Tennyson and Browning to Carlyle and Thackeray (Johnson, 1953/1986: 119), who enjoyed privileged access to Dickens as his closest friend for thirty-three years and who, at various times, acted as his unofficial literary agent, proofreader, copy editor and critic. Forster includes a footnote, quoting letters from Dickens in which the latter states: 'I desire no better for my fame ... than such a biographer and such a critic ... You know me better than any other man does, or ever will' (Forster, 1872–1874/1969, I: 455). Sadly, Forster fails to exploit this intimacy. Lacking the Boswellian touch (there are no dramatised 'scenes', few telling details from Forster's own observation, and little in the way of personal reminiscence), Forster's text has the dull sobriety of his lawyer's training. He was able to draw upon three decades of letters, documents and personal papers; he knew the genesis and development of Dickens's writing, enjoyed the regular company of Dickens's family and friends, and was the trusted confidant over the two main traumas of Dickens's personal life – his childhood experiences at Warren's Blacking Factory and the break-up of his marriage to Catherine. Yet, Forster's sense of Victorian propriety, exacerbated by information overload and failing health, combined to dull the life out of his biography. The vibrancy when it occurs is Dickens's own: for example, in his letters to Forster excited about his visits to America, or in the edited highlights Forster quotes from Dickens's 'Autobiographical Fragment' accounting for his time at Warren's and his experiences of the Marshalsea Prison.

One obvious indicator of the nineteenth-century mores is in how Forster handles (or fails to handle) Dickens's marriage breakdown. The biographer's uncertainty is signalled in the relevant chapter title. Whereas all the other chapters signify their content with book titles, places visited, countries travelled in, readings given and so on, Book 8, Chapter 2 coyly announces 'What Happened at This Time (1857–8)'. Forster omits to tell the story of Dickens's separation from Catherine in anything but the vaguest outline. He comments: 'I give only what is strictly necessary to account for what followed, and even then with the deepest reluctance' (Forster, II: 198), and then goes on to quote extracts from letters to him in which Dickens expresses a sympathy for Catherine and an acknowledgement of his own faults which are hard to reconcile with his harsh treatment of his wife and the self-righteousness of his public self-justification in the press. Although Forster knew her well, Catherine finds little place in his biography; and Nelly Ternan is omitted altogether save for a mention in Dickens's will which Forster prints as an appendix.

Forster is more forthcoming on Dickens the writer than on Dickens the man. His account of his own involvement in the decision over the title of *David Copperfield* (Forster, II: 78–79) evokes the novelist for whom names acted as a necessary catalyst to characterisation; and Dickens's alterations to Chapters 22 and 32 of the novel in respect of the character of Miss Mowcher (Forster, II: 99) open up the issue of basing fictional characters on living originals about which Forster's comments are astute and fair-minded, particularly over the appearance of Leigh Hunt, thinly disguised as Harold Skimpole in *Bleak House* (Forster, II: 100–102). Here, as elsewhere (for example, over his claim that he alone knew the contents of the 'Autobiographical Fragment' – a claim that Dickens's wife and son subsequently rejected (Slater, 1983: 156–158)), Forster is keen to stress his own unique relationship with Dickens, the importance of which is unquestionable, particularly in respect of *David Copperfield* and the 'Autobiographical Fragment'. Forster was the recipient of the much-quoted letter from Dickens written when the novel was almost finished:

> I am within three pages of the shore; and am strangely divided, as usual in such cases, between sorrow and joy. Oh, my dear Forster, if I were to say half of what *Copperfield* makes me feel tonight, how strangely, even to you, I should be turned inside out! I seem to be sending some part of myself into the Shadowy World. (Letter to John Forster, 21 October, 1850, in Forster, II: 98)

Forster goes on to discuss how, in prose fiction, autobiography enters 'largely in disguise', leading him to refer back to the use he had made earlier of Dickens's 'Autobiographical Fragment' that the author had given him (Forster, I: 20–33). Dickens's 'Fragment' is a construct of a child of 11 or 12 by an author in his late thirties seen inevitably through the haze of memory that blurs the distinction between fact and fiction. In drawing explicitly on the 'Fragment' in *David Copperfield*, Chapter 11, Dickens is transforming his boyhood experiences of 1824 into writing a quarter of a century later (Bodenheimer, 2007: 63; Fleishman, 1983: 205; see Chapter 12). Forster is properly cautious in assessing the results, seeing the writing as a pale reflection, dulled by time, of the traumas of Dickens's youth.

> The *Copperfield* disclosures formerly made will forever connect the book with the author's individual story; but too much has been assumed, from those revelations, of a full identity of Dickens with his hero, and of a supposed intention that his own character as well as parts of his career should be expressed in the narrative. It is right to warn the reader of this … many as are the resemblances in Copperfield's adventures to portions of those of Dickens, it would be the greatest mistake to imagine anything like a complete identity of the fictitious novelist with the real one, beyond the Hungerford scenes; or to suppose that the youth, who then received his first hard schooling in life, came out of it as little harmed or hardened as David did. The language of

> fiction reflects only faintly the narrative of actual fact; and the man whose character it helped to form was expressed not less faintly in the impulsive impressionable youth, incapable of resisting the leading of others, and only disciplined into self-control by the later griefs of his entrance into manhood. Here was but another proof of how thoroughly Dickens understood his calling, and that to weave fact and fiction unskilfully would be only to make truth less true. (Forster, II: 105)

Fine though Forster's sentiments and insights are, he remains the one biographer who could have taken them further beyond the common distinction between factual truth and fictional truth. In what ways did 'the language of fiction' help to form Dickens's character? This potentially intriguing idea is left floating, as is the equally intriguing reference to Dickens's 'later griefs' (his unrequited love for Maria Beadnell?) which mysteriously confer discipline and self-control on this impressionable youth. Here and elsewhere, Forster hints at the answers, but shies away both from using his personal knowledge and from speculative interpretation. He defines his role as historian, one moreover who has been entrusted with portraying the life of one of the great men of his time, a role that fulfilled the Victorian principle of biography as defined by Carlyle, 'whose dicta ("History is the essence of innumerable biographies"; and "The History of the world is but the Biography of great men") became high-ranking Victorian platitudes' (Altick, 1965/1979: 82). Looking back at this role forty years later, Lytton Strachey is explicit in his attack upon the general run of Victorian biography: 'Those two fat volumes, with which it is our custom to commemorate the dead – who does not know them, with their ill-digested masses of material, their slip-shod style, their tone of tedious panegyric, their lamentable lack of selection, of detachment, of design?' (Strachey, 1918/1986: 10). While this description would be a caricature of Forster's 'Life', there are enough hints here to explain why 'it [Forster's biography] has now come to be regarded less as a book to be read than as a work of reference' (Fielding, 1966: 10). Forster's 'Life' has a Boswellian fullness without his flair. More importantly, his picture is not the 'warts and all' variety that Boswell and Johnson both favoured; in the portrait of the 'Victorian Dickens', the warts have been carefully air-brushed out.

The Modern Dickens

Edgar Johnson's book is modern but not modernist. *Charles Dickens: His Tragedy and Triumph* (1953/1986) has all the characteristics of modern scholarship, its subject authoritatively researched and scrupulously presented;

but it has none of the modernist features that we associate with literary experimentation post-1914, and which, in biography, find their counterpart in Lytton Strachey. Strachey's modernism parallels that of his contemporaries, Eliot and Joyce; his *Eminent Victorians* (1918/1986) revolutionised biography as irrevocably as *The Waste Land* and *Ulysses* did poetry and fiction. 'I am … beginning a new experiment', he wrote to Ottoline Morrell on 17 October 1912, 'in the way of a short condensed biography of Cardinal Manning – written from a slightly cynical point of view' (quoted in Strachey, 1918/1986: viii). Strachey's modernism was the art of brevity: it entailed selecting the significant characteristics of a life and accepting the redundancy of much of its detail; it subverted the uncritical praise of the public images of his four subjects with an ironic wit trained upon their private attitudes and beliefs. In Stracheyean terms, Johnson's 'Life' is distinctly old-fashioned. It is substantial, densely detailed and conventionally ordered; and the tone and vocabulary of its Preface would be enough to make Strachey raise an eyebrow if not curl his lip. For the fact is that biography is such a conservative genre that formal changes, let alone experimentation, evolve slowly. Only in the 1990s, a generation or more after Johnson, has biography begun to exhibit stylistic and formal changes which reflect the instabilities of its subject matter. But this is to anticipate Ackroyd.

Johnson begins rhapsodically with Dickens, the 'great man' of literary history: 'Charles Dickens belongs to all the world. He is a titan of literature, and his own moving life story, with its radiances of laughter, its conquests of genius …', and he follows up by immediately fictionalising his subject. The second paragraph starts:

> Dickens was himself a Dickens character, bursting with inordinate and fantastic vitality. His everyday world was identical with the world of his novels, brilliant in hue, violent in movement, crammed with people all furiously alive and places as alive as the people. (Johnson, 1953/1986: 7)

A modern biography this may be, but the traces of unconstrained eulogy are still there. The old-fashioned, Chestertonian streak in Johnson's writing is tempered by the grid-like structure that contains it. His 'Life' is organised in ten parts, each titled, and each consisting of four or five chapters of similar length also individually titled. Biography thus imposes its rigid framework on the fluidity of life, curtailing its random nature into a series of discrete episodes. Dates, places and the sequencing of events are invariably clear; biographical memory is much sharper than that of actual life. This framework is held in place by opening and summative accounts (Johnson, 1953/1986: 11–12, 562–570) which, respectively, signal Johnson's theme of

Dickens's 'tragedy and triumph' and provide the traditional closing set-piece summarising Dickens's character and unique achievements. Both in attitude and structure, then, Johnson has not departed very far from Forster, even though his prose is infinitely more accessible. What is modern is the way he integrates his accounts of the novels with Dickens's life, the openness of his discussion of Dickens's private life following the revelations of Thomas Wright and Gladys Storey, and his preference for the 1850s novels of social criticism over Dickens's earlier work.

The first of these issues takes us back to the relationship between fact and fiction that Johnson had raised in his Preface quoted above. Mid-century biographers and critics were not as sceptical as those of today about reading the writer's life in his fictions. Hence, Humphrey House (1941/1960), while acknowledging 'the process of imaginative transformation' that changes a supposed original in real life into a fictional character, can still offer the biographer unlimited freedom.

> The novels themselves are, of course, a primary source for the life. Charles Dickens was the child of Mr Micawber (with a touch of Dorrit) and Mrs Nickleby. He lodged for a time with Mrs Pipchin. As a youth he fell in love with Dora, who grew up into Flora. For the biographer such identifications as those are of greatest value ... (House, 1941/1960: 11)

Present-day biography would replace 'greatest' with 'limited' and treat 'such identifications' with scepticism. Edgar Johnson uses this interpretative freedom in a particular way. According to an exchange of letters with fellow biographer J. L. Clifford, Johnson 'does claim to be using a very special kind of biographical criticism'. Clifford continues:

> For example, when he came to *David Copperfield* in the life of Dickens, he examined it as an evocation of Dickens's own personality. There is a constant projection to be seen of Dickens in his own works. So many of the characters in his novels are orphans, and in this fact Johnson sees his unconscious rejection of his own parents. There is, then, a back-and-forth relationship between Dickens and his characters. (Clifford, 1970: 98)

Clifford overstates the case for Johnson's biographical criticism. Johnson is appropriately tentative in deducing life from art and, in fact, offers very little that can plausibly be called literary criticism. His brief Chapter 32 on *David Copperfield* certainly refers to 'Dickens's feelings of being rejected by his natural parents' and concludes that the chapters dealing with Dickens's childhood are 'a profound and tremendous achievement in coming to grips with his own past' (Johnson, 1953/1986: 349), but this scarcely amounts to literary criticism, biographical, psychological or otherwise. Johnson is similarly cautious in his comments on *Great Expectations*, merely associating the emotional tenor of Pip's feelings for Estella with Dickens's for Ellen Ternan rather than assuming any facile identification as other biographers had done (Slater, 1983: 212–213).

> It is inevitable that we should associate Pip's helpless enslavement to Estella with Dickens's passion for Ellen Ternan. Never before had he portrayed a man's love for a woman with such depth or revealed its desperation of compulsive suffering. David Copperfield's heartache for Dora is an iridescent dream-grief compared with Pip's agonised nightmare-reality. (Johnson, 1953/1986: 491)

This association of aspects of Dickens's life and his fiction is as far as Johnson goes. What is missing from Johnson's 'Life' is a discussion of the psychological patterns that recur in Dickens's life and works; patterns such as the preoccupation with the image of young, virginal women; the idealised brother–sister relationships; the portrayal of children, orphans especially, in relation to the adult world. Johnson integrates his comments on the novels seamlessly with the external events of Dickens's life, but the internal life which one expects modern biography to probe is left largely unexplored.

At least Dickens's personal life is part of Johnson's agenda in areas that Forster had avoided. Nowhere is the contrast more marked than over the issue of Dickens's relationship with Nelly Ternan. On this, of course, Forster was silent. As was noted in Chapter 4, Johnson judged that 'it seems not unlikely' that at some point in the winter of 1861–1862, Nelly gave in and became Dickens's lover (Johnson, 1953/1986: 500). He is more forthright and speculative, however, when he views Nelly through the prism of Dickens's fiction, seeing her reflection in the novels of the time, from Lucie Manette in *A Tale of Two Cities* to Helena Landless in *The Mystery of Edwin Drood*. 'Did he [Dickens] suspect her [Nelly], like Bella Wilfer, the heroine of *Our Mutual Friend*, of being calculating and mercenary, and, unlike Bella, of having remained so? Was his tenderness for her, too, shot through with bitterness and disillusion?' (Johnson, 1953/1986: 554). He presents the Dickens of the 1860s as an unhappy man, acknowledges that there is no evidence of the contribution Nelly made to his emotional state, but then concludes that 'there can be no doubt that in some way she, too, failed his need'. Claire Tomalin's (1991) biography of Nelly Ternan has forever silenced such a censorious and simplistic conclusion. What Johnson's handling of this issue illustrates is the difficulty mid-century biography found, especially one like this written on the traditional, non-Stracheyean model, in accommodating the seemingly limitless growth of information and interpretative possibilities once the intimacies of the interior life of the subject became an accepted area of the biographer's territory. One cannot help but regret Johnson's limitations in this respect. Equally, one cannot help wishing that Strachey had chosen Dickens as one of his eminent Victorians.

Less contentious and more significant for the modern estimate of Dickens's status as a novelist is Johnson's preference for the novels of the 1850s over their predecessors. 'In the books that followed *David Copperfield* he [Dickens] was to attempt nothing less than an anatomy of modern society' (Johnson, 1953/1986: 385). Whereas earlier commentators had responded more readily to what Chesterton termed the 'old atmosphere of a democratic optimism' (Chesterton, 1906/1975: 10–11) characteristic of the earlier novels, Johnson's advocacy of Dickens's later books helped to form modern thinking. '*Bleak House*, *Little Dorrit* and *Our Mutual Friend*, all masterpieces of his [Dickens's] maturity, are dark and tremendous structures reaching almost epic magnitude' (Johnson, 1953/1986: 569). It is this additional emphasis on Dickens the serious social thinker, as well as popular entertainer, that marks out the 'modern Dickens'. Johnson claims that: 'By the time he had reached the middle of his career he understood capitalist industrialism at least as well as most nineteenth-century political economists' (Johnson, 1953/1986: 564). The modern Dickens emerges as a man of ideas whose thinking about individual personalities and the good government of society went far deeper than its initial appeal through humour, caricature and melodrama would suggest.

The Post-Modern Dickens

To call Ackroyd's *Dickens* 'post-modern' requires immediate qualification. As with Johnson's 'modern' 'Life', the label is suggestive of changes in a conservative genre rather than, in Ackroyd's case, of an affinity with, say, Borges or Barthes. Certainly, Ackroyd's belief in constructing a convincing historical description of Victorian England and of Charles Dickens as its 'emblem' resonates throughout from Prologue (p. xv) to Postscript (p. 1143). There is no post-modern attempt to collapse the distinction between history and fiction. Indeed, the two are kept strikingly apart, the seven Interludes marked off by Roman numerals and a larger typeface. Yet, the very presence of such fictional constructions within a biography is unprecedented and significant, for it indicates a willingness to juxtapose the historical with the fictional, the serious with the playful, and, by implication, to challenge, if not subvert, the easy self-confidence that conventional biography has assumed in its ability to recreate the past on the basis of unstable evidence. The post-modern character of Ackroyd's book lies in this deliberate blending of literary genres and in its stylistic innovations which, together with his skill in maintaining the uniqueness and separateness of Dickens's novels while relating them to his life, enable him to claim biography as 'an agent of true knowledge'. Ackroyd summarises this view of biography in his Postscript:

> To see Dickens day by day, making his way, the incidents of his existence shaping his fiction just as his fiction alters his life, the same pattern of emotion and imagery rising up from letters and novels and conversations, the same momentum and the same desire for control – to see Dickens thus is to turn biography into an agent of true knowledge, even as we remember that the greatness of his fiction may lie in its absolute *difference* from anything which the life may show us. But once we have made that leap, from the man to his works, then we can also begin to carve out that unimaginable passage from the single human being to the age in which he lived. (Ackroyd, 1999: 1143)

The penultimate paragraph of Ackroyd's book from which these sentences are taken begins with a justification for biography derived from David Copperfield's words, 'trifles make the sum of life' (a key idea which Ackroyd quotes three times on pp. xvi, 640 and 1143), and ends with some rhetorical flourishes which see Dickens as an individual 'whom we have come to understand', one in whom are reflected 'the lineaments of the age itself'. Biography, then, conceived as purposeful eclecticism building up a portrait of the man from diverse materials and sources; as a detailed, composite, textual construct that figures as the emblem of the age; and as a quest for knowledge and understanding of the man and his times. These are big claims. How have they been fulfilled in the thousand pages or more that precede them?

Size matters, it seems, since Ackroyd has produced a long, expansive, Dickensian book. Yet, for all its generous proportions, it avoids the biographical obesity that besets many recent biographies through its stylistic nimbleness. The narrative continuity makes light of the exhaustive research that Ackroyd carried out (pp. ix–x, 1145–1214). Customary conventions are dispensed with – there are no chapter titles, no part divisions, no running heads with dates, no clear pointers to sources and footnotes. Ackroyd's prose is set to catch Dickens in motion. To this end, sentences, paragraphs, even chapters begin with 'And …'; sentences lose their verbs; unattached phrases and single words add pace and colour to the text. Everything is geared to capturing Dickens's restless energy.

This strong narrative drive is complemented by Ackroyd's frequent use of several rhetorical devices calculated to bring the image of Dickens, his family and friends into our mind's eye. He often resorts to open, rhetorical questions in order to involve the reader. For example, of Mrs Lirriper, he says: 'Surely it is possible to see in this contemporaneous portrait some kind of oblique, posthumous tribute to Mrs Dickens which her son could not give her in her lifetime?' (p. 988). Or again, discussing the possibility that Lucie Manette in *A Tale of Two Cities* may be a partial portrait of Nelly Ternan with Dickens casting himself in the role of Sidney Carton, Ackroyd asks: 'is there some image of himself as a similar hero who must love without hope? Who must be patient unto death?' (p. 909). Or again, noting Dickens's 'constant interest in the imprisoned and the mad', Ackroyd queries whether it reflected more than mere philanthropy: 'is there not also something darker, and deeper, something to do with his own feelings of anxiety and guilt expressed in what Putnam called his "nervous manner"?' (p. 366). The biography is frequently dotted with questions such as these which probe Dickens's motivations and emotional attachments.

A different rhetorical device, that of imitating Dickens's style, is sometimes used to evoke places. For example, the deliberate, repetitious build-up at the start of *Bleak House* is echoed in Ackroyd's description of the London of the 1840s. An initial sequence of mounting, incantatory phrases – 'a city of small shops and trades, a city of dirty red brick, a city ... of fog and decay' – is followed by another: 'Poured into the narrow streets; poured into the jerry built houses ...; poured into the cellars ...' (p. 402). But in neither Dickens nor Ackroyd is it merely empty rhetoric for descriptive effect, for Ackroyd continues by quoting official health reports from the period describing the living conditions of the poor and by absolving Dickens from the charge of 'fantasy or melodrama' in his harrowing accounts of disease and poverty in *Bleak House* or *Oliver Twist*.

Ackroyd's portrayal of Dickens's state of mind immediately after his father's death at the end of March 1851 is created through a variation of this device. He quotes short extracts from Dickens's essay 'Night Walks', alternating them with his own brand of Dickensian rhetorical repetition. Hence:

> And, as he walked the streets after his father's death, 'the wild moon and clouds were as restless as an evil conscience in a tumbled bed and the very shadow of the immensity of London seemed to lie oppressively upon the river'. Dickens walked on. Past deserted theatres. Past the stone walls of Newgate. Past the King's Bench Prison where he had once imprisoned Mr Micawber, so sad a simulacrum of his Father. Past Bedlam ... (Ackroyd, 1999: 656–657)

Then, after dipping into a quotation from 'Night Walks' again for a strange image of the dead rising from their graves, a change of tense brings Dickens closer to us: 'he was walking endlessly, as obsessively as those characters of his who labour under some great affliction. Still he walks on ...' (p. 657). Here, as in his evocation of London, the consciously adopted Dickensian tone aims to bring Dickens alive for us.

He is Dickensian, too, in his use of mental images. Taking his cue from his subject's eidetic imagination in which he claimed to see and hear his characters as though they were beside him (Ackroyd, 1999: 422–423) – Buss's painting, *Dickens's Dream* (see Chapter 6 (vii)), captures the idea of what Dickens called his 'Mental Museum' (p. 334) – Ackroyd constantly places images of Dickens before us. We are encouraged to keep in mind two pictures of the author as a child:

> This is the other significant image of Dickens's childhood, to be placed beside that of the young boy singing and acting upon a tavern table – it is the image of the solitary child, lost in his book, preoccupied with his own fancies, creating his own world. (Ackroyd, 1999: 51)

Dream images, images of fear and loss are identified as significant in Dickens's formative years:

> There is something in Dickens's infancy, something which cannot now be recovered or understood, some primal fear which left him casting about for images with which to express it and which gave him as a novelist that sensitivity to the adult world which is most often to be found in the eyes of a frightened child. (Ackroyd, 1999: 54)

This fear is associated with one image above all others: 'the image of the Marshalsea never left him', Ackroyd says. 'The high wall with the spikes on top of it, the shadows cast by the prison buildings, the lounging shabby people – all of these images return again and again in his narratives' (Ackroyd, 1999: 79). This power of visualising people and scenes becomes, for Ackroyd, the key to Dickens's art:

> For him the important things are the *pictures*; they are more significant to him than ideas or themes or even, sometimes, words. He talks of his fiction on occasions as a 'picture frame' but his pictures within the frame are not like the still lives of an artist; Dickens sees objects and images as if they had suddenly been illuminated by lightning. A character 'came flashing up ... and I had only to look on and leisurely describe it ...'. (Ackroyd, 1999: 589–590)

And what Ackroyd identifies as the key to Dickens he, in turn, exploits as his biographer. Dickens's ability to make characters and places vividly present in the reader's mind's eye is emulated by Ackroyd's ability to bring Dickens forward in time, to bring him into our present. So, after discussing the elements that went into the chapter concerning Edith Dombey's elopement, he pictures Dickens, travelling by train to Scotland and imagining Carker's death beneath an express train, and he links this image to the Staplehurst disaster and to the present-day reader's conception of speed:

> As he travelled up by train to Scotland with Catherine, he was thinking of the train that would destroy Carker; the train which plunges upon him and turns him into blood and 'mutilated fragments'; Dickens thinking of all this, not knowing that in eighteen years time he would experience a greater railway disaster; all of us thinking of Dickens as we read this, and realising how great a distance separates his world from our own when we learn that the speed of an express train was then twenty-six miles per hour. (Ackroyd, 1999: 567)

Here Ackroyd's Dickens is shown as moving imaginatively into an episode in his current fiction, then into one in his own future life when he and Nelly Ternan nearly perished; and then he is suddenly distanced as we look at him across the chasm of 150 years. Time becomes a variable dimension as fact and fiction are entwined.

In the Interludes, Ackroyd goes further. Dickens steps out of the biographical frame altogether; he moves from being an authenticated historical person to become a character in a series of seven fictional scenes. We encounter him meeting Little Dorrit and her (and his) father in the Marshalsea; as a young man observing and being observed in Kingsland Road; in conversation with Ackroyd's other biographical and fictional creations – Eliot, Wilde and Chatterton; as the creative power behind a host of Dickens's characters at Greenwich Fair who insist on their immortality; at a 'strange meeting' with Ackroyd in the Geffrye Museum to discuss his fiction in relation to his life; as the biographical subject when Ackroyd is formally interviewed about this biography; and as a figure in 'a dream of the present', the biographer's hallucination that Dickens still lives. Of these, the meeting of Ackroyd and his subject in the mid-Victorian Room of the Geffrye Museum is the most subtle in its representation of Dickens, its oblique look at biography, and in the implications of the setting. The appearance and manner of this fictional Dickens are calculated to remind us of the 'real' one elsewhere in Ackroyd's pages: his dandified clothes, his humming of an old song, his restless rearranging of small objects in the room. The conversation turns on the concept of self-knowledge, in particular, of Dickens's relationship to his characters and of Ackroyd's access to his subject's identity. Ackroyd playfully blends authentic details – Dickens's 'direct glance', his fiddling with his signet ring – with imaginative speculation about his subject's inner life; but biography is a serious game of trying to reconstitute the past for the present. Biographical writing, as the Museum setting implies, becomes part of the heritage industry, a reconstruction in all its cluttered details of the mid-Victorian drawing room with a plaster figure of Charles Dickens in period costume.

Here, as throughout the book, Ackroyd is a highly self-conscious biographer. He is well aware not only of his own agenda but also of those of Forster and Johnson and that 'Every biography is a prisoner of its time' (Ackroyd, 1999: 944). He acknowledges that his Dickens is a blend of documented data and fictional invention. He is explicit about the thoroughness of his academic research, yet he is sceptical about the 'scientific' validity of biographical scholarship (Ackroyd, 1999: 941–942). In all these respects, the confident reconstruction of the past that formed the traditional mission of biography is shown to be unstable. A post-modern Dickens can be invented but his true self ultimately eludes the biographer. As Ackroyd has his fictional Dickens conclude: 'The mystery is too deep to fathom … The mystery of my own self' (Ackroyd, 1999: 796).

Lives and Times

Given that this 'mystery' is beyond the reach of biography, is the modern biographer better able to create a more authentic Dickens than his Victorian predecessor? We have noted how the friend, the academic and the novelist each reflect their personal and professional characteristics in their works, but the issues around 'lives and times' not only concern the concept of biography and its purposes, they also raise the problems of contemporaneity and historical distance. Forster, as a participant in Dickens's life, may suffer a myopic foreshortening of his subject; Johnson and Ackroyd may gain from their more distant spectatorship. The Leavises are no doubt right to emphasise Forster's advantages of 'his intimate personal knowledge of his friend' and his ability to give us the sense of 'being really inward with Dickens's personality and character'. They are no doubt wrong in scornfully dismissing modern biographers who are deemed guilty of 'interpreting', 'misrepresenting', 'assembling irrelevant data' and 'insinuating, through critical stupidity, false assumptions about the subject's art, character, personality and history' (F. R. & Q. D. Leavis, 1972: 10). The Leavisite preference for Forster and dislike of Edgar Johnson merely reflect their prejudice against a genre which they see as valid only as a 'source', a contemporary archive for the literary critics to use in pursuit of their higher calling of literary appreciation and critical analysis. Life-writing as such, certainly any that finds interest and significance in aspects of the life reflected in the works, is deemed worse than useless – it is a distortion. The Leavisite view is plainly self-serving and, even in the early 1970s, let alone after forty years of literary theory, often seen as anachronistic. For what historicist criticism and modern biography have amply demonstrated is that both our knowledge and interpretations of history and individual lives are not fossilised exhibits in some time-exempt museum arranged for the benefit of literary critics. They are changing constructs created from the discipline of research into primary sources and represented according to the predilections of their times. Looked at in this way, the rewriting of a literary life in different periods offers a multi-faceted portrait of the subject, a historicised view of the genre, and an insight into how particular cultures and societies saw themselves. In Holmes's words, it is in becoming aware of the 'shifts and differences – factual, formal, stylistic, ideological, aesthetic – between early and later biographies' that the benefits of comparative study lie. Readers can 'discover how reputations developed, how fashions changed, how social and moral attitudes moved, how standards of judgement altered as each generation one after another continuously reconsidered and idealised or condemned its forbears in the writing and reading of biography' (Holmes, 2002: 15–16). We have seen something of this process in these three biographies of Dickens. It has enabled us to appreciate Forster's and Johnson's strengths and account for their shortcomings; and to acknowledge that, in Ackroyd, Dickens has found a creative biographer for today whose empathy with his subject is at least the equal of that of modern literary critics, who is less susceptible to imposing his own pet theories than many of them, whose book deserves critical appraisal as a work of art alongside his and his subject's fiction, and whose self-awareness of the respective territories of biography and the novel is evident throughout.

8

Literary Auto/Biography

> *The biggest obstacle to an account of Wordsworth's self-creation is his own self-portrait in* The Prelude.... *It is not Wordsworth's biography, but neither is it his autobiography: his early life was both the same as, yet different from,* The Prelude's *account of it.*
>
> (K. R. Johnston, *The Hidden Wordsworth*, 2000: 7)

> *His [Joyce's] work is 'history fabled', not only in* A Portrait *but in* Ulysses *as well. He was never a creator ex nihilo; he recomposed what he remembered.*
>
> (R. Ellmann, *James Joyce*, 1959/1983: 364)

Acts of Self-Creation in Wordsworth and Joyce

'Auto/Biography' is a composite term, its two capitalised words hinged at the middle. The forward slash is introduced in order to connect the subject's own versions of self as they develop continuously and modify over time to the constructs of the subject's biographers. Lacking Lewis Carroll's auditory playfulness, this portmanteau word nonetheless offers an invitation to unpack the contents of its two compartments and poses a number of questions. What does the biographer do when faced with the subject's autobiography cast in literary form? Say 'thanks for the memories', while judiciously analysing the author's self-censorship? Celebrate the technical and aesthetic accomplishment of the author in transmuting life into art? Fill in the gaps, contextual and substantive, that help to complete a fuller picture of the author's life? The answer, of course, is all of these things.

Acts of self-creation in poetry and fiction take many forms. The implied author is always with us, however discreetly; and sometimes blatantly in the self-promoting Byron or the self-mythologising Sylvia Plath. Fleishman

(1983: 195–196) has shown the prevalence of the autobiographical novel in Victorian times, examining among others *David Copperfield* and *Villette*. The present emphasis is upon those rarer instances of self-creation, ones dedicated to probing the making of the artistic life. Wordsworth's *The Prelude* and Joyce's *A Portrait of the Artist as a Young Man* are seminal texts. Both the poet and the novelist are writers 'writing themselves'. Both texts are constructions of memory. Both plot a narrative of their lives punctuated by what they regard as significant experiences – Wordsworth's 'spots of time', Joyce's 'epiphanies'. Both seek a sense of artistic identity, a coherent self-concept, through creating a literary persona. Both focus on the formative experiences of childhood and youth, stopping their life stories in their early twenties. Both texts were born out of other writings (*The Recluse* and *Stephen Hero*) revised and reworked over time, indicating a process of self-discovery as well as of self-creation. In both texts the author reads as well as writes himself, finding in this self-reflexive act a personification in language gazing narcissistically back at him. This is Paul de Man's point in his well-known essay, 'Autobiography as De-Facement' (de Man, 1979). In this post-structuralist view, autobiographies are texts that generate fictions or figurative images rather than the self-knowledge they purport to seek. De Man accepts such fictions and figures as necessary autobiographical metaphors but regards them as 'de-facements', or masks, which conceal the subject rather than as projections that are true to life, or representations aiding a process of self-discovery. The autobiographical subject becomes a figure of rhetoric: everything is determined by 'the resources of his [the writer's] medium' (de Man, 1979: 920). Language is thus the central issue in these acts of self-creation.

What can we learn about 'auto/biography' from a consideration of these works? How do the elements of mask and metaphor manifest themselves and how do the biographers react? This chapter is in three parts:

(i) The first part focuses on Wordsworth's self-creation in *The Prelude*, the poem which, more than any other, represents the Romantic notion of the unified self, and upon the responses of two recent biographers to a literary life seen through an autobiographical screen.
(ii) The second part considers Joyce's *A Portrait*, the novel which represents the self in modernist, fragmented form, and Ellmann's classic biography.
(iii) The third part draws some conclusions about literary auto/biography, triangulating the temporal qualities of narrative, the synthetic operation of memory, and the role of literary forms and language as they combine into the creation of a sense of 'self'.

Wordsworth's 'biographic verse'

Wordsworth's description at the end of *The Prelude* (XIII, 341) of his poem as 'biographic verse' echoes his alternative title at the start, 'the Growth of a Poet's Mind'. His end is also his beginning in a further sense. *The Prelude* was conceived as the integral first part of a longer philosophical poem, urged on him by Coleridge, *The Recluse*; but the latter grandiose project faded as the personal significance of Wordsworth's spiritual biography increased, *The Recluse* remaining a mere fragment. Beginning and ending are also more than external narrative markers. Structurally, the poem starts and finishes in the Vale of Grasmere. In between is the journey, told in thirteen Books in the 1805 version (to which all references relate: Wordsworth, 1805/1960), of Wordsworth's first twenty-three years from Hawkshead to Cambridge to the Continent to the West Country and back to the Lake District. But the more important journey is inside the poet's head. Autobiographically, its loose, meandering structure – reflecting Wordsworth's wonderings as much as his wanderings – sacrifices the momentum of linear chronological narrative to the circularity of a mind that is constantly working over past experiences. As he puts it with uncharacteristic succinctness: 'each man is a memory to himself' (III, 189). This interplay of memory and the growth of selfhood is fundamental to *The Prelude* in which three features are prominent: the voice and manner in which the narrative is developed; the relationship between memory and imagination; and the literary language and form in which the life story is cast.

The first question must be: Who is the 'I' of this narrative? To identify the 'I' as either Wordsworth the man or as Wordsworth the implied author is unsatisfactory. *The Prelude*'s protagonist is not the well-documented figure from literary history, nor is he as ill-defined as the author's 'second self' (that idea of the author that we deduce from a literary text) (Booth, 1961: 151). The 'I' of *The Prelude* lies somewhere between the two, a projection of the Poet-self which Wordsworth self-consciously creates as he explores his own life narrative. Wordsworth's persona takes up a tricky autobiographical stance: his Poet-self appears knowledgeable, intimate, privy to profound personal feelings and high-flown thoughts, yet we know that the voice that is addressing us is both editing and aestheticising the experiences it describes. The 'I' both draws us in by its intimacy and keeps us at a distance by its art. Biographically, the life story that it tells becomes its own subject; that is to say that *The Prelude* is not the record of Wordsworth's life but a continuous attempt to discover the springs of his own creative personality through the invention of an autobiographical fiction (Denzin, 1989: 35).

The asymmetry of the literary narrative and the life narrative reflects this motivation in several unusual ways. The coverage of Wordsworth's life in *The Prelude* is little more than a quarter of his actual life of eighty years. His compositional process started in 1798 when he was 28 and was completed in 1805 when he was 35. However, *The Prelude* was revised constantly for over forty years until his death in 1850. This retrospective revisionism did not extend his history; Wordsworth's persona remains perpetually young, so that the constant presence of *The Prelude* throughout his adult life and the tinkerings with the text mean that the poem's composition itself becomes an integral part of his biography (Wordsworth, 1979). The narrative 'I' becomes both a mask and a metaphor. The 'red thread' of the poem, the pervasive notion that, for Wordsworth, the natural world is not just an object 'out there' but a presence within, a powerful guide to the essence of human nature, has been repeatedly analysed. In *The Prelude*, Book VIII, Wordsworth reviews his early life and summarises what he sees as its threefold development: the 'animal activities' and 'trivial pleasures' of boyhood; the years of adolescence when 'Nature did / For her own sake become my joy'; and his more mature state of young manhood after his sometimes traumatic experiences in post-Revolutionary France have widened and deepened his sympathies for humanity and sharpened his creative sensibility. (A similar development is described in his *Tintern Abbey*, lines 66–111.)

Yet, there are deliberate omissions and evasions in this tracing of his personal history, the most striking of which is that, although we hear much about his time in France after the Revolution – his initial euphoria (X, 693–694) and later disillusion (X, 792–795) – nowhere does he acknowledge the existence of his mistress, Annette Vallon, or their daughter Caroline, a child whom he did not see until she was 10 years old and then only briefly on a visit to Calais. Instead, in a classic example of psychological displacement, he gives us the tale of 'Vaudracour and Julia' (IX, 555–934), which tells a Romeo and Juliet story of the ecstasy of young lovers, the frisson of 'stolen interviews' together (line 632), the anguish of parting (lines 727–728), and the birth and death of their baby (lines 780–907). Why did Wordsworth so disguise such significant events in his own history, ones which certainly must have had a bearing upon 'the growth of a poet's mind'? Wordsworth was no Byron and perhaps felt a natural inhibition against revealing the misdemeanours of his youth to the world. Or, as a sensitive biographer, he may well have wished to avoid causing pain to living people, especially to the families involved. Or again, by 1805, Wordsworth is married to Mary Hutchinson, Caroline is a young teenager and, with hindsight, Wordsworth may have realised the essentially transient nature of an affair that did not fit into his development as a poet. This episode more than any other exposes the differences, on the one hand, between Wordsworth the man whose powerful feelings for Annette (whether of short-lived passion and subsequent guilt, or of genuine love that took a decade to fade (Gill, 1990: 66–67)) were a casualty of post-Revolution turmoil, differences in religion and political allegiance, and war between their two countries, and, on the other hand, Wordsworth's self-personification as the Poet, concerned to comprehend and articulate the workings of his literary mind.

In Wordsworth's act of self-creation in *The Prelude*, such lacunae are perhaps less important than the focal points, his celebrated 'spots of time', those 'moments of being' in Virginia Woolf's phrase, which stand out from the routine and function as a form of revelation (Woolf, 1939–1940/2002: 86). She elaborates this idea in her 'Sketch of the Past' which, at one point, reads like a gloss upon Wordsworth's notion of bringing the past alive in the present moment – his double consciousness. Looking back to boyhood, Wordsworth says:

> ...so wide appears
> The vacancy between me and those days,
> Which yet have such self-presence in my mind
> That, sometimes, when I think of them, I seem
> Two consciousnesses, conscious of myself
> And of some other Being.
>
> (II, 28–33)

Virginia Woolf not only shares the eidetic vividness of memory, she also hints that the perception of the present narrows and heightens the focus upon particular incidents in the past, investing them with autobiographical significance. 'It would be interesting', she says, 'to make the two people, I now, I then, come out in contrast. And further, this past is much affected by the present moment' (Woolf, 1939–1940/2002: 87). The synthetic operation of memory produces a sense of continuity between present and past, offering a unifying pattern to the otherwise ordinary and disparate experiences of life and, with it, the potential to meet the basic human need for a consistent sense of identity. Despite the view in modern theory that this sense of continuity reflects the Romantic illusion of a unified self, it remains a fundamental feature of auto/biography. It is dramatised, celebrated and analysed repeatedly in *The Prelude* – from Wordsworth's accounts of his boyhood activities, stealing a boat, skating at night, kite-flying, and fishing in Book I, to those of his apocalyptic experiences in the Gondo gorge when crossing the Alps with Robert Jones in 1790 (VI, 556–572) and during their ascent of Snowdon the following summer (XIII, 1–84).

Wordsworth is explicit about the role of synthetic memory in the famous lines recalling his walks near Penrith Beacon (XI, 258–343). His announcement that,

> There are in our existence spots of time,
> Which with distinct pre-eminence retain
> A vivifying Virtue …

suggests that Wordsworth was conscious of a recurring schema in his mental life, one with a particular memorial character. Here, the 'ordinary sight' of the Beacon, of 'a girl who bore a pitcher on her head' struggling against the wind, and of a 'naked pool' in the hills, is charged with autobiographical significance through the layers of personal history that time has laid down. Wordsworth's lines assume the status of willed dreams, pictures in a mental landscape, framed by memory, coalescing as dreams do. Three images of Wordsworth are set at angles, as it were, to create the spot of time: the 'I' of the mature poet aged 34 or 35, the youthful Wordsworth aged 18 walking the Beacon with Mary Hutchinson, and the boy 'not six years old' becoming lost and frightened in the mountains, leading his horse past the gibbet-mast beneath which was carved the murderer's name in the turf. The reader is given a verbal triptych; three viewpoints in one, comprising a graphic sense of place and an inscribed sense of time. The lines framing the picture stress the importance of the individual's reflective imagination, the power of the mind to which 'outward sense' is the mere servant, and the restorative function of memory. Here, as throughout *The Prelude*, such experiences are accorded the highest value. They are protected as capital assets, locked away in his memory bank. Wordsworth lives off the interest.

The inscribed sense of time becomes one of layered memories. These spots of time are miniatures of the whole poem, one constructed from an adult's perspective but geared towards returning to the sources of his own poetic power in childhood. Yet, Wordsworth's account is not just a narrative of his journey and return to a paradise lost in the Vale of Grasmere; nor is its theme merely that of mental recovery – Wordsworth's psychological restoration through memories of past times. 'Return' and 'restoration' are principal ideas here as throughout *The Prelude* (Jay, 1984: 54–55) but, as modern commentators have stressed, the key element lies in Wordsworth's autobiographical act of writing itself and the consequent invention of a rhetorical identity. As Hartman points out, Wordsworth's longing at the start of *The Prelude* for the great theme that eludes him is easily explained: 'Wordsworth cannot find his theme because he already has it: himself' (Hartman, 1962/1993: 49). The lifelong rewriting of the poem integrates the structure of composition, language and the passage of time in a peculiar intimacy – one which Wordsworth himself hints at in the concluding lines of the episode discussed above:

> ... and I would give,
> While yet we may, as far as words can give,
> A substance and a life to what I feel ...
> (XI, 339–341)

As Fleishman (1983: 102–103) remarks, 'The completing stage of Wordsworth's life as conceived in *The Prelude* is the writing of the poem itself'. The poem becomes an 'extended epitaph ... written by the poet for himself, from a perspective that stems, so to speak, from beyond the grave', obliging us, according to de Man, 'to imagine a tombstone large enough to hold the entire *Prelude*' (de Man, 1987/1993: 63)!

Memory not only feeds the imagination with incident, it also resonates through Wordsworth's mode of composition and influences the form and language of *The Prelude*. It underlies Wordsworth's sense of identity and is the most pervasive influence upon the creation of his Poet-self. Wordsworth's habit of reciting or memorising verses as he walked is well known, particularly his account of composing *Tintern Abbey* in his head during a four- or five-day ramble between Tintern and Bristol where he committed all 159 lines of the poem to paper without altering a single one. With a rare touch of humour, *The Prelude* records similar occasions in the Lake District where Wordsworth describes how, when walking the dog in the evenings, it would give him 'timely notice' to stop 'murmuring / And talking' to himself by running on ahead whenever someone approached (IV, 101–120). His mode of composition is clearly both a powerful form of memory-training and a direct influence upon the rhythms of his verse. Walking and talking lend a steady, regular rhythm to his internal reverie for which the iambic pentameter of his blank verse is the natural carrier. Wordsworth hints at this at the outset when he says, 'I paced on ... with careless steps', and

> My own voice chear'd me, and, far more, the mind's
> Internal echo of the imperfect sound;
> To both I listen'd; ...
> (I, 64–66)

Wordsworth listened, too, to his inheritance from earlier poets. Memories of his reading invest *The Prelude* whose 'biographic verse' has a mixed ancestry – the eighteenth-century pastoral, contemplative verse typified by

Thomson's *The Seasons*, and the high seriousness of the Miltonic epic. In Book V, 'Books', he records the period when, as a 13-year-old, he first experienced how 'words themselves / Move us with conscious pleasure', and

> My ears began to open to the charm
> Of words in tuneful order, found them sweet
> For *their own sakes*, a passion and a power.
> (V, 577–579, Wordsworth's italics)

This love of language translates into a distinctive diction in *The Prelude*. His recurrent keywords, abstract nouns such as 'being', 'forms', 'shapes', 'images', testify to the continuous interplay between the outer world of scenes in nature and the inner world of the poet's mind; rather as if objects from the natural world have been drawn in through the power of his 'inward eye' to become generalised as part of his essential identity. He appears to indicate this process as fundamental to the origin and development of his personality:

> How shall I trace the history, where seek
> The origin of what I then have felt?

His answer is that,

> I forgot
> That I had bodily eyes, and what I saw
> Appear'd like something in myself, a dream,
> A prospect in my mind.
> (II, 365–371)

Wordsworth's extended meditation on his own life in *The Prelude* stems from his realisation, continuously re-experienced in the composition of the poem, that he did not choose his calling but was the chosen one. He was destined to create, in writing the Poet-self he describes, 'a dedicated Spirit' (IV, 344). Wordsworth's *The Prelude* is simultaneously an example of biographical self-projection and a disquisition on how his sense of identity demands to be articulated in poetic form. In de Man's terms, it is both 'mask' and 'metaphor'.

* * *

Wordsworth's self-creation is a challenge, 'for the biographer of Wordsworth's early years must confront his subject's own account of himself at every turn' (Johnston, 2000: 6). Two recent biographers, of whom Johnston is one, provide strikingly different perceptions of the poet's life. Johnston's *The Hidden Wordsworth* tacitly perpetuates the common view that there is little of interest in either the life or the poetry after the publication of *Poems in Two Volumes* in 1807 when Wordsworth was 37. Johnston's time-frame coincides roughly with that of *The Prelude* and he sets out to rescue the young Wordsworth from the staid image of the revered old man of Haydon's portrait (1842) where Wordsworth is shown brooding against a background of Lake District mountains in the year before he became Poet Laureate to Queen Victoria. In contrast, Juliet Barker's *Wordsworth: A Life* (2000) examines the second half of Wordsworth's life as fully as the first. Its scholarly documentation is remorseless; and emerging from the data is a Wordsworth who, far from the solitary 'loner' isolated in the Lakes, is a much-travelled man who, when at home, was surrounded by family and friends and a continual stream of visitors. Johnston is on a mission – to penetrate behind what he calls 'the Wordsworthian cover-up' (p. 3) of the 'facts' about the poet's political life and sex life and, therefore, his poetical life, especially as evidenced in *The Prelude*; Barker refutes these so-called facts as unwarranted guesswork, resting her case upon the solid foundations of documentary evidence about which she is reluctant to speculate.

What, then, are the main contentious issues for these biographers and how do they respond to their subject's own literary account of himself? As might be expected, Wordsworth and his biographers differ on the issue of fidelity to the truth. Wordsworth the autobiographer was disarmingly dismissive of any would-be biographer's efforts:

> The obstacles which stand in the way of the fidelity of the Biographer and Historian … are incalculably greater than those which are to be encountered by the Poet who has an adequate notion of the dignity of his art … there is no object standing between the Poet and the image of things; between this, and the Biographer and Historian there are a thousand. (Wordsworth, 1802/1968: 257–258)

Safe behind his mask of 'the Poet', he can dictate the agenda and claim a clarity and honesty denied to others. Not surprisingly, his biographers have demurred at this, pointing out *The Prelude*'s omissions, especially of his social life as a Cambridge student and, of course, the major lacuna of his relationship with Annette Vallon. In swashbuckling style, Johnston enthuses: 'With its urban revolutions and Alpine scenery, French mistresses and passionate sisters, secret agents and furious guardian uncles, Wordsworth's young life was a most exciting one: Byron might have envied it' (Johnston, 2000: 2). Surely, this is way over the top, yet Johnston does do much to rehabilitate Wordsworth from his conventional stuffy image, showing how his boyhood adventures in the Lake District, his school years at Hawkshead, the influence of his teacher William Taylor, his wide reading, and his circle of friends, all fed into his self-creation in *The Prelude* and into his image of himself as 'the Poet' in the great decade from 1797 to 1807. Johnston is convincing when challenging *The Prelude*'s partial picture of Wordsworth's time at Cambridge, less so when promoting him as a government spy. Biographically, the two most pertinent and contentious issues are Wordsworth's 'lost months' of late summer and autumn 1793, and the treatment of the poet's passionately expressed love for his sister, Dorothy. On both counts, Barker's scepticism hardens into scornful rejection as Johnston is relegated to her endnotes. Their differences are typical of those between two main approaches to literary biography: that of the literary scholar and that of the historian. Whereas Johnston quotes copiously from the poetry and discusses it in relation to the life, Barker rarely ventures into literary appreciation or analysis, preferring to situate Wordsworth's writings within the meticulously documented context of the rest of his day-to-day existence. There are strengths and weaknesses in both approaches. The literary scholar is more willing to interpret, to create possible scenarios for the subject's behaviour; in effect, to treat the 'life' as a text to be deconstructed. The historian is more cautiously tied to the evidence, scrupulously amassing the data and presenting it with balanced judgement and objectivity as the principles. The one is vulnerable to over-dramatising the life, the other to failing to making the subject live.

Hence, Johnston's reconstruction of Wordsworth's unproven return to France in 1793, in a dangerous and failed attempt to see Annette, just at the time when Robespierre's Reign of Terror was beginning, is based on suppositions from four sources detailed in his Chapter 15: Carlyle's account of talking with Wordsworth in 1840 about the Revolution; Wordsworth's annotations to his copy of Burke's works; and on suggestions in an early biography and in Annette's letters (Johnston, 2000: 264–270). Johnston becomes convinced of Wordsworth's 'Return to France', the title of Chapter 16 with its provocative and paradoxical sub-heading, 'The Evidence of Speculation'. Johnston has Wordsworth crossing to Normandy in mid-September 1793, reaching Paris by 7 October and witnessing the execution of Antoine Gorsas, a journalist of the Girondin party, escaping from the capital as Robespierre's moves against English residents increased and, despite heroic efforts to reach Annette in Blois later in the month, being forced back to England by the intense fighting in the Loire region. He backs his claims by arguing that in *The Prelude*, Book X, Wordsworth gives a 'sequential but disguised account of his adventures in France' (Johnston, 2000: 284); and that this textual record is further substantiated by one of the many Miltonic analogies in *The Prelude*, this time in Wordsworth's imaginative parallel between his situation and that of *Samson Agonistes*. Johnston then extends these intertextual links to *Tintern Abbey* and finds Wordsworth sublimating his passion for Annette in the figure of his sister, Dorothy – a reading that, Johnston claims, 'makes sense in the most rudimentary terms of psychological biography' (Johnston, 2000: 292). He is explicit about his stance: 'We cannot separate these kinds of evidence neatly into the biographical and the literary: for Wordsworth, the "literary", especially if it were Miltonic, *was* biographical' (Johnston, 2000: 290).

Barker will have none of this. She rehearses the scenario, acknowledges the available evidence, and expands Stephen Gill's questions in his more balanced assessment of the possibilities into an uncompromising rejection of Wordsworth's return to France, finding that the visit presents 'so many insuperable difficulties that it defies belief' (Barker, 2000: 136; Gill, 1990: 77–78). She reaches the 'boring and unglamorous conclusion' that Carlyle's memory was mistaken. After all, 'He was recalling a conversation which had taken place at least twenty-five years previously, with a man remembering events of almost fifty years before that' (Barker, 2000: 137). Her endnote comments tartly: 'Johnston leads the field in imagining a glamorously novelesque return to France but fails to offer any valid motive or argument to prove it' (Barker, 2000: 837). She is equally scathing about Johnston's attitude to Wordsworth's and Dorothy's relationship. Both biographers agree that there is no evidence of incest: the one speaks of Dorothy's 'emotional dependency' (Barker, 2000: 83), the other of intimacy and sexual abstinence (Johnston, 2000: 458). But Barker is clearly unsympathetic to Johnston's psychological interpolations of Wordsworth's poetry. Again, her endnote is brusque. She erects implicit boundaries around her sense of biography in her remark that such interpretations remain 'principally the domain of literary critics rather than biographers'. And she dismisses Johnston as someone 'desperate to believe there was an incestuous relationship but [who is] unable to convince even himself' (Barker, 2000: 849–850).

This particular battle of the books is helpful in revealing the historical and literary stances of the two biographies: Barker stresses the 'empirical' Wordsworth, Johnston the self-creating Wordsworth in his poetry. This accounts for the relative absence of poetry in Barker's 800 pages and its preponderance in Johnston. Granted their differences, what do these biographies tell us about the sort of life-writing that has an autobiographical antecedent standing between them and their subject? Three interrelated points are suggested. First, as data, the autobiographical text is partial, unstable, circumstantial evidence to be handled with care, if not scepticism.

It is self-centred to a degree that vitiates the wider context of the life; and it is self-serving in promoting a personal construct in which character is mediated by deliberate literary technique. Secondly, the self-projection in an autobiographical poem is as selective an interpretation of the life as that of a biography; it just selects on different principles. Its agenda is governed by the urge for self-realisation through art, not by the desire to tell a life story through the presentation and interpretation of evidence. Thirdly, the 'biographer as spectator' and reader of the life will see things that the 'autobiographer as participant' and writer of the life does not. Reading the life at a distance from the outside complements reading the life as a close-up from within. Self-definition by the subject is no more fixed than the biographers' repeated attempts to capture the life. Auto/Biography, in its doubleness, offers a partial corrective to the singular perception of the subject that can otherwise restrict our concept of the life.

Joyce's 'artist, like the God of creation'

What does Joyce add to our understanding of how a literary text represents the growth of its writer's sense of self and the development of its writer's mind? Joyce's famous description of the artist, the finished portrait as it were, comes towards the end of his book:

> The artist, like the God of creation, remains within or behind or beyond or above his handiwork, invisible, refined out of existence, indifferent, paring his fingernails. (Joyce, 1916/1960: 215)

This image is the culmination of Joyce's aesthetic theory, expressed through his fictionalised self in the character of Stephen Dedalus. It represents what he calls the third and final phase of artistic development, the 'dramatic' phase, when the work of art stands clear and autonomous, impersonal, independent of its author. The forms of literature that precede this phase, the 'lyric' and the 'epical', are seen as still invested with the personality of the artist, the second adding a meditative dimension to the simple emotional responses recorded in the lyrical form. Autobiographically, this formulation has two significant ramifications: the traditional metaphor for the artist as God is a conception given a particularly painful birth in the narrative of Stephen's Catholic upbringing and education; and the account of this history in fictional form, opening with its impersonal, objectified, 'Once upon a time ...' and ending with Stephen's diary entries, leaves the reader in biographical limbo, uncertain whether, in the blunt words of one influential critic, the portrait is 'an objective rendering of reality, looked at from a respectable aesthetic distance, [or] ... a mere subjective indulgence' (Booth, 1961: 332). More generously, *A Portrait of the Artist as a Young Man* can be seen as its author's thinly disguised representation of his growth towards maturity as a writer in whom the ambiguities and uncertainties of his youthful experiences are reflected in the shifts of tone, viewpoint and forms of expression. The variety of ways in which Stephen is depicted, from the contrasting opening and ending, the dialogue he is given, the visions and dreams he experiences, and the constant changes of viewpoint from his movements in the external world to the perceptions of his inner world, create a multifaceted portrait with elements set at angles like a Cubist picture. Both in his account and analysis of Stephen's development and in the innovative form he adopts, Joyce breaks new ground. In what proved to be a significant decade in auto/biography, the first English edition of *A Portrait* was published just a year before Strachey's *Eminent Victorians* (1918). A century on from Wordsworth, this act of self-creation has a distinctly modernist character.

The narrative is a self-projection of the first twenty years of Joyce's life: five chapters like five acts of a drama, with the climax coming at the end of Chapter 4 and, instead of a narrative closure with a denouement resolving the action, a final chapter which opens up the life ahead. Each chapter has its epiphanic moments, those 'sudden spiritual manifestation[s]', as Joyce described them in *Stephen Hero* (Joyce, 1904/1973: 50), triggered by some scene, incident, object, 'gesture or ... memorable phase of mind', of which twelve appear in *A Portrait* (Beja, 1973: 52–57). This history, punctuated by such moments, plots the development of the artist, a *Künstlerroman* that portrays him as a 'loner' who becomes increasingly repelled by his surroundings, who becomes psychologically alienated from his family, who as an adolescent becomes bewildered and aggrieved by the conflict between his sexual awareness and Jesuit education, and whose artistic identity can only be realised through self-exile. In background, substance and response, Joyce's factual history could hardly be more different from Wordsworth's; but, in the literary representation of this history, though the genres differ, the autobiographical personae have points of similarity. In both, the hero is spotlighted. The insistent narrative 'I' of Wordsworth is replaced in *A Portrait* by the Hamlet-like Stephen, always on stage, with the other characters mere foils to his thoughts and experiences. His father emerges briefly on their visit to Cork (Chapter 4), but the rest of his family scarcely figure; Stephen himself is unsure about how many siblings there are and feels 'the mystical kinship of fosterage' (p. 98) rather than any genuine affection. His Ophelia is a shadowy image; 'E_____ C_____' (p. 70) (aka Emma Clery) is more a creature of Stephen's imagination than a real woman. Cranly, Davin, Lynch, his student friends, are differentiated as personalities but all are confined to Chapter 5 to role-play their minor parts in dialogue with the hero. And the Jesuit priests at Clongowes Wood College (Chapter 1) and Belvedere College (Chapters 2, 3, 4) are little more than authority figures with the power to invade his body (the pandybat episode, Chapter 1), mind (the Director's pressure to enter the Order, Chapter 4) and soul (the Hell-fire sermon, Chapter 3). Yet, beyond the superficial similarity of textual self-representation in Wordsworth and Joyce, marked differences exist. Where Wordsworth stresses the notions of 'return' and 'restoration', and the continuity between past and present, Joyce's evocation of the past implies resistance and deliberate discontinuity, a break with the past in order to forge a future self. Jay (1984: 140) comments that the strategy in *A Portrait* is 'opposed to Wordsworth's, since it does not intend to recapture the past for the purposes of a recovery but to overcome the past for the purposes of making a wilful new beginning in exile from it'.

One feature which Joyce shares with Wordsworth is the sensory power to evoke early childhood experiences – as in the opening of *A Portrait*, the impressionistic scenes at Clongowes and the child's-eye view of the Christmas dinner party in Chapter 1, all of which, like the outdoor activities in *The Prelude*, Book I, seem, in the solidity of their presence in the author's mind, to form the imaginative foundation for the life that is to follow. Wordsworth's life narrative brought him back to the Lake District as a young man; after the travels of his early life, this became his base where he was surrounded daily by the scenes of his boyhood. The paradox of Joyce's life narrative as a writer in exile is that, although he left Ireland after graduating from University College, Dublin, in 1902 and composed his fictions in Paris, Trieste and Zurich, they all centre on Dublin. The autobiography of his early years feeds his fictions; the external surroundings in three fascinating continental cities never intrude. Memory is the motor of Joyce's imagination.

As with Wordsworth, it is this retrospective play of mind on the formative memories that provides the substance of his autobiographical fiction. So, at Stephen's moment of truth when he has to choose between the safe, predictable vocation on offer to become 'The Reverend Stephen Dedalus, S.J.', or the vagaries of a future as a writer, it is the memories of childhood at Clongowes that crowd his mind:

> Some instinct, waking at these memories, stronger than education or piety, quickened within him at every near approach to that life [i.e. of the priesthood], an instinct subtle and hostile, and armed him against acquiescence. (p. 161)

Stephen's 'moment of being' is extended in a sequence of external events and internalised thoughts. He walks away from the interview with the Director, turns away from his impoverished home life where his brothers and sisters 'all seemed weary of life even before entering upon it' (p. 164), watches his rejected future pass before his eyes as 'a squad of Christian brothers' crosses a bridge over the river, and questions what it is about words that commands his loyalty as a writer. Wordsworth's language, as we have seen, was an integral part of his identity. Joyce takes this further. He locates the power of words not in their colour, associations and rhythms as they reflect the external world, but from the way they hold a mirror up to the nature of the world within his head. 'It has come increasingly to be recognised that the process of personal growth traced in *A Portrait* is largely a linguistic one, as is appropriate to the portrait of an artist whose art is writing' (Fleishman, 1983: 413; see also Jay, 1984: 128–131, 137). And Fleishman goes on to trace this language pattern in Stephen's development. This artist paints what he knows, not what he sees. As Joyce puts it:

> ... he drew less pleasure from the reflection of the glowing sensible world through the prism of a language many-coloured and richly storied than from the contemplation of an inner world of individual emotions mirrored perfectly in a lucid supple periodic prose. (p. 167)

This realisation leads Stephen directly to his sense of vocation as symbolised in his name: 'Now, as never before, his strange name seemed to him a prophecy' and he sees a vision of his future as an artist as he stands on the bank of the Liffey:

> ... a hawk-like man flying sunward above the sea, a prophecy of the end he had been born to serve and had been following through the mists of childhood and boyhood, a symbol of the artist forging anew in his workshop out of the sluggish matter of the earth a new soaring impalpable imperishable being. (p. 169)

Stephen Dedalus's life is associated with that of his namesake, the 'fabulous artificer', Daedalus, in the creation of a dangerous future – the artist as Icarus. The figure of Icarus-Stephen has long been a source of controversy, seeming to promise, ambiguously, both artistic aspiration and the fall, if not death, of the author. Yet, in the fiction of Stephen, as in Joyce's actual life, the choice of becoming an artist is not really a choice at all. Art chooses him. This vision at the end of Chapter 4, above all other epiphanies, is his most significant 'spot of time' and it climaxes in the image of the girl-cum-seabird (p. 171), his Muse gazing out to sea, symbolising that, as for Wordsworth, he has now become 'a dedicated spirit'.

After which, we are back with Chapter 5, with Stephen as the self-absorbed student who plays the role of intellectual dandy with his college friends; but it is self-consciously done by Joyce as first Lynch and later Cranly counter this poseur, the one challenging his aesthetic theory with earthy cynicism, the other questioning his capacity to live in future without human or divine love, 'Alone, quite alone' (p. 247). Awkward though Chapter 5 may appear in relation to the coherent narrative that precedes it, and insufferable as we might find Stephen to be in his superior and naïvely romantic effusions, Joyce's counterpointing of Stephen's intellectualism with his friends' probings and subversions leaves us with a hero who is much less secure than the protestations of his mind and the symbolism of his imaginings would have us believe. In this ambivalence lies the paradox of Joyce's act of self-creation: fictional Stephen is as vulnerable as the Wordsworthian 'I' to bouts of what Keats called the 'egotistical sublime' (Keats, 1817/2002: 147); yet, Joyce shows considerable courage in his retrospective search to represent a portrait of himself which is true to the ideals of his immaturity, and considerable artistry in constructing this representation as a succession of episodes, written in a variety of styles, to reflect the fragmentary nature of the growth towards selfhood.

* * *

What light does Ellmann throw upon this self-portrait in his biography? His *James Joyce* (1959; revised edition, 1983) is widely regarded as the most complete example of the genre in the past half-century, not least because it integrates the life and the art of its subject so successfully. In doing so, Ellmann is also emulating his subject, who acknowledged that 'When your work and life make one, when they are interwoven in the same fabric', then the autobiographical novelist is in unique, creative circumstances. Ellmann glosses this remark by Joyce as follows:

> The fact that he was turning his life into fiction at the same time that he was living it encouraged him to feel a certain detachment from what happened to him, for he knew he could reconsider and re-order it for the purpose of his book. At the same time, since he felt dependent for material upon actual events, he had an interest … in making the events through which he lived take on as extreme a form as possible. (Ellmann, 1959/1983: 149)

Ellmann is here writing about *Stephen Hero* and one of the strengths of his biography, allied to this reciprocal relationship between art and life, is to show how *A Portrait* was conceived and born. The pregnancy lasted ten years. Conception became evident with the sketch 'A Portrait of the Artist' (1904), part essay part story, which Joyce submitted unsuccessfully to a new journal. This sketch grew into a life-sized study, *Stephen Hero*, and was reworked in shortened form a decade later to appear eventually as the finished painting in *A Portrait*. The comparison with birth is no idle metaphor. In Joyce's rewriting *Stephen Hero* as *A Portrait* in five chapters, Ellmann shows that '*A Portrait of the Artist as a Young Man* is in fact the gestation of a soul, and in the metaphor Joyce found his new principle of order'. He locates an 'atmosphere of biological struggle' throughout the book's language and symbolism until, in Stephen's diary at the end, 'the soul is released from its confinement, its individuality complete, and the style shifts with savage abruptness' (Ellmann, 1959/1983: 296–297). Ellmann was the first to understand the significance of Joyce's metaphorical rebirth (Jay, 1984: 120–121).

Ellmann also suggests a different configuration of time and memory in *A Portrait* which is germane to autobiographical writing and analogous to what was said above about *The Prelude*. He argues that, 'The episodic framework of *Stephen Hero* was renounced in favour of a group of scenes radiating backwards and forwards', and he exemplifies this from the interrelated 'clusters of sensations' in three such scenes in Chapter 1 – the memories of infancy at the start, Stephen's sickness at Clongowes, and the pandybat episode. While the reading eye is ineluctably processing the text as 'a linear succession of events', the effect on the reader's mind is that the sequence becomes 'primarily one of layers rather than of years' (Ellmann, 1959/1983: 297). Ellmann implies that by reconfiguring narrative time so that its forward drive is mediated by a contemplative stillness that probes the interrelatedness of these events – ones occurring at different times and places in the life history – Joyce is reflecting the way consciousness deals with memories. They are apprehended as being superimposed on each other, thus facilitating an autobiographical reading of them which, in turn, becomes a means of access to a sense of selfhood. This notion of consciousness permeates both Joyce's self-concept and his style of articulating it. The opening paragraph of his original 1904 sketch, in effect the first draft of *A Portrait*, begins with the assertion that the past has no 'iron memorial aspect', but 'implies a fluid succession of presents'. What we are to seek is the 'individuating rhythm': 'a portrait is not an identificative paper but rather the curve of emotion' (Joyce, 1904/1973: 41). Joyce's self-portrait looks behind the identikit likeness to the interconnected memories that constitute personality. Portraits in words, as much as those in paint, seek to represent the aggregate of the past in the features of the present image, interpreting their temporal presence as 'fluid', one in which elements merge, unfixed and freely associating as in a river, quite unlike the unchanging solidity of some 'iron memorial'. Although Ellmann identifies Stephen's diary entries at the end of *A Portrait* as Joyce's first 'interior monologue' (Ellmann, 1959/1983: 358), it is here in the early sketch that one can detect the beginnings of the idea of a 'stream of consciousness' which Joyce was to make such a feature in *Ulysses*.

Vital to the fluidity of this 'succession of presents' is Joyce's concept of epiphanies. Again, Ellmann is helpful in plotting their course from Joyce's first idea of collecting these moments into a small book of what might be called 'prose poems' (Ellmann, 1959/1983: 85), to their eventual inclusion in *Stephen Hero* and *A Portrait*. In fact, in *A Portrait*, there is no specific reference to this term, but the concept is embedded in Stephen's aesthetic theory where he describes it as the sudden revelation of 'the whatness of a thing' and characterises it, with heightened vocabulary, as 'radiance', 'luminous', 'spiritual', 'enchantment', and with Shelley's image of the mind at the creative moment as a 'fading coal' (Joyce, 1916/1960: 213). This allusion to atheist Shelley's *A Defence of Poetry* seems particularly pointed as a way of indicating the artist's experience of the creative process as a slow fading away of divine inspiration as the business of making the art-work with words takes over. This literary process, as we have seen, is also that of Joyce's life as he outgrows his Catholic upbringing. 'Epiphany', with its religious connotation of Christ's appearance to the Magi, is redefined in secular terms as Stephen faces his future. Perhaps this is as close as we can come to Joyce's autobiographical image of the 'artist, like the God of creation'.

Masks and Metaphors

At the outset, I raised the issue, via Paul de Man, of whether autobiography should be seen as mask or metaphor. Subsequently, I have noted it operating in both modes in *The Prelude* and *The Portrait*. From a theoretical point of view, the mask is undeniable; the Poet-self and the Artist-self are literary inventions. But, considered psychologically as a way of constructing a personal history, such autobiographical figures are valid metaphorical means of understanding selfhood. Paul de Man is again helpful in the distinction he draws between 'the performative' and 'the cognitive' dimensions of autobiography where the former is always dominant: 'the textual "I" seeks out excuses to perform itself; it creates dramas in order to stage the "real" drama of the "self"' (de Man, quoted in Anderson, 2005: 51). De Man seems ready to stress the role-playing but reluctant to acknowledge the insights that can accrue from the creation of a metaphorical figure in the interpretation of the self. Undue emphasis on the mask, with its implications of concealment if not of dissembling, risks neglecting the metaphor and its effort at understanding through figurative representation. The two are not mutually exclusive, but in reconciling them, literary biographers are faced with uniquely difficult issues when attempting to come to terms with literary lives already explicitly encoded by their subjects in particular texts.

The doubleness of the term 'auto/biography' not only encompasses two images – the self-portrait and the biographer's portrait; it also indicates the particular problems of the *literary* biographer whose subject has self-consciously married the lived-through experiences of daily events with the compulsion to write, making the ordinary strange by translating it into poetry or fiction. Stephen Gill expresses the biographer's need to resist the seduction of literary 'truth' masquerading as historical 'fact':

> In the *1805 Prelude* Wordsworth thus presents a teleological account of the formative years of his life. With his interpretive key everything can be seen as contributing to his growth into what he was already destined to be, a great poet of a particular kind. But we must resist the proffered key. (Gill, 1990: 7)

Joyce's celebrated 'biografiend' (his playfully derogatory label in *Finnegans Wake*) is only too aware of the implications of this resistance. Ellmann begins his book by suggesting that a writer's life differs from those of others since 'events are becoming artistic sources even as they command his present attention'. He goes on:

> Instead of allowing each day, pushed back by the next, to lapse into imprecise memory, he shapes again the experiences which have shaped him.... In turn the process of reshaping experience becomes a part of his life, another of its recurrent events like rising or sleeping. The biographer must measure in each moment this participation of the artist in two simultaneous processes. (Ellmann, 1959/1983: 3)

Literary lives, particularly ones like those of Wordsworth and Joyce, are a continuous blending of events and composition. Words are their catalyst, whether as single images or in animating the whole business of writing. A murderer's name carved in turf beneath the gibbet, or school graffiti carved in the wood of a desk lid – each carries its creative charge from childhood into the literary life (*The Prelude*, IV, 101–120; *A Portrait*, 1916/1960: 90). Similarly, words are shown on the move in both books. Whether it is Wordsworth's *sotto voce* mumbling as he composes while rambling the country lanes, or Stephen's inner speech or conversations with friends around the streets of Dublin, walking and talking are endemic in the lives of these two artists. While their self-created narratives are loosely characterised by a temporal ordering of experiences, it is the verbal exploration of those 'moments of being' that give insight into this blending of events and composition. The two features which we have noticed as central to this process are the synthetic operation of memory and the drive to articulate a sense of selfhood in words.

The shift from the apprehension to the articulation of memories involves the interplay of word and image. Curiously, this seems to necessitate a merging of literary genres where poetry inclines to the prosaic and prose to the poetic. Wordsworth attested as much in his 'Preface' to *Lyrical Ballads*, arguing that 'a large portion of the language of every good poem can in no respect differ from that of good prose ... there neither is, nor can be, any *essential* difference between the language of prose and metrical composition' (Wordsworth, 1802/1968: 253). Conversely, Joyce, as we have seen, invokes Shelley's *A Defence of Poetry* in his account and, at the visionary moment of his life when he becomes the artist, he resorts to poetry:

> He drew forth a phrase from his treasure and spoke it softly to himself:
> – A day of dappled seaborne clouds.
> The phrase and the day and the scene harmonised in a chord.
> (Joyce, 1916/1960: 166)

Wordsworth's 'spots of time' within his poem are represented narratively; that is, he tells the story of the creative process of uncovering the layers of memory laid down in his history – a sort of psychological archaeology. Joyce's 'epiphanies' within his novel are represented poetically; that is, he pinpoints these 'most delicate and evanescent moments' (Joyce, 1904/1973: 50), seeing the task of the artist as focusing on the aesthetic image in his mind and capturing it in words. Wordsworth's 'spots of time' are recollected as images in the tranquillity of the compositional act and developed as integral parts of his narrative; Joyce's 'epiphanies' were pre-formed 'prose poems' whose prior existence affects both their own translation from image into words and their integration into the texture of his novel. Here, more than anywhere, the reciprocity between the life narrative and the literary narrative is acutely felt. Faced with these acts of self-creation, the singular task of the *literary* biographer is not to seek the man behind the mask, but to accept the persona as a coded version of the subject and to elucidate the relationship between the textual self and the life as it was lived.

9

Biography in Practice

An Interview with Dominic Hibberd, author of *Wilfred Owen: A New Biography*

Dominic Hibberd is the leading authority on the life and poetry of Wilfred Owen. His many publications include an edition of Owen's poems, Wilfred Owen: War Poems and Others *(1973), a critical study,* Owen the Poet *(1986),* Wilfred Owen: The Last Year *(1992) and, with John Onions,* The Winter of the World: Poems of the First World War *(2007), as well as two biographies,* Harold Monro: Poet of the New Age *(2001) and* Wilfred Owen: A New Biography *(2002).*

This interview, conducted in April 2007, focused on this last publication. The conversation was guided by some notes of issues and questions, sent in advance, designed to illuminate the complementary purposes of this book: to gain insights into the genre and to contextualise the literary subjects. Following Holmes's notion of biography as both a 'pursuit' and a 'haunting' (see Chapter 3), the first and third sections of this interview are about the practice of biography and the issues it raises. In between, the second section discusses the biographer's perceptions of the main themes of Wilfred Owen's life.

(i) ***Living with the Subject:*** *practical matters of how Dominic's interest in Owen developed, the sources and management of information, and the process of writing the biography.*
(ii) ***Imagining Wilfred:*** *the main themes in Wilfred Owen's life story, in particular the two strands in his sense of vocation as a poet – religion and reading; the class consciousness and growing awareness of his homosexuality during his formative years; and the uncertainty surrounding his fatal decision to return to France in September 1918.*

(iii) ***Matters of Life and Death:** wider issues arising out of the biography: the tidy ordering of life-writing versus the messiness of living; the biographer's role as historian and/or storyteller; the justification for a 'new' biography in respect of the existing ones; and the relationship that develops between biographer and subject.*

This was the agenda. Here is the conversation.

Living with the Subject

MB: Dom, I thought we'd begin with how you got interested in Wilfred Owen, when and how it came about. Could you say a bit about that?

DH: It was simply that I was a schoolmaster at Manchester Grammar School [MGS] and had to teach Owen's poems for A-level from the old 1931 Blunden edition, which we were still using in 1968. It so happened that the *Collected Letters* had been published the year before and I realised, reading through the letters, that here was a research subject. If you put the letters next to the poems, you could say all sorts of new things that nobody had said before. So that's where it all grew from; and by chance, at Manchester University, there was Dennis Welland, who was the only person who had written a book about Owen. He was very kind and helpful, gave me an introduction to Chatto & Windus, and between us we hatched the idea of doing a school edition of Owen's poems, which I duly did in the end.

MB: This was all in the 1960s, then?

DH: Yes, it was 1968/69, when I started teaching the poems, and my edition of the poems came out I think in 1973. With the publication at least in progress, I was able to leave MGS and go to America for a year to a job in a University which gave me a chance to do huge amounts of reading. I read all the stuff that Wilfred had read, or might have read, and lots of other war poetry as well, and gave myself a good grounding in it. Then I came back to do a PhD and then, I think in the second year of that, suddenly my hopes of doing the great edition of Owen's poems collapsed because I discovered that Jon Stallworthy had been appointed to be the official biographer and editor. It wasn't his fault at all, of course; he didn't know I existed. But it was the end of that particular line.

MB: But you must have recovered because you obviously published a lot of articles and books, not only on Owen but, for example, the Macmillan *Casebook* on World War One Poetry, and so on, in subsequent years.

DH: Yes. Well, I went to see Jon and he suggested that I could do a critical book on Owen, which I duly did eventually. He gave me unrestricted access to the manuscripts, which was very kind of him, but on condition that I didn't publish anything until his edition was out. So his edition came out, I think, in 1983, and my book *Owen the Poet: A Critical Study* came out in 1986. By that stage, I'd also read a lot of other First World War poets, so in that same year I produced, with one of my research students, John Onions, an anthology of First World War poetry as well. And there ... I felt at the time, I'd probably come to the end of all that.

MB: So what prompted this particular biography then, ten years or more on from that stage?

DH: Well, 1993 was Owen's Centenary and it occurred to me that I might do a picture book to mark that. And it grew into rather more than that and became a biographical study of his last year. In fact, it was very frustrating to do that because, you know, there were lots of things in his early life that make sense in the later life, and you can't start at the beginning if you're only writing about the last year. So I found it quite ... not exactly a tiresome book to write, but clearly not satisfactory in several ways. But I still didn't really think of doing a biography. Jon Stallworthy had done one and ... but eventually I was talked into it by friends, publishers, by the need to make some money ... and so, in the end, I agreed.

MB: So how long did it take to actually put the biography together?

DH: I reckon it took about five years' full-time work. It was slightly embarrassing because I had also done a biography of Harold Monro which had come out in 2001 and the Owen biography came out in 2002. It looked as though I had just written a biography in a year, but actually the Monro book had been written long before that and was delayed by the publishers.

MB: Can we move on to the sources that you used, Dom? I'm wondering, given the fact that in the 1960s there would be family and friends and descendants, and maybe former comrades in arms still living, whether or not you actually interviewed anybody who had first-hand knowledge of Wilfred, or if any have emerged since the publication of your book? Did any issues crop up from these sorts of connections?

DH: Sadly, little, because of course at the beginning I never thought of writing a biography and so I didn't pursue the links. If I had done in the late 1960s, yes, I might have found fellow soldiers and all sorts of people; but, alas, by the time I got round to thinking of doing a biography seriously, the only person that I'd ever met was Wilfred's first cousin, Leslie Gunston, whom I did get to know quite well and quite often used to go and see, but he was not actually at all communicative about Wilfred. He didn't tell me anything that I couldn't have found out from other sources. I only met one other man, in his nineties, who had been in the army with Wilfred and who didn't think much of him. Those were the only two people I ever met who had actually known him personally.

MB: So you never met Harold? [WO's brother]

DH: No. I corresponded with Harold briefly at the end of his life, but he died in 1970 or '71.

MB: I love the bit in the book where you begin one paragraph, 'And here Harold Owen interrupts the story, scissors in hand'. I thought that was perhaps the sharpest example, literally, of the fact that he was a very unreliable source – cutting up his brother's letters, mixing fact and fiction in his own memoir [*Journey from Obscurity*, 3 vols, 1963–1965], and even doctoring Wilfred's MC citation, I gather.

DH: Well, it seems so. I can't think who else could have done it. Yes.

MB: In practice as a biographer, how do you deal with an unreliable source who is nonetheless clearly a very important one whom you can't ignore?

DH: In a way, it was very much to my advantage, because until I came along everyone had assumed that Harold was telling the truth and so at least I could do something new. Because it seemed perfectly obvious to me that he wasn't telling the truth on a great many matters; and, when one actually did a bit of digging, one could see quite clearly that he had rewritten the past as he saw it. So, for example, he claims in his book that the family had to spend all its spare money on Wilfred's education, which was quite expensive, so there was nothing left for Harold, who just got what free education he could. Actually, that's quite untrue, because the course that Wilfred did as a pupil-teacher was itself free; and Harold, later on, joined it on the same terms. Harold was, not intentionally I think, cooking the books. I mean everybody says that he was a very honest, honourable man and that he was doing everything for the best but, in my opinion, he wanted people to see the Wilfred that he thought people ought to see, not the real man.

MB: But that must have put you in a funny position every now and then, having to sort out truth from fiction; and also, I suppose, it was an encouragement to you to speculate, to interpret the evidence of *Journey from Obscurity*.

DH: Well, I liked to think, until I read your notes, that I hadn't speculated very much, or only on the basis of very strong probability, only when there was no other way of completing the story. Because you can't just leave the reader with a nothingness to jump over; you've got to suggest something that might have happened, at any rate. Maybe I have imposed my own views on things rather more than I realised, but no …, I think I really was honest as far as one possibly could be. But then on some matters you do have to use some kind of instinct.

MB: What about the letters, because those were another important source? Most of them were written home to Susan, his mother, weren't they? Yet Harold also had a hand in editing those, of course.

DH: I think there's no doubt that Harold did destroy quite a few. It's quite noticeable when you get to a key point, for example, on the two occasions when Wilfred goes to the Western Front at the end of 1916 and then again in 1918. There must have been some more letters then, and one doesn't know exactly what happened. Was Wilfred ordered to go, or did he decide to go? Did he jump or was he pushed? There's no way of being absolutely sure about that; and I think that's due to Harold's intervening. And there are certainly other areas where you can see this ... you know, where Wilfred says, 'What did you think about the momentous events described in my last letter?' and the last letter isn't there, so you don't know what the momentous events were.

MB: Frustrating, yes. But there must be examples, too, of the way in which he slanted or edited his letters back from the Front to Susan, so that, in a way, he was glossing his experiences, horrific as they were, for home consumption, so as not to worry her too much.

DH: Well, no, I'm not sure about that. I think he was extraordinarily ... well, not exactly unkind to her but quite ruthless in a way. Some of the things he said about religion, which was very dear to her heart after all, as she was a deeply committed Christian, she must have found quite hard to cope with. Wilfred is very sceptical about religion in his later letters. Similarly, some of his descriptions of the Western Front and the flooded dug-out and so on are as vivid as anything in letters by soldiers; and I think the reason why Wilfred was writing like that was because he wanted to get at his two Gunston cousins who both stayed at home. They remained as civilians, under slightly questionable circumstances, and Wilfred wanted to get at their consciences, I think, through writing home.

MB: Did you pick up any of that when you met Leslie Gunston?

DH: No. Leslie never referred to that kind of thing, no.

MB: OK. If we can move on, Dom. Obviously, there's a lot of data from these sources we've been talking about, and I was wondering how you actually managed the information in practice. I remember reading somewhere in Paula Backscheider's book [*Reflections on Biography*, 1999] that, as a biographer, she spent something like 80–90 per cent of her time on research, travel, data collection, filing, all this sort of stuff, and only 10–15 per cent on actually writing the book. So I was wondering what your experience was, how you operated with the data available and did you use a filing system, card indexes, computer files? Did you write in longhand and then on to a word processor? Did you write it continuously as a narrative, or do bits in a different order and then put them all together?

DH: I like working very much from primary sources. I'm not interested in what X has said about what Y has said about what Z has said about the subject. I like to know about the subject. So, I've worked a lot from manuscripts and that often means American libraries, and always in pencil. I use spiral-bound notebooks with lots of pencil notes in; I should think I've got a dozen of them. The last thing one wants to do is to copy it all out again, so I use those and I always leave the front two pages empty so that I can write an index when it's all full. The other thing I had for both biographies I did was a lever-arch file which I called 'Chrono'.

MB: Chrono?

DH: Chrono – which was the chronology of the life. I had a page per year with two lines for every month, and wrote into that anything that could be dated, whatever it was, while I was reading round.

MB: That's fascinating.

DH: And gradually then the life took shape. It was especially useful for Harold Monro actually, because the records were much more scattered there. Then, in a really detailed area, like Wilfred's time at the Western Front, I would have a page per month and a couple of lines per day, you know, just to work out exactly where he was and what was going on. When you've got that structure, then you can follow it through and start drawing a story from it.

MB: So you were, in effect, writing Wilfred's diary for him, weren't you?

DH: Well, almost, yes, that kind of thing. And as for the actual writing – longhand always: twice in biro, in rough, and then writing it out again in longhand with a fountain pen. Then I'd type it on to a computer.

MB: But did you write it forwards?

DH: Yes, chronologically, from the beginning right through. That was something I learned from doing the book about Wilfred's last year; that it was so frustrating then not to be able to talk about, for example, Wilfred's sexuality. You know, you need to start at the beginning and work through, and if you can't do that, goodness it's difficult. So yes, I began with the first page.

MB: I suppose it's natural to write it forwards when you've got all the diary elements set out for you.

DH: It's all there, yes.

Imagining Wilfred

MB: If we can move on to the actual Wilfred you've created for readers. One of the things that I noticed, of course, straight away, is that it's 200 pages into your biography before Wilfred actually gets to France in uniform at the very end of 1916. In other words, over half your book deals with Wilfred's pre-war experiences which, in themselves, with the best will in the world, are probably not the reasons for most people going to read about Wilfred Owen. So, I wondered whether you felt there was a problem of balance between the pre-war years and the 1917–18 period?

DH: Well, I didn't at all. Some readers have objected that the book is far too detailed, and every now and then a reviewer would say that they got a bit impatient with the early chapters; but I don't see how you can possibly make sense of Wilfred's life unless you know what happened at the beginning. After all, although half the book is devoted to 1917–18, that's a great deal less than half his life, although he only lived to be 25. I wanted to tell the whole story, so I thought, 'Well, there are going to be readers who aren't going to like this, but they can go hang; they can just go and read another book somewhere'.

MB: Excellent. I mean that was my feeling, too. But the corollary to this for me was the sense I had of reading a foreshortened life, especially through the frequent forward references to the war. The sort of things I'm thinking about are the Bordeaux church bells that sound in 'Anthem for Doomed Youth'; or the recurring image of the terrifying face and fixed eyes during his depressing time at Dunsden which are later used in 'Strange Meeting' and elsewhere; or again, the electric lights at the flower show in Shrewsbury which appear in 'Disabled'. I thought these might be conscious attempts on your part to keep me, the reader, aware of the fact that the war was coming, as it were. Was this me, or is this you?

DH: Yes, absolutely deliberate, yes. (laughter)

MB: I thought it must be.

DH: And, of course, there's the great luxury of being able to write a full-length book about somebody who only lived to be 25. There's nothing about old age and all that kind of thing; that doesn't happen. It stops, quite literally, with a bang; which has considerable advantages, I think, everything is highly concentrated.

MB: On Wilfred's sense of vocation, there are two strands that I picked up from your biography: his religious upbringing and his own growing literary experiences. If we can talk about the religion first, in a way, I felt from reading your book that this was the key to Wilfred's own sense of identity. There's this sense that there's an uncomfortable, triangular relationship within him as the growing poet, the increasingly sceptical Christian, and the military officer; and that somewhere in the relationships between these three, there is the key to who Wilfred Owen actually was. Am I right about this? They seem to be things that crop up over and over again, and religion is clearly a major factor through his very early years and upbringing.

DH: Yes. I don't see it as a triangle, more as parallels. In the way he was trained [as a child and as a parish assistant at Dunsden], you are initiated into knowledge which non-Christians don't have and you have to master Biblical texts so that you've got them absolutely to hand. So that's why I used the phrase 'mystery and mastery' from 'Strange Meeting'. Your job is to go out and spread the Gospel, spread the Word, and love other people. Then again, if you're a poet, you are in a mysterious brotherhood, like a kind of priesthood, cut off from other people, once again, knowing your subject inside out having studied for a long time, which is what Wilfred wanted to do and was never able to do. Again, your task is a practical one, to improve society through loving other people by putting yourself in their position. The key to this is, I think, Shelley rather than Keats. He seems to me a very important figure. Then again, as an officer, you're cut off from civilians. You're in a separate world of your own, again a band of brothers, and you have to be an absolute master of everything military. As Colonel Shirley told cadets in the Artists' Rifles, 'An officer has to be able to do everything his men can do, only do it better'. It's not 'spreading the Gospel' in quite the same way, but fighting in a war is a bit similar in its need for mastery.

MB: So these terms, 'mystery' and 'mastery' which you use at least twice in the book – it's the mystery of Christianity as well as the mastery of it; the mystery of being a poet as well as the mastery of the technicalities of poetry. But is there much mystery in being an officer? I can see there's certainly mastery.

DH: Well, when you're cut off from civilians, it's the same as being a Christian or a poet, you're in a band of brothers, a kind of priesthood, as it were. So it does have a sort of religious connotation all the way through, I think, that makes you quite special and separate, different from ordinary people.

MB: Does this actually fit with what you say fairly late on in the book? On the one hand, you say he spent the afternoon of his 25th birthday at Ripon Cathedral, speculating that, and I quote, he was 'perhaps praying to the God he had never quite ceased to believe in' (p. 306). And yet, four pages on, you quote him as writing in a letter home, 'God so hated the world that He gave several millions of English-begotten sons, that whosoever believeth in them should not perish, but have a comfortable life'. That's pretty bitter stuff, and I wondered whether his faith in what he is describing as a hateful God actually survived the horrors of war.

DH: You are a most ruthless reader (laughter). I'm not sure whether you've caught me out on that entirely or not. Clearly, I should have explained it more. I think, perhaps, I'm working from my own experience here, which

I haven't talked about at all yet, but when I was at Cambridge I was caught up in evangelical religion and thought I was converted. I signed the card and all the rest of it and was actually a college representative for the Christian Union. Then I realised in my last year that it didn't really add up and it all fell away very quickly as soon as I left Cambridge and I've never gone back to it. But I've never quite been able to find it in my heart to say there is no God; that's going further than I'm willing to go. Maybe there is, maybe there isn't; and I think Wilfred was the same, only much more so, because it had been built into him from such an early age; so that to make a complete, total break on the basis of what, after all, can only be guesswork, was, I think, more than he would have ever been willing to do. But I am inevitably speculating from my own position here and perhaps I shouldn't have done.

MB: Well, not at all. I mean it's an interesting phenomenon, I think, the way in which biographers associate themselves with their subjects. So that when one reads, 'perhaps praying to a God he never quite ceased to believe in', in a way, you're going beyond empathy. Here is something which is part of your experience which you are bringing to the experience that you imagined Wilfred, on all the evidence that you've got, may have shared.

DH: That's why the Dunsden chapters I found particularly interesting to write because they are all about his experience of evangelical religion which I felt I understood in a way that nobody had ever done before. When he talks about going to the PM, for example, I know exactly what the PM was. It stands for Prayer Meeting, a key event in the parish week.

MB: You use the phrase 'a kind of priesthood' more than once; there's this sense of a priestly calling both in the poetry and in the military, and that religion underpins everything.

DH: Yes. That way of thinking about it does seem to me to be crucially important there. So when he says, 'God so hated the world ...', he may have been perhaps mocking Easter worshippers and his mother too. You know, even if you are a believer, you can sometimes say that kind of thing.

MB: Oh, yes. But the thing he seemed to take from his religious upbringing, once he moved into the military, was this notion of service, wasn't it?

DH: In a way, he thinks of war as an evil and un-Christian business. Being a pacifist would perhaps be OK in theory, but in practice the more important thing is service to his men.

MB: Yes.

DH: You've got to fight this thing through and ... you know, so many of them did feel that. This was a war which had to be fought. Nowadays, we think of it as futility and all that. The futility myth has got hold of so many people's understanding of war, but at the time they thought that this was a desperately important war that simply had to be fought.

MB: If we can switch, Dom, to the other strand which you follow through in his vocation, that is his literary development, I'm a little surprised that you identify Wilfred's earliest influence as Wordsworth rather than Keats, which is what I'd always assumed. Is this a lasting influence? Does it show itself in any of his poems?

DH: I think so, yes. If you think of his very last poem, 'Spring Offensive', and the little brambles that cling to the soldiers to try to stop them going into battle, that sort of thing seems to suggest a kind of 'Wordsworthian' understanding of nature. Then, when the attack happens, and it's a spring offensive in the sense that it's against the spring as well as during it, the landscape responds with fury. There is that interchange of action from within and from without that Wordsworth talks about of a very violent and terrible kind. I think Wordsworth is there a lot but, of course, Wilfred's enthusiasm for Keats was the overwhelming thing in his early years.

MB: And again, something I didn't know, was that although he read and marked rhymes and phrases in Keats's poems, he was also a great reader of biographies, of the literary lives of writers.

DH: Yes, yes.

MB: And that suggests to me again a sort of Wordsworthian thing, now I think about it, that he was clearly wanting to develop his literary sense of self, not only through technicalities but through a way of life, through a vocation. It's like Wordsworth's phrase for himself in *The Prelude*, 'a dedicated spirit'. This sense of wanting to live the life of a poet maybe was fed by the biographies he was reading.

DH: Yes, it certainly had a lot to do with it. I think he was always looking for parallels between his own life and those of writers. Of course, one has to remember that there was very little in the way of what we would now call literary criticism and, if you wanted to find out about a writer, you really had to read about his life because there wasn't much else on the whole.

MB: Later literary influences that you discuss are the 'Decadents', especially Laurent Tailhade, and yet the major influence on the war poems is that of Siegfried Sassoon in 1917 and 1918. Can you expand a bit on these two contrary influences – the romantic inheritance and the tough realism of Sassoon's poetry? What did he learn from these two sources?

DH: Well, remember that Sassoon himself was, before the war, a romantic and decadent poet. His verses were considerably more limp than Wilfred's, I think, and less distinguished; but this was the kind of world he belonged to as, of course, all of them did. And then you have to remember that in the romantic tradition, there is Shelley; and there's Oscar Wilde who writes rather bad decadent verse, I think, but speaks out strongly on social issues, especially prison reform ...; if you meet something that is horrifying, well you've got to tell people about it. So you tell them the actual vivid detail, in just the same way as if you meet something beautiful you tell them about that as well.

MB: I suppose it's more the style of writing that I was wondering about. I mean 'Dulce Et Decorum Est' is always cited as the Sassoon-like poem. But what about 'Anthem for Doomed Youth', which still shows many characteristics of romantic verse but, nonetheless, is a sort of elegy and about something very terrible. Is it right to think of it as a transitional poem?

DH: Oh yes, yes, I think so. But then you've also got to think of 'Dulce' as a transitional poem as well; and it's interesting that both were written within, perhaps, three or four weeks of each other.

MB: Really?

DH: Extraordinary that he could have done both. But he's moving from 'Anthem' where there are lots of echoes of patriotic literature, the traditional sonnet and Keatsian language, to 'Dulce', which is a very harsh reaction against the sort of heroic poetry that you kept finding in the newspapers. Then again, if you compare that with, say, 'Strange Meeting', or 'Insensibility', or 'Spring Offensive', the great 1918 poems, he's clearly moved a long way from those Sassoon-ish satires he wrote at Craiglockhart. It was partly to do with the politics of the thing. Sassoon had given him a new way of understanding the war and of thinking, as a lot of pacifists did in 1917 – though modern historians say they were actually mistaken – that the war could then be stopped by peace negotiations, if only negotiations could be got going. So the crucial thing was to get at the people's conscience and tell them what this business was about, and you did this by harsh satire and realism.

MB: But you are really saying that, in the great 1918 poems, Wilfred had moved on from that.

DH: Yes, because after the German 'March Offensive', there was no longer any possibility of peace negotiations.

MB: So, is it possible to characterise the style that he moved on to, to characterise his development over what is just a matter of months? In the later poems, has he become more symbolic, or more resigned to accepting the inevitability of human nature at war?

DH: I think the poems become more elegiac. They're less concerned with kicking the reader in the stomach and more with moving you to pity. He is realising what his men are really suffering, and writing about war in general rather than this particular war; writing for the future, not for the immediate public at the time. You know, he was aiming for future generations, people like us. His canvas has become much larger, I think. Some people think that the 1918 poems are less good than the 1917 ones, but I think he's got to be judged more by the 1918 ones.

MB: You're really suggesting that by that stage, he's becoming a poet of warning, a poet of prophecy, a 'poet as witness', as Seamus Heaney called it.

DH: Yes.

MB: If we look at this period though, this is the great modernist decade in poetry, isn't it? But Wilfred's only brush with modernism appears to have been Edith Sitwell's *Wheels* in 1917. Eliot and Pound seem to be unknown by him, and yet *Prufrock and other Observations* was also published in 1917. So, I wondered on the broader literary canvas whether you felt this label of 'war poet', just like those other labels, 'Georgian poet' or 'modernist poet', is a sort of limiting factor. Is he just, as it were, a 'war poet' who is remembered perhaps for a dozen very good poems?

DH: Well, first of all, I think academics grossly overestimate the importance of modernism at the time. Very few people were aware of modernism at all and many who were aware of it thought it was a lot of rubbish anyway. So, you have to be careful. I read very recently an interesting book by Peter Howarth [*British Poetry in the Age of Modernism*, 2006] in which he talks about 'non-modernists' including Wilfred and people like de la Mare and Edward Thomas and a number of other poets – Hardy, for example, who was, of course, still alive and at the height of his powers during the war. The modernists' contribution to First World War poetry seems to me to be really very limited indeed. But, I'm quite sure that if Wilfred had read *The Waste Land*, he would have absorbed all that and learned from it. As for being 'a war poet', yes, he did, I think, accept that label. He wrote in his 'Preface' originally, something like 'Why a true war poet must be truthful'; he then crossed out 'war', but nevertheless he accepted, I think, that for as long as the war lasted that is what he would have to be. After it, he could branch out and do something wider and different.

MB: Can your research for the biography tell us anything about the way he wrote? I don't mean the inner workings of Wilfred Owen's mind; we can't know that with him or anyone else, but you may be able to say something about the sources of his imagery, his mode of composition, what is revealed in his manuscripts and drafts and revisions, where he wrote and so on. Did he write in the trenches, or did he wait until he got back to base behind the lines? Or was it all recollected in tranquillity in Craiglockhart and Ripon?

DH: It was all recollected in tranquillity. I don't have any evidence that he wrote any war poems in the trenches or anywhere near them. When he was in France in early 1917 he was writing sonnets on subjects that he'd agreed with Leslie Gunston about 'Golden Hair', topics of that kind. He'd written some poems about war of a heroic, conventional kind, but it was Sassoon who got him going; and one has to say, I think, that if he hadn't met Sassoon in

1917 the great war poems would not have been written. It was Sassoon who gave him the impetus and the ideas on which to base his writing. But he always needed peace and quiet and a room to himself; and in Ripon, especially, he had to get a room in a cottage up under the roof, very secluded and shut away, without interruptions. That was how he kept going. He put poems through many different drafts, I mean 8, 9, 10 or more, before he got something that he liked, and all that took time. I don't know that anyone can explain quite what happens in that moment when raw words are somehow forged into a poem …

MB: I suppose the nearest we get are those manuscripts annotated with Sassoon's pencil, his comments on alternative words in the drafts of 'Anthem for Doomed Youth'. Does this occur elsewhere?

DH: No, that's the only example I can recall.

MB: Which I've always found fascinating, but rather tantalising. It gets you fairly near the point where the mind and the pen and the paper are together, but you don't actually know what's happening.

DH: You never quite solve it, yes.

MB: Two themes which occur frequently in the biography are the class consciousness that seemed to pervade both civilian and military life during what were Wilfred's formative years, and secondly, his growing awareness of his own homosexuality which, at this time, of course, he had to keep secret. When he gets to Craiglockhart, his confidence seems to increase about his 'gayness', and when he does well as a military officer, again his confidence seems to develop. So, is it right to say that these are pretty crucial, fundamental elements in forming his character and the ways in which he developed as a man and as a poet?

DH: Yes, they're two very big questions. This is my one big regret about the book, because so many reviewers said, in effect, 'Shock, horror, Wilfred Owen was a snob!', and I bitterly regretted that I hadn't said that, of course, at his end of the lower middle class, everybody was a snob. It was terribly important to keep up appearances, to have good table linen, a nice piece of silver, that kind of thing. And to know the difference between Esquire and Mister and so on, in a way that was not the case at all at the upper end of the middle classes where Harold Monro was who didn't care a bean about that kind of thing because he was much more secure in his position. But, for Wilfred's family, it really mattered and everybody in the street would have been the same. It wasn't something peculiar to Wilfred. But, once you put on the King's uniform, you are automatically a gentleman, no matter what your background is. That gave him quite a bit of stability once he got used to it.

MB: What about his growing awareness of his homosexuality? How significant is it in his development as a man and as a writer?

DH: Very hard to tell. This is one of the points on which I differ fundamentally with Jon Stallworthy because in his biography he hardly mentions Wilfred's homosexuality at all, he avoids it. Even now, when he writes about Owen, he will always say, 'Well, there's absolutely no evidence that he had any sexual experience etc. etc.' I don't know what evidence he would expect to find. You can hardly expect Wilfred to be writing home to his mother saying, 'Darling Mother, I spent last Saturday night with a beautiful French youth, I'm sure you'll be pleased to know'. Of course, there isn't this kind of evidence, but I think it is crucial that he was gay. Meeting Sassoon, who was also gay of course, and with whom he shared confidences, was very important to him. If anything, he was rather more at ease about it than Sassoon himself was, I think. Then, in 1918, meeting other gay writers and realising that this whole thing could actually be to his advantage; that the gay poet is more likely to feel pity and sympathy towards other people, you know, that actually might mean that he could be a better poet than he might otherwise have been.

MB: And the issue of shell-shock and his return to France. He was called 'cowardly' by one of his senior officers, wasn't he? It seems unjust to modern minds, hearing about Gulf War Syndrome and post-traumatic stress disorders, that he would be automatically under suspicion as a physically unwounded convalescent living at Craiglockhart and having, as it were, an easy war by comparison with those in France. Yet, the evidence is that he did suffer from neurasthenia and needed months and months of treatment – a judgement which your tentative reading of his mental state in his poetry seems to support. His condition laid him open to suspicions of malingering and of not wanting to go back; and yet, of course, he does feel the call to return to France in September 1918. Can you say a bit about this decision to return? Would he have been happy staying in England?

DH: Well, let's say first of all that we don't know for sure that he did decide; he may have been pushed rather than jumped. But clearly he was willing to go and did volunteer to put his name on the draft. I think that if he had got the chance that he thought he was going to get earlier in that year, through Scott Moncrieff, of a permanent home posting, well, as a human being, I think he would have probably taken it. But I also think that he would have felt terribly guilty forever afterwards, especially with the stain on his character, if that's what it was, of the accusation of cowardice. We can't be absolutely sure that happened. We really only know through Robert Graves and one or two other sources. Wilfred doesn't say anything about it.

MB: So this notion of his Christian conscience, 'seared' though it was, actually was finally the strongest motivation and overcame what might have been the conscientious objector in him at that stage?

DH: Well, duty was hugely important and that's what he'd been trained to think by Colonel Shirley in the Artists' Rifles; as an officer, that's what you had to do. You couldn't duck out, or at least you ought not to. Lots of people did of course but it was not an honourable thing to do. And when Sassoon was sent back wounded, then Wilfred felt his duty, as a poet as well, was to go back to the Front. When these two duties, as poet and as soldier, coincided, then the decision was made.

Matters of Life and Death

MB: Maybe this leads to the sense I got from reading your book a second time, this sense of fatalism. Here was the portrait of a young man with a literary vocation, cramped by social conventions, inhibited by class consciousness and secrecy over his homosexuality, limited in educational opportunities; then the war comes and, at that point in my reading, I felt this life story that I've had for 200 pages or more is now becoming a death story. There was this feeling of inevitability at where it was leading. Picking up on what we've just been discussing about his return to France in September 1918, you comment at one point that he 'knew his chances of survival would be slight'. There's this sense of fatalism about the whole life story becoming a death story. I'm trying to get at what your feeling was in writing the biography, whether there was this sort of changeover from a life that was growing in France, in Bordeaux before the war, to a climax in 1917 or so and then the steep descent to his death.

DH: Yes, it's like a tragedy, isn't it? You know from the beginning the hero is going to be killed in the end.

MB: Yes.

DH: I always knew that and, right from the beginning, I wanted the book to end with three words: 'Wilfred was dead.' I think I'm right in saying that the penultimate chapter does end there. That was how I presented it to the publisher and the publisher then said, 'Well, this is fine, but you do need one more chapter to tie the story up'. And I was glad he did because, of course, it was good advice. But I knew that … I mean, this is very personal … I've written two books about Wilfred before and both of them ended with his death, but this time I knew it was going to be final and that a companionship which had lasted for, I don't know, 35 years or so, was this time really going to come to an end. I just dreaded it. It was a very painful thing to have to write the end of it. And so by the time I got into 1917, I was already beginning to feel that it was inevitably coming to an end. But, at the same time, I also had a very strong feeling about Wilfred's life, which may be me imposing a pattern of completeness, that everything belongs, everything fits, in the most extraordinary way. It has that quality for me that, although war gets him in the end, he's achieved so much in that time that, in a way, it's hard to see what more he could have done. And, although I'm sure he would have done a great deal more, there is this extraordinary sense of completeness to me about his life. So, it was desperately sad and, at the same time, it's something to be pleased about.

MB: I wonder whether that means that there's a sort of mythologizing of the life. I don't mean in any derogatory sense. I'm thinking that there are many precedents and some subsequent examples of writers who have died young and whose lives have been mythologised: the romantic poets particularly, but later, Sylvia Plath, Dylan Thomas, B. S. Johnson. They are all writers who died before their time and myths grew up about the nature of their lives which gather a sort of completeness as myths tend to. Myths carry meanings beyond mere narrative, and maybe the pattern of Wilfred's life in particular lends itself to that.

DH: Yes, I think there's much truth in that and, as I've said to you before, until I read your notes, I would have thought that I was simply the detached historian, but now I'm not so sure. (laughter)

MB: Well, if we can move on, the detached historian, if that is what you are, seemed to me to show itself in the way you structured your biography. It's a very tidy life, meticulously ordered. Each chapter is given a title, a place, a time, and from the reader's point of view, this is all aesthetically satisfying and reassuring. But, of course, life is much messier than that, so I was conscious that you'd imposed a narrative shape and a narrative continuity. Inevitably, there's no way you can't do so. But it does leave open questions like, 'What do you do with any gaps in the record?' I'm thinking back to your 'diary' now. Presumably, there were holes in it. Do you leave them, or do you fill them with speculations and possibilities? Are you aware of things that have been left out that you simply can't get at, or things that ought to be there but you're not able to use them?

DH: To some extent, of course. It was quite a tidy life and things do break down into sections. If you look at Jon Stallworthy's chapters, for example, on the whole they correspond with mine, although in places I've broken the mould a bit. But I couldn't break it as much as I would have liked to, because that's just the way the shape was. I'm not conscious of having left anything out, not knowingly anyway, except details that seemed to me to do nothing to help the story along. So, to an extent, yes, I was certainly intervening and controlling the flow of evidence. But gaps? I think it's legitimate to speculate where you can do so on the basis of strong probability. But where you really just don't know at all, you just have to say so and there are some places where I do say that. But the story seemed to me to hold together pretty well.

MB: You've used the word 'story' a couple of times, which reminds me that biography is often viewed as a hybrid between your 'detached historian' and the narrative storyteller, between history and fiction. Standing back from the two biographies you've done, do you have a sense of what sort of biographer you are?

DH: While I was writing both the books I did realise that the thing I was enjoying most of all was actually storytelling. Telling a narrative was fascinating – getting stuff into the story early on that you knew was going to make sense later, and maybe leaving it out if it wasn't going to add anything. One of the criteria for including things was: Does this contribute to the story or doesn't it and how is it all going to come together at the end? That was fascinating and the reason why, I suppose, I wrote it chronologically. But, at the same time, I did take pride in sticking strictly to the evidence; and using lots of it! I did actually gather huge amounts of it; I think that if I have any strength at all it is that I'm quite good at collecting detail and organising it. Some people don't like that and don't want that sort of book. Well, that's their look-out; I'm not interested in them terribly. But to tell a story that holds the reader's attention ... One of the reviewers of my Monro biography described it as 'gripping'; that was a wonderful treat. I was delighted; I've always wanted to write a book that somebody would say was 'gripping'! That does matter enormously and so, I suppose, thinking of myself as an historian I was perhaps mistaken since I was being much more nearly an artist – not necessarily a good one of course – than I realised at the time.

MB: Your biography's subtitle is 'A New Biography', indicating that new truths will be revealed. I wonder where you felt the newness comes. Is it to do with Wilfred's character and personality? Is it to do with his experiences on the battlefield – I'm thinking of those diagrams you give about the Western Front? Or both?

DH: For a time we considered the subtitle 'The Truth Untold', a quotation from 'Strange Meeting' and that unfortunately got on to the publisher's website.

MB: Ah, that explains why it was at the head of Roy Hattersley's highly complimentary review in *The Observer* (22 September 2002).

DH: Yes. It's rather embarrassing because it won't quite do. One of the things I did do was to write about Owen's homosexuality, which hadn't been written about before. And nobody had traced the battles before. Stallworthy simply says, 'Somewhere near Beaumont Hamel' for the crucial battle. But, if you actually go back into the military archives, you can read it all. It's a hell of a job! You've got to look at all the Battalions in the Brigade and then at the Brigade Diary and the Division Diary and the Corps Diary and the Army Diary and the Medics and the Machine-Gunners and all the rest of it. You've got to look at all that and pick up little bits here and there and reconstruct the battle. You can then actually work out, broadly speaking, what actually happened. All that is entirely new. Also, the whole business of Wilfred's shell-shock and Dr Brock, that's new; there's nothing of that in Stallworthy.

MB: Yet, clearly, Stallworthy is a major figure. How did you negotiate your way through, or past, his account to establish your own version? He gets just one index reference on your last page. Did you deliberately put him aside and write afresh?

DH: Yes. I ignored him completely but, when I had written a chapter on, say, Dunsden, I then read his chapter on Dunsden just to make sure that I hadn't missed anything out. Every time I did that I couldn't help noticing how inaccurate he was. All sorts of little things weren't right, and large areas of Wilfred's activities and experiences he had nothing to say about at all. And there was his ready belief in Harold Owen's testimony, so that I became more and more confident as I went on that I was really writing a new account of Wilfred's life.

MB: Getting this newness involved you in a lot of library work, in London presumably?

DH: Masses, yes.

MB: And actually walking the ground in France?

DH: Yes. I went with two very kind friends in the Wilfred Owen Association, Philip Guest and Helen McPhail, who had made several explorations in France. They were preparing to take coach tours out there so they went on a 'recce' first and took me with them several times. It was absolutely fascinating because Philip had done quite a lot of work on military records already and, at that stage, knew more than I did, and he was very ready to share his researches.

MB: One last thing, Dom, is you and the subject, particularly as you have lived most of your professional life with Wilfred. Did you choose the subject or did it, in some strange way, choose you? In your Introduction, you talk about writing from the feeling of 'companionship'; and writing about his death as being 'an ordeal that you put off for many weeks'. You hinted earlier at a vicarious friendship, 'companionship', whatever, over the years which I can well understand. So you learned a lot about Wilfred. Did he teach you much about yourself – or is that an unfair question?

DH: Well, I don't know ... Let's say it's a very personal question. I've talked about the religious thing already, and that was a way-in and one of the first things I understood when reading the letters. And then, as time went on, I ... well, I'm gay myself, of course, and have been reluctant to admit it all my life really, and still am. But, as I studied Wilfred, I realised that he was gay and, as I went on, I came to realise more and more that I was. He did, I am sure, force me out of the closet in so far as I ever have come out.

MB: Well there can hardly be a closer empathy than this … rather wonderful in a way.

DH: Yes, it was. I really don't think I could say that I was in love with Wilfred. I've met one gay man who really claims to be physically in love with Wilfred and I find that fairly revolting … especially if you've heard the details of what he has to say about him. (laughter)

MB: I think you'd better spare me those.

DH: I did become very fond of Wilfred and it was a very close companionship. And, of course, it was a wonderful research subject. There was always something new to look for. Even now, when I open the Letters, it doesn't take me more than a couple of pages to find something and I think, 'Well, that's fascinating; I ought to follow that up'. And, of course, I can't do it any more, so it was very sad coming to the end of the book. He is … well, I mean he was a great friend but he's 'dead' in a way – no deader than he was before, but the companionship isn't there anymore because I really have finished my researches; and that's a great gap.

MB: That almost suggests that in writing the biography you're writing two 'Lives': his 'Life', of course, but in a way you're also rehearsing and writing your own 'Life' to an extent.

DH: I was doing something like that, which is a bit terrifying.

MB: Well, it is curious, isn't it?

DH: I've never written poetry, I haven't been in a war, I don't know …

MB: No, but I'm reminded of what Richard Holmes says in his book, *Footsteps* [1985]. He describes biography as two things: a 'pursuit' and a 'haunting'. The pursuit is the biographer actually doing the historical work; and then there is the haunting where this imagined figure sits in your head and you have a very close and intimate relationship because you know so much about this person. You're haunted, not in any Gothic horror sense, but in the sense of there always being a permanent lodger up there in your head somewhere.

DH: Yes, a haunting in the sense of a close companionship, that's certainly right. And I did love the research, it was just fascinating; all sorts of stuff that I had to dig up all over the place, some of it useful, some of it not. I think it really is 'a new biography' because there is so much in it that had not been discovered before, even though the basic framework of the story is well known and can't be changed.

MB: Thank you very much, Dom.

10

Authorised Lives

The truism that writing history requires distance is nowhere more pertinent than when writing 'Lives'. For biographers of contemporary subjects, proximity may produce not sharpness of definition but myopia, a blurred or foreshortened image which may distort judgement. These issues were touched upon earlier in discussions of Boswell, Johnson, Forster and Mrs Gaskell. In the late twentieth century, the situation was exacerbated through the information explosion: writers became more aware of the worth of their literary and personal data and of the variety of media in which they exist; and biographers became keener to access primary source material, either to establish their account of a recent author as the one to beat in a competitive market, or to substantiate a new slant on the life of a subject from an earlier period. Knowing the whereabouts of data, judging its relevance, assessing the weight to give to it have all become more exacting. Writing the biography of a contemporary author has always laboured with such difficulties but, in recent decades particularly, the accessibility of information in a cultural climate in which there are few qualms about publicising intimate details has often provoked protectionism from those who control the source materials of the biographer's art: the gate-keepers of the literary estates. The most notorious is the Estate of Sylvia Plath, where the skirmishes between Olwyn Hughes, gate-keeper of the Estate, and those mostly feminist commentators, the 'hostile Plathologists', have been acutely plotted by Ian Hamilton (1992: 293–304; 2003: 303). And where there are gate-keepers, there are also gate-crashers – the writers of unofficial 'Lives' who ignore or contrive to circumvent the legal restrictions. We will see instances of both in what follows.

This is not the place to scrutinise the ways in which literary estates perform their prime duties of safeguarding an author's works, carrying out their author's wishes, and generating income, usually for the author's family. Important matters without doubt and ones that may have a bearing upon how and when a biography is produced, as the two examples at the end of this chapter demonstrate. But the unique, not to say idiosyncratic, nature of each 'Life', whether authorised or not, suggests a different emphasis. This chapter reviews five present-day biographers' accounts of twentieth-century subjects – four authorised and one unauthorised. It gives a critical assessment of these biographical portraits and sets each within the context of how the biography was commissioned, the comments of the biographer and, when appropriate, how the literary estate exercised its role. The emphasis falls upon the process of compiling the biographies. It offers some insights into the formative influences surrounding these 'Lives' and glimpses of how these books came into being.

The Life of Graham Greene by Norman Sherry

Do we really want to know that the infant Graham Greene 'cut his first tooth on 6 July 1905' (Sherry, 1989, I: 8)? One of the problems of the authorised biographer is that privileged access to all the documents and, in Sherry's case, to his apparently cooperative if elusive subject, offers a temptation to prolixity that is hard to resist. Yet this turned out to be the least of Sherry's difficulties for, as his 'pursuit' of Graham Greene developed into a thirty-year marathon, his project proved increasingly debilitating and, on occasions, life-threatening.

This biographer's tale has become a notorious sequel to that of his subject's restless and risky life. Sherry himself outlines its plot in the Prefaces to the three volumes of his biography. He first met Graham Greene in 1974. Initially, he encountered some ambivalence from him about 'anyone looking into my life' (I: xiii); then, in a portent of their unpredictable future relationship, he nearly lost his subject when Greene was almost run over by a taxi as they crossed St James's Street to see where Greene used to drink with Kim Philby. Greene liked the literary detective work Sherry had done in his books on Conrad, especially his willingness to follow his subject's tracks in different parts of the world, and, in 1976, he authorised Sherry to be his official biographer. In subsequent decades, Sherry travelled in his master's footsteps, 'risking disease and death as he had done' (I: xv): he contracted dysentery in Mexico and, according to one interview, gangrene of the intestine in Panama and tropical diabetes in Liberia (*Guardian Review*, 11 October 2004) in the course of what can fairly be described as heroic efforts to fulfil his obligations to Greene's wishes. Greene himself became concerned for his biographer's safety when Sherry narrowly escaped being caught up in the revolution in Liberia and declared himself 'terrified' at the idea of Sherry visiting a leper colony in the Congo (Letter, 16 December 1984, III: 820).

Sherry's position as the biographer who is authorised yet independent is, on the face of it, an enviable one. Greene had sent him a map of the world with all the places he had travelled to marked in red, asked him not to interview certain women, and exhorted him to 'Tell the truth, Norman … the truth, or else I'll haunt you'. Volume 1 was published in 1989 and received wide approval. Two years later, on his deathbed on 2 April 1991, Greene signed a brief document confirming Sherry's status and granting him exclusive permission to quote from his published and unpublished material (III: 815). Yet, only a few weeks after Greene's death, his son Francis, literary executor of the Estate, contacted Sherry and demanded to see every chapter from now on to judge whether or not it was publishable. Protected by his subject's deathbed statement, Sherry could proceed freely. Official authorisation from Greene, allied to an obsessive conscientiousness in the biographer, created a ruling passion in Norman Sherry which has dominated his whole life. It has had mixed results for the biographical 'Life'.

Volume 1 covers Greene's childhood with a distant mother and a nanny substitute; the trauma of his schooldays, especially his relationships with his tormentors Carter and Wheeler at Berkhamstead School where he first encountered the betrayals that feature prominently in his novels (I: 81–83); his early suicide attempts in his notorious efforts to counter boredom with Russian roulette (I: 154–158); and his conversion to Roman Catholicism (I: 254–256). These experiences – his craving for affection, his early awareness of human beings' potential for evil as well as good, his need to take risks, and his personal struggle with religious belief – permeate both his life and his writing. On the latter issue, for example, Sherry effectively juxtaposes Greene's account in *A Sort of Life* (1971) with letters from the time and passages taken from Greene's version of events: here, access to all the documents serves him well. This is not the case with the excruciating and profuse quotations from Greene's sentimental love letters which chart his courting of Vivien Dayrell-Browning who became his wife, and which continue remorselessly into Volume 2 in the relationship with Catherine Walston. Independence would have been well tempered with some editorial blue pencil. By contrast, Sherry's stamina and commitment in retracing Greene's journeys, his first-hand accounts and his use of documentary materials combine well in the two most compelling episodes: the Liberian adventure in 1935 and the travels in Mexico in 1938. The harrowing details of Greene's journey into the uncharted hinterland of Liberia are enlivened with Greene's own account (*Journey without Maps*, 1936), well-judged links with Conrad's *Heart of Darkness* (I: 563), and extracts both from Greene's diary and from the account of his travelling companion, his 23-year-old cousin, Barbara (I: 509–566). Less than three years later, Greene was off again, this time to Mexico. Again, Sherry weaves together the reflections, forty years on, of Greene's wife Vivien from whom he became separated but never divorced (I: 665); passages from *The Lawless Roads* (1939); and comments from interviews carried out in 1978 when following in Greene's footsteps. But his real biographical coup was in identifying and meeting the 'original' of the mestizo, the Judas figure in *The Power and the Glory* who betrays the whisky priest, as one Don Pelito, a down-and-out on the streets of Yajalon (I: 717–722).

Perhaps Sherry's crispest assessment of Greene's character is in his brief Preface to Volume 2, 'Seeking Greene', which begins, nonetheless, with a sense of fatigue: 'As this work bears down quickly on the twentieth year, I am aware of the expense of spirit ...'. Volume 2 covers the years 1939–1955 when Greene produced his best work (*The Power and the Glory*, *The Heart of the Matter*, *The End of the Affair*), was supervised in MI6 by a master-spy, and experienced the most significant love affair of his life. Norman Sherry provides useful contextual commentary on the ways in which the conditions Greene suffered during his travels entered into his fictions (see, for example, II: 41 on *The Power and the Glory*), but here, as in the other volumes, there is far too much cloying detail on Greene's love life. Against a background of seemingly continual visits to strip clubs, prostitutes and sleazy bars around the world, Greene played out an emotionally charged drama with his five great loves: Vivien was succeeded by Dorothy Glover, Catherine Walston, Anita Bjork and Yvonne Cloetta. And the greatest of these was Lady Walston – a relationship that permeates *The End of the Affair* (II: 333–336). To his credit (or perhaps in his own defence), Sherry quotes a letter of Greene's from 21 July 1949: 'if anybody ever tries to write a biography of me, how complicated they are going to find it and how misled they are going to be' (II: 320).

This sentiment could apply equally to Greene's relationship with the double agent Kim Philby, which began during the Second World War when Philby was the much-admired leader of a group of MI6 agents of which Greene was a member (II: 166–183). Greene continued his unpopular public support for Philby after the latter's defection to Moscow in January 1963, and Sherry records their discussion of Philby's activities as the only occasion when Greene became angry (II: 489). The friendship between Greene and Philby lasted until the latter's death in 1988. He is certainly not uncritical of Greene in this area of his life – he uses phrases such as 'ludicrous statement' (III: 746) and 'deliberate political folly' (III: 748) – but he seems as puzzled as anyone in trying to explain Greene's stance in relation to the Soviet Union: 'anarchist? socialist? near-communist?' (III: 743), and resorts, as his 'last word', to repeating the episode of Greene's anger at his linking of Philby's betrayals to those Greene himself had endured at the hands of his schoolboy tormentors (III: 750–752).

The Philby story is not the only one that continues to appear intermittently in the years 1955–1991 covered in Volume 3. Greene's affairs with Catherine Walston and the Swedish actress Anita Bjork maintain Sherry's interest as he raids Greene's letters and diaries for evidence. He seems helplessly ensnared even when he senses the reader's boredom: 'If we are tiring of Greene's ardent correspondence ...', he begins, trying to enlist our sympathy for the biographer's plight (III: 105). The fatigue noted at the start of Volume 2 is even more marked in his final volume. It is often badly written ('Greene was a sponge ... he soaked up information at the speed of sound', III: 616). There are some quaintly phrased judgements ('What a cad Burgess could be', on Anthony Burgess's criticism of *The Honorary Consul*, III: 549). And there are too many personal intrusions, ranging from snatches of Sherry's verse and his appearance in the first photograph in the book, to his own protracted and difficult labours as a biographer (III: 702). Despite such flaws, Sherry's official status together with his commitment to follow in Greene's tracks enable him to provide significant contextual information. His account of *A Burnt-Out Case*, Greene's harrowing novel set in the Congo, is well documented from interviews and correspondence with Dr Michel Lechat, director of the Yonda leprosarium, illuminated by intertextual references to Conrad's *Heart of Darkness* which Sherry is well qualified to give, and thoughtfully developed by juxtaposing entries from Greene's 'Congo Journal' with passages in the novel. Sherry's status is less helpful as he nears the end of the 'Life' when he tries to sum up Greene's religious belief. Chapter 48 asks, 'What Did Greene Believe?' and follows this title with an epigraph from Greene: 'The trouble is, I don't believe my unbelief.' Sherry gets little further than this gnomic comment and relies on extracts from an interview conducted by John Cornwell for the *Tablet* in which Greene describes himself ambiguously as 'a Catholic Agnostic' – an oxymoron if ever there was one (III: 691).

In his epilogue on 'Leaving Greene', Norman Sherry admits, 'Reaching the end had often seemed beyond my strength and spirit' (III: 803). Given the scope and demands of his project, this is hardly surprising. Sherry was inexorably set on producing a biography in the 'tombstone' mode. His three volumes total 2,251 pages; their aggregate weight is 3.75 kg, which raises the question of whether the desire for Boswellian fullness has grown into Sherryean obesity. Certainly, if any biography needs both the perspective of a longer history and a sharper focus by being condensed into a single volume, then this one does. (Curiously, Sherry himself has given an agenda in the crisp 'capsule' biographies that preface each volume.) It remains to be seen how the Greene Literary Estate will respond to such needs. Yet, while it is easy to find fault, Norman Sherry's labours provide invaluable documentation on Greene's life and travels for which future biographers will have reason to be grateful. If his three volumes make a flawed biography, one suspects that Greene himself would have enjoyed the irony of the 'Life' imitating the life. For, unwittingly, Norman Sherry has created a fragmentary, uneven biography to match the fractures and fault-lines in the life of his subject.

Bernard Shaw by Michael Holroyd

Unlike Norman Sherry, Holroyd was unable to interview his subject. Shaw died twenty years before his appointment as official biographer. Yet, although Holroyd says that he spent fifteen years on this biography, the contractual ambiguities and the sensitivities of others connected with the Shaw Estate meant that almost twice that time elapsed before the project was complete. Even as early as Volume 1, Holroyd is commenting wryly on his 'eloquent explanations' for not finishing 'such a marathon' sooner (I: 466). Subsequently, he has written about the daunting scale of the research needed and, not least, the problems he encountered from an unauthorised potential rival (Holroyd, 2003: 169–183) to which we turn presently. But first, the 'Life'.

Volume 1 covers the years from Shaw's Irish upbringing to his marriage to Charlotte Payne-Townshend in June 1898 when he had already turned 40. Michael Holroyd's construction of 'Shaw' shows how the ambiguous *ménage à trois* in which he spent his formative years (I: 26–33) helped to produce the childhood identity of 'Sonny' who was to live on throughout his adult life inside the self-consciously manufactured identity of 'GBS'. This dual sense of self affected all his love affairs throughout his twenties and thirties. For example, Holroyd comments on the emotional tug-of-war in Shaw's reactions to his first serious girlfriend, Alice Lockett: 'Sonny had wanted love; GBS soared wittily above it; and Shaw was pulled between the two' (I: 109). Shaw follows his mother to London, attempts to write fiction, and becomes an early member of the Fabian Society (I: 132–133) to which he introduced Sidney Webb (I: 174). Music criticism, political journalism, public speaking, a busy social life, and Shaw still found time to write his well-known *Plays Pleasant and Unpleasant* (1898), his first real success in the theatre coming with *Arms and the Man* in 1894 (I: 298–306). By the end of the century he was not only a well-known and controversial public figure but also a man embarked on what he called the 'terrible adventure' of marriage.

Volume 2 sees Shaw at the height of his powers in both the main arenas of his public life: the theatre and politics. The two, as Michael Holroyd shows, are intimately connected; and both are invested with a disconcerting wit that is the essence of Shavian art, most clearly seen in the first of his middle period plays, *Man and Superman* (1903). Holroyd comments shrewdly on Max Beerbohm's remarks on the text of the play, on a caricature Beerbohm drew of Shaw, and on his review of the stage performance that he saw two years later (II: 68–71), showing how Beerbohm came to acknowledge that the Shavian revolution in the British theatre, aided and abetted by Shaw's close friend Harley Granville-Barker, was to bring about the theatre of ideas: a 'modernist' theatre analogous to, yet different from, the radical changes taking place in the other literary and visual arts. The international arms trade (*Major Barbara*), Anglo-Irish relations (*John Bull's Other Island*), medical ethics (*The Doctor's Dilemma*) and an idiosyncratic take on gender politics (*Caesar and Cleopatra*) – all saw controversial ideas, ones still 'live' today, brought on to the stage. In discussing these plays, Michael Holroyd embeds them tellingly in the mores and politics of the period in such a manner that their messages still challenge us nearly a century later.

Shaw's private life was exhilarating for different reasons, his passion for the motor car exceeded only by that for Mrs Patrick Campbell. Holroyd gives an amusing account of Shaw behind the wheel, 'extraordinarily reckless', like his contemporary Mr Toad. Shaw was 'academically fond' of the temperamental De Dietrich – 'a philosophical vehicle' – and 'for serious holiday-making its humorous potential made it an essential item of equipment' (II: 206–207). His adoration of Mrs Pat (or Stella as she was known) had no such humour. Holroyd presents Shaw's romance with her as confirming all his beliefs about love – 'a hideous business' (II: 317); and Holroyd's analysis of the personal cross-currents in *Pygmalion*, both of Shaw's family history and of his relationship with Mrs Pat who played Eliza, brings out the serious hurt that lies beneath the surface of the comedy (II: 325–340). This is biographical criticism at its best, reading the life and the literature in tandem. Equally illuminating is Michael Holroyd's account of Shaw's earlier biographers (Henderson, Chesterton and St John Ervine), and particularly of Shaw's 'secret collaborations [through which] he learned how to ghost his own life through later biographers, from Frank Harris to Hesketh Pearson. So he became the very author of himself' (II: 212–213) – a phrase that could serve as the subtitle for the whole biography.

Volume 3 picks up this biographical theme twenty years later with the completion of Pearson's 'Life' in 1939. Holroyd comments: 'Shaw's method of ghostwriting his "Lives" involved borrowing something of the character of his biographer. As Pearson's "uninvited collaborator", he was faced with an intriguing linguistic exercise of impersonating someone who was Personifying him' (III: 369). Shaw's 'ghostings', 'corrections' and 'rewritings' were so extensive that it is not surprising that he was more pleased with Pearson's biography than with the efforts of others. Equally, this could have been reason enough for the Shaw Estate to commission a 'Life' uncontaminated by the subject.

Earlier in discussing the significance of *Back to Methuselah* in Shaw's life, Holroyd makes an analogy with literary biography that reveals a profound empathy with the philosophical stance of his subject:

> As subjects of literary biographies will collaborate with their unknown biographers in the future writing of their lives, so our general history may be considered as part of an unfinished narrative that did not cater for our self-interest, but would be influenced by our acts and thoughts. This collaborative hypothesis would bring back our self-respect and sense of responsibility, emphasise the importance of collective self-help, and restore the value of instinct and the use of intelligence as controls for human destiny. (III: 37)

Literary biography as a collaborative act becomes a metaphor for the Shavian view of evolutionary history, one that he dramatised in *Back to Methuselah* which, with its 'machinery of ghosts and miracles ... a hooded serpent that whispers, a terrifying Oracle, and hairless Ancients and She-Ancients', Shaw described as his 'Ring' (III: 43).

In the theatre, this final period is notable for *Heartbreak House*, Shaw's bleakest play reflecting his opposition to the First World War, Chekhovian in manner and styled by Shaw as his *Lear*; and for *St Joan*, one of his most enduring plays. As with his commentary upon *Pygmalion* above, Holroyd illuminates the play with a mixture of background information about Shaw's sources, the tantalising influence of T. E. Lawrence on his portrayal of an outsider, the theatrical context (which saw the unlikely combination of Sybil Thorndike, who played the lead, and a middle-aged Fabian, Mary Hankinson, as the twin inspirational models for the role) and some sharp criticism: 'it is this swanking and fun ... that makes Shaw's Joan into the Principal Boy of pantomime, and the play into a charade' (III: 87).

As GBS's fame increased, the roll call of famous names among his friends grew ever more varied, from Nancy Astor and Edward Elgar to the enclosed nun, Dame Laurentia McLachlan, and the heavyweight boxer, Gene Tunney (III: 217). But Holroyd shows how, despite all these potential distractions, Shaw remained true to his two professional worlds – his Fabian world and his theatre world (III: 141–142). In literature, in social life and in international travel, Shaw was indefatigable. Michael Holroyd distinguishes GBS's travels at the end of the 1920s as 'a sequence of romantic flights and theatrical explorations' (III: 169) from those he undertook in his late seventies as 'a series of evangelical missions' (III: 271). South Africa, India, China, Japan, North America and even two visits to New Zealand – nowhere was too distant for a man driven by the belief that he had seen his conception of the good society born in Soviet Russia, 'a cause of embarrassment to even the most devoted Shavian', as Robin Cook remarked (*Guardian Review*, 2 October 2004).

Shaw's last decade, in Michael Holroyd's account, is dominated by his battles with Hollywood and his remarkable document, *Everybody's Political What's What*, published in his eighty-ninth year. The ease with which Holroyd's wit about the former sits with his empathy for the latter is typical of this prime example of life-writing and offers an appropriate summation of this brief summary. The Shavian wit of both subject and biographer is caught in Holroyd's choice quotations and dry comment about the efforts of film-maker Gabriel Pascal, who tried to raise money from General de Gaulle in order to make the film of St Joan with Greta Garbo: '"instead of Garbo," Pascal reported to Shaw, "de Gaulle wanted to play the Saint himself." "If the heroine had been the Blessed Virgin," commented GBS, "they would probably have suggested Mae West."' To which Holroyd quotes the apocryphal line: '"We never met," regretted Mae West, "but I would have been happy to entertain the gentleman."' And on negotiations with Hollywood, he remarks wryly, 'The speed with which absolutely nothing happened was often breathtaking' (III: 473). A few pages later, he is generous in his comments upon Shaw's 'political schoolbook', quoting a passage which captures Shaw's socialist credo and locating its power in the eloquence of Shaw's rhetoric: 'Socialism is not charity nor loving-kindness, nor sympathy with the poor, nor popular philanthropy ... but the economist's hatred of waste and disorder, the aesthete's hatred of ugliness and dirt, the lawyer's hatred of injustice, the doctor's hatred of disease, the saint's hatred of the seven deadly sins' (III: 481). Here, as in his comments in 1912 about 'the Americanisation of the whole world' (III: 304), his prophetic address in Cape Town in 1932 about the inequalities between the black and white populations (III: 275–277) and, after Hiroshima, his warnings of different wars in the future, 'wars of religion ... fundamentalists and atheists, Moslems and Hindus, Shintos and Buddhists' (III: 482), GBS, as Holroyd demonstrates repeatedly, is our contemporary.

Michael Holroyd completed his one-volume abridgement of his biography – what he called his 'GBEssence' (Holroyd, 2003: 182) – in 1997. It is a distillation of the three-volume 'Life' that had appeared between 1988 and 1991 to which had been added a fourth volume in 1992 about Shaw's 'afterlife' in the legal battles over his wills and the aftermath of his unsuccessful efforts to reform the English alphabet. But the apparent speed of Holroyd's hare compared with Sherry's tortoise is illusory since, as Holroyd himself has pointed out, he was invited to be Shaw's authorised biographer as early as 1969 (Holroyd, 2003: 170). His biographer's tale is a shaggy dog story to rival Sherry's. But here the comparison ends, for the intrigues of the plot are different, the lessons for the biographer more significant, and the resulting 'Life' incomparably more sophisticated. The reason is not hard to find: whereas Greene appears to have appointed a casual acquaintance rather than a close friend or experienced biographer to write his 'Life', the Society of Authors, when asked by the Shaw Estate to identify an appropriate biographer, invited a known practitioner whose writing demonstrated a verbal dexterity to match the Shavian wit of his subject. And thereby hangs the tale of the 'Life' of GBS; for, years before Michael Holroyd accepted the role of official biographer, Professor Dan Laurence at New York University – already literary and dramatic adviser to the Shaw Estate – had been working towards an edition of Shaw's *Collected Letters* and, with Holroyd's appointment, was in effect passed over for the plum job of authorised biographer. From Michael Holroyd's account, he took this badly since, in his 'pursuit' of Shaw, Laurence appears to have been single-minded to the point of obsession. Unwittingly, the Shaw Estate had discovered a man with Sherryean tendencies within its own ranks. Only this was worse: a 'would-be' biographer, with a formidable knowledge of his subject, a passionate sense of grievance, yet no contractual status to write the 'Life'.

Michael Holroyd presents the struggle between the authorised biographer and the would-be biographer as a series of skirmishes during the 1970s and 1980s, with the Shaw Estate acting as occasional referee. The 'personal animosity' Laurence felt towards his usurper and the difficulties Holroyd felt in working with a man of such a 'complicated nature' rendered collaboration impossible. The emotional climax as well as an impasse was reached in 1975 when Laurence resigned his editorship of Shaw's *Collected Letters*, threatened to work on his own 'so-called unofficial biography' and to burn all his data in his garden in 'the largest conflagration of literary documents since Dickens's bonfire at Gad's Hill' (Holroyd, 2003: 177). Holroyd sees Dan Laurence's 'lonely obsession' as a warning to biographers, both for their own psychological health and for the knock-on effects that such rivals might have on their own work. For Holroyd was asked to suspend work on his biography and was put on a retainer for over a decade while the Shaw Estate wooed Dan Laurence back to editing Shaw's *Collected Letters*. The delivery date for Holroyd's manuscript slipped even further into the late 1980s.

In so far as anyone outside this rivalry can judge, Michael Holroyd is scrupulously fair to Dan Laurence in his account, 'The Making of *Bernard Shaw*'. He confesses to 'an exasperated admiration' for Laurence and acknowledges both his 'academic integrity' and the 'great value' that Laurence's publications have been to him in writing his 'Life'. The lesson from this conflict is clear: authorisation is a mixed blessing. While the imprimatur confers security on the chosen one, it may come at a cost, as well as bringing insecurity and all its attendant bitterness into the lives of the losers. Thankfully, Dan Laurence did not pursue his unofficial biography. Instead, he devoted himself to becoming 'the great patron of Shaw studies', as Michael Holroyd generously acknowledges (Holroyd, 2003: 182). Yet, there is a wider lesson: because authorisation implies exclusion, naming the elect is culturally divisive; and the literary estates, which increasingly are the regulators of literary 'Lives' (Hamilton, 1992), thus become the unintended agents in the formation of the canon of literary biography. One way to judge the effect is to turn to an unauthorised biography where, despite the eminence of both the subject and the biographer, access to unpublished work and documents controlled by the estate remains blocked.

T. S. Eliot by Peter Ackroyd

In death as in life, T. S. Eliot was at pains to guard his privacy. As early as 1925 he decided that he did not want a biography (Ackroyd, 1985: 310); and later in life he added a memorandum to his will: 'I do not wish my executors to facilitate or countenance the writing of a biography of me.' His widow, Valerie, has done his bidding and not sanctioned a 'Life' (Hamilton, 1992: 292). Twenty years on from Eliot's death, Peter Ackroyd ends his Acknowledgements at the start of his book with the statement: 'I am forbidden by the Eliot Estate to quote from Eliot's published work, except for purposes of fair comment in a critical context, or to quote from Eliot's unpublished work or correspondence' (Ackroyd, 1985: 10). The most noticeable effect of these legal restrictions is that here we are offered a literary biography without quotations. Moreover, Ackroyd seems to compound his difficulties with a brief 'Prelude' in which he refers to Eliot's remark that the best of his poetry had cost him dearly in experience, and adds: 'the connection between the life and the work is here explicitly made, and it will be the purpose of this book to attempt to elucidate the mystery of that connection' (Ackroyd, 1985: 13). Thus the unauthorised biographer appears to face up to the acknowledged legislators of the literary life; but, in fact, far from challenging or trying to circumvent the Estate, or even to quote a few lines for fair critical comment, Ackroyd simply turns his back on it and, with a nod and a wink to the reader, implies that it is a good idea to have *The Complete Poems and Plays of T. S. Eliot* readily to hand.

Because of the eminence of his subject and the mass of available archive material, Ackroyd's task was not too severely limited; most would agree with Ian Hamilton's comment that Ackroyd has 'managed to come up with a detailed, plausible and widow-proof account of Eliot's life' (Hamilton, 1992: 304). But the portrait of Eliot that we have from Ackroyd, Gordon (1998) and others remains contentious and open to speculation while the Estate continues to mount police guard over the poet's papers. The portrait was most recently besmirched in a 'Life' of Eliot's first wife, Vivien (Seymour-Jones, 2001), which Hermione Lee, after a brilliantly succinct account of the cases for the prosecution and the defence of Eliot over his treatment of Vivien, has characterised as 'biography as blame' (Lee, 2008: 132). Until the ban on Eliot's correspondence is lifted (originally scheduled for 2015, but likely to be extended), fair judgement about Eliot's first unhappy marriage and much else will contain a good deal of speculation. Meanwhile, Ackroyd's 'Life' remains the best guide.

The shape of Ackroyd's biography is indicated in his 'Prelude', where he quotes a letter to Ezra Pound in which Eliot declares that he experienced only two periods of happiness in his life – his New England childhood and his second marriage to his secretary, Valerie. Each was under a decade long and they are allotted the opening and closing chapters respectively in the biography. The half-century in between has two pivotal periods: 1914–1915 and 1925–1927. In the first, Eliot made three crucial commitments: he decided finally to become a poet rather than a philosopher; he entered into what proved to be a disastrous marriage; and, despite the war and with Pound's encouragement, he adopted England as the most conducive environment for the literary life he wished to lead. In 1927, this last decision was formalised when he became a British subject and, in the same year, he was confirmed in the Church of England. This latter period also saw two other life-shaping events: his professional life was secured with his appointment at Faber & Gwyer (later Faber & Faber), while at the same time his personal life with Vivien was falling apart and he was actively considering a separation (Ackroyd, 1985: 152, 159). This shape reflects Ellmann's entry in the *Dictionary of National Biography*, a model of how life-writing and literary criticism can mutually illuminate each other even in so small a compass (Ellmann, 1981, reprinted in Sutherland, 2001: 101–108), and may well have been in Ackroyd's mind when he set out his aims in his 'Prelude'. This is the narrative shaping that, as discussed in Chapters 2 and 11, the biographer recognises in the key events and phases of the subject's lifetime and subsequently delineates in the aesthetic pattern of the biographical text. Structurally, the shape of Eliot's future 'Lives' is unlikely to alter significantly; the details, however, are sure to be modified and interpreted afresh when the embargo on his papers is eventually lifted.

The question, then, for this unauthorised 'Life' is: How far does Ackroyd fulfil the promise of his ambitious goal of elucidating the mysterious connection between the life and the work? His opening chapter claims that, 'by indirection, a portrait of the young Eliot emerges – and of the child in the man' (Ackroyd, 1985: 23). He argues that Eliot's early environments – his urban upbringing in an increasingly shabby St Louis, his garden adjacent to the schoolyard where from over the wall he could hear children's voices, the nearness of the Mississippi River, the summer holidays on the Atlantic coast – all invest his poetry from the early 'Preludes' to 'Burnt Norton' and 'Dry Salvages'. Later, discussing 'Ash Wednesday', Ackroyd quotes Auden's belief that the inspiration for most of T. S. Eliot's poetry came from 'a few intense visionary experiences, which probably occurred quite early in life' (p. 180). Throughout, there is the sense that 'the voice of the lost child' is never far away from the centre of Eliot's life and poetry.

Another aspect of childhood that seeps into his poems is that, as a delicate infant born with a congenital double hernia which meant that he had to wear a truss for most of his life, Eliot was brought up in a household full of caring and sympathetic women: his mother, sisters and nurse. Ackroyd notes the curious paradox that in his early poems such as 'Prufrock' and 'Portrait of a Lady', there is a 'brooding dislike, or fear, of women' (p. 44). The implications are of feelings of sexual and social inadequacy transmuted into the characters of his verse; of the over-protected child struggling to find an identity as a man. How far this accounts for the unhappiness of his marriage to Vivien Haigh-Wood is one of the main issues that access to his unpublished writings may eventually help to resolve. Certainly, Ackroyd makes a connection: 'I believe that he went towards her [Vivien] with a kind of child-like trust' (p. 63). Yet, he repudiates any suggestion that the collapse of the marriage can be read into the game of chess sequence in *The Waste Land*, 'since the element of artifice and fictional creation must play a large part in the creation of the anxious, harried woman in that section', a section against which Vivien wrote 'wonderful' on the typescript (pp. 114–115). It was over a decade later, after years of bizarre behaviour from a desperately unhappy woman, that Eliot finally decided to leave his wife. No-one, as Ackroyd points out, 'not even members of Vivien's own family, criticised him for it at the time' (p. 206). With the agreement of both Eliot and her brother, Vivien was committed to a private mental hospital in 1938 where, after a further decade of confinement, she died unexpectedly in January 1947, aged 58.

No aspect of Eliot's life has attracted more attention than the story of his first marriage. Ackroyd is necessarily circumspect about the effects this prolonged trauma and sense of guilt in Eliot's personal life had upon his works. 'Fair comment in a critical context' precludes plotting the details of such effects in Eliot's lines. Nonetheless, they emerge in the writing. Ackroyd generalises: 'The image of the man who believes himself to have committed a crime, and the notion of a secret which leads to guilt and feelings of worthlessness, are significant aspects of his later drama' (p. 208). And, on *The Family Reunion*, written as the process of committing Vivien to mental hospital was underway, Ackroyd is more specific – and ambivalent. For, on the one hand, he outlines the plot and its 'classical' character of crimes and a curse within a family, the machinery of the Furies, and its focus on a protagonist who believes he has murdered his wife and whose description, he concedes, 'is very close to contemporary accounts of Vivien herself'; yet, on the other hand, he also withdraws from any facile identification, saying that 'although such theatricality does not preclude self-examination ... it does hinder the kind of self-revelation which a banal identification of author and character assumes' (p. 246). His stance is similar to that of Lee's when commenting on the violent misogyny in *Sweeney Agonistes*: 'even when Eliot's cruel perversity scares me to death, I don't want to collapse his writing entirely into autobiography. I want to recognise the life in the work, *and* to see how it's transformed' (Lee, 2008: 138). Autobiographical elements infiltrate the works in many ways. Ultimately, the question is not whether such writings function as psychological therapy, but whether they succeed as effective drama.

Ackroyd's portrait of Eliot is of an inhibited, lonely, melancholy man whose self-concept was beset by uncertainties and whose philosophical position was defined by its scepticism. Eliot's most frequent description of himself was as a 'resident alien' (pp. 24, 88, 166, 272), one which leads Ackroyd to describe his subject as developing 'a consciously created identity', and of having a personality that was 'a made thing, a construct' (p. 89). These instabilities and the lack of rootedness in Eliot's life (Ackroyd says, 'he was never completely at home anywhere') lie behind the aggressive dogmatism of his well-known statement about himself as 'classicist in literature, royalist in politics, and Anglo-catholic in religion' (p. 174). In his poetry and drama, as in his working life, Eliot needed a sense of order, a shaping pattern, to hold together what otherwise would be scattered pieces of an unmade jigsaw. Ackroyd sees this in the image of the banker-cum-poet: 'The man who wrote *The Waste Land* was a man behind his desk, a bank official' (p. 78); and he extrapolates from this need and this image to locate Eliot's 'true voice' in the 'principle of literary organisation' which holds together the 'heterogeneous fragments' that characterise these early poems. He finds a similar connection between life and art in Eliot's growing religious faith (expressed in his mundane activities as a churchwarden and in other ecclesiastical duties, and in his essays on religion and culture in the 1930s) and its reflection in *Four Quartets* and *Murder in the Cathedral.* Again, in respect of the latter, Ackroyd stops short of autobiographical specificity with a devious 'not un-' formulation that would have made Orwell wince. Ackroyd says: 'The play is typical of Eliot's work in the sense that it is concerned with a figure, not unconnected with the author himself, who has some special awareness of which others are deprived' (p. 227). Even the Christian names match. Ackroyd argues that Eliot 'was deeply preoccupied with the nature of this solitary and ambivalent figure but ... too close to that character to be able to objectify him in dramatic terms.' Thus, the literary critical questions that the play poses are given a biographical edge: 'Is "Tom" vain or holy, a martyr or a self-deluded man, a pariah to be avoided as the Chorus suggests ... or a saint to be venerated?' (p. 227).

One of the photographs Ackroyd includes is of Eliot at the blackboard demonstrating the action of *The Cocktail Party* via a flow diagram (opp. p. 208; p. 289). Ackroyd sees the connection between Eliot's plays and *Four Quartets* in both this formal structuring and in 'the emphases and cadences of speech' that characterise his last great poems. (pp. 230, 270). Recognising the preoccupations of the life transmuted in the works; observing in the organisation of the works the need for literary order; and finding the language to represent how this order can hold together the disparate, fragmentary nature of human experience – Eliot's life and works have a challenging unity. Ackroyd captures this paradoxical nature in his final summative comments:

> We are confronted with a number of paradoxes: Eliot proclaimed the impersonality of great poetry, and yet his own personality and experience are branded in letters of fire upon his work. He was a poet who insisted on the nature and value of a tradition, and yet he had no real predecessors or successors. He was a writer who attempted to create order and coherence, and yet his central vision was of 'the Void'. His poetic voice is unmistakable, and yet it was composed from a number of other poets' voices which he adapted or borrowed. He was a strange, private and often bewildered man who was raised into a cultural guru, a representative of authority and stability. (Ackroyd, 1985: 334–335)

Ackroyd ends by quoting Eliot's own remark about Edwin Muir. It can stand as a justification for an unauthorised biography such as this, researched and written with such insight into 'the mystery of that connection' between the life and the work. Eliot said: 'We also understand the poetry better when we know more about the man.'

Orwell: The Life by D. J. Taylor

With George Orwell, we encounter a dramatic death-bed statement and another second wife cast in the controversial role of a young literary widow. For his biographers, the statement is arguably one of the most significant of Orwell's life – his 'I do' from his bed in Room 65 of University College Hospital as he married Sonia Brownell just over three months before he died. His widow, fifteen years his junior, to whom he left everything, has inevitably been seen by earlier biographers as a gold-digger who married for mercenary motives, who spent the fortune that accrued from the royalties from *Animal Farm* and *1984*, and mishandled his Estate. Sonia Orwell's biographer and friend, Hilary Spurling, has attempted a rehabilitation (Spurling, 2002), one which Taylor, as one of Orwell's two centenary biographers, appears to accept, rejecting as nonsense the portrait of Sonia as a 'high-class literary groupie' (Taylor, 2004: 364), or as 'an impenitent gold-digger' (p. 413), and affirming her role as 'a diligent guardian of Orwell's interests' (p. 421). Certainly, the facts of her history bear this out. She deployed Orwell's posthumous income helping young writers such as Jean Rhys in ways he would have approved, edited with Ian Angus the four-volume *Collected Essays, Journalism and Letters of George Orwell* (1968/1970), profited only modestly herself from his Estate, and died in 1980 in relative poverty (Taylor, 2004: 422).

This is not to say that Sonia's concern to protect Orwell's life from the incursions of biographers was always carried out with consistency and sound judgement. Gordon Bowker, the other centenary biographer, even suggests that Orwell's request in his will for 'no biography' was Sonia's doing (*TLS*, 15 September 2006), and he characterises her dealings with would-be biographers as capricious and inconsistent. No doubt he would share Taylor's assessment of Sonia as 'an odd woman and an even odder literary widow: loyal, protective, keen to do the right thing, but simultaneously erratic in her judgement and capricious in her personal likes and dislikes' (Taylor, 2004: 6). Her death, coming at the mid-point in the almost sixty years since her husband died, marked a significant change in Orwell's lives and afterlives. Taylor attributes 'the tortuous history of Orwell biography' to its subject but, while Orwell's supposed wish for 'no biography' may be its origin, for the ensuing thirty years it was the subject's widow who was at the centre of this history. The development of Orwell biography both pre- and post-Sonia's death has been outlined many times (Collini, *TLS*, 20 June 2003; Taylor, 2004: 5–6; Bowker, *TLS*, 15 September 2006); behind the various accounts, the most revealing primary source is the *Collected Essays, Journalism and Letters*.

Sonia Orwell's Introduction to these four volumes artfully attempts to subvert the need for a biography. She emphasises that Orwell 'was not given to keeping notebooks, diaries, sketches or outlines of projected books or work-in-progress and threw away the drafts and manuscripts of his books when they were redundant. In fact he left very few of those "papers" which writers always seem to leave, providing such marvellous hunting-grounds for critics or biographers. He left no personal papers: there is nothing either concealed or spectacularly revealed in his letters' (S. Orwell, 1970, I: 14). And, in explaining the reasons for presenting the material chronologically, she says this is 'to give a continuous picture of Orwell's life as well as of his work', and she reminds the reader that 'In his will he asked that no biography of him be written' (p. 17). He gave no reasons but his widow does so, advancing the usual argument that Orwell is to be found in his works, and pointing to the autobiographical element of much of his writing, as if this somehow absolves the need for a biography. Clearly, she sees the *Collected Essays, Journalism and Letters* as a surrogate 'Life' and hopes it will be the last word: 'With these volumes the picture is as complete as it can be.' Her editorial arrangement of the material is designed to 'give an idea of how his life and work developed. To him they were one' (p. 18). The sincerity of her feelings for Orwell's memory and the naïvety of her sense of the cultural demands of biography make an uncomfortable combination. Though far from unique, it offers a clear example both of the dilemmas and sensitivities that can occur when a writer's estate is controlled by the bereaved family and of the need to view the subject at some historical distance from the life and the works.

Taylor's book enjoys several advantages: he writes from a perspective fifty years distant from his subject; he is free from the earlier restraints imposed by the Estate; and he admits to being a long-time admirer of Orwell who, he tells us, 'has obsessed me for the best part of a quarter of a century' (Taylor, 2004: 1). Here, then, is a biography that has grown from a singular passion over many years, one more akin to the literary relationship between Dominic Hibberd and Wilfred Owen (see Chapter 9) than to that of the professional biographer who moves from subject to subject. Taylor locates Orwell's appeal in two features: 'the sense of sheer personality that rises from his work – that urgent need to communicate vital things'; and the 'moral force' of his writing, 'a kind of ethical litmus paper' which, in turn, became the test of how to respond to totalitarianism, fascism, and consumer capitalism which in various guises and regimes were the substitutes for the decline of mass religious belief in the mid-twentieth century (Taylor, 2004: 2).

Yet, for all his obsession, Taylor's constant refrain is of Orwell's elusiveness. Sonia Orwell's remark about the absence of personal 'papers' was clearly both a discouragement and a warning to biographers of potential frustration. And so it proved. Taylor notes that there is no record or formal account of Orwell's four and a half years in Burma (p. 68). He laments that when one asks what Orwell was like in his early twenties, 'Nobody knows' (p. 73); and he summarises the character of Orwell's whole pre-1930 life with the words, 'Orwell himself is impossible to pin down' (p. 89). The frustrations deepen towards depression: 'vast areas of his [Orwell's] personal life stretch out into impenetrable blackness' (p. 98). And Taylor is forced to work with what he calls Orwell's 'elusive presence', confessing 'how little we know about him and how few verifiable facts remain. His day-to-day existence, routines – even his whereabouts – are a mystery for months on end' (p. 107). Even in autumn 1939, at the start of the Second World War when one might expect to find Orwell on record, Taylor comments: 'It is also a period when Orwell is at his most elusive, when the trail goes intermittently cold' (p. 273). One can see why the widow might feel that the *Collected Essays, Journalism and Letters* could serve as a biography, and why Taylor finds himself biographically challenged.

What, then, is the image of Orwell that is created? Does it inevitably owe more to fictional creation than historical recreation, more to inference from the works than evidence of the facts? The questions arise not only through Orwell's elusiveness but also because a sense of personal identity was itself a key issue that Orwell himself faced. Its most obvious manifestation was his decision in 1932 that 'Eric Blair' should become 'George Orwell'. Taylor rejects the idea that the need for a pseudonym represented some 'change of personality, motive or resolve' in favour of the more prosaic explanation that he did not want to embarrass his parents over the seedy subject-matter of *Down and Out in Paris and London* (Taylor, 2004: 126). Yet he hints elsewhere that there may be more subtle implications to be drawn.

Earlier in the 'Life' when writing about Orwell's childhood, he comments that 'Orwell went through life in ceaseless cultivation of what might be called his personal myth' (p. 24), a phrase that he repeats in his description of Orwell's retrospective account of himself at Eton (p. 53). Orwell's formative years certainly encourage this idea. Born in India before returning to England as a 4-year-old, five years at a private preparatory school, a similar period at public school, the same period again in the Imperial Police in Burma – Eric Blair by his mid-twenties had the impeccable middle-class background, education and training for an administrative role at home or abroad. He had grown up with little normal family life, experienced a privileged school life, and embarked on a working life helping to run the Empire. He knew little or nothing about the lives of ordinary people in his 'home country'. He was, albeit for quite different reasons, rather like Eliot – a 'resident alien'. He needed to reinvent himself both in order to relate to the England he returned to and to find himself as writer. His well-known 'tramping exploits' into the seedier areas of London and the industrial North, embarked upon from his parents' home in respectable Southwold in the early 1930s, were by a man who was 'introverted, detached, literally vagrant' (Taylor, 2004: 110). They were his means of coming to terms, through a self-administered culture shock, with the contrast between his privileged past and the realities of 1930s England. Given the documentary basis of his writings about Burma and England up to the mid-1930s, the change from Blair to Orwell signals the invention of a literary self through which he can be the detached observer of the human condition yet also retain the literary freedom to select, embellish and shape his accounts into aesthetic forms. Indeed, it has been argued that all Orwell's writings up to 1937, including his 'fictions' and 'documentaries', should be seen 'as sketches towards the creation of his most successful character, "Orwell"' (Williams, 1971: 52; see also Crick, 1980: xxii). Hence, the journal writer of *Down and Out in Paris and London*, the fictional Gordon Comstock, the angry young man in *Keep the Aspidistra Flying*, the narrator of *Shooting an Elephant* and the contrasting voices of the two parts of *The Road to Wigan Pier*, where Orwell first casts himself in the spectator role before becoming overtly autobiographical in part two – all constitute projections, with differing emphases, of Orwell's literary persona. Then came Spain. And another change was wrought in the literary persona: to the role of detached observer was added that of the committed participant.

Taylor is explicit about the significance of Orwell's decision to go to Spain to fight against Franco and the fascists:

> Spain, it can safely be said, was the defining experience of Orwell's life. Much more emphatically than the disillusionment of Burma, his trips among the embankment sleepers or his journeys among the unemployed, it gave him a sense of what he wanted from life and the goals that he wished to achieve. (Taylor, 2004: 201)

Orwell himself recognised the significance of his time in Spain. *Homage to Catalonia*, written six months after his return, includes a chapter where he reflects upon his first 115 days in the line which 'from the point of view of my own development ... were less futile than I thought [at the time] ... they taught me things that I could not have learned in any other way'. He identifies 'the workers' militias' as the key. They were 'a sort of microcosm of the classless society'; they gave a 'foretaste' of what socialism could be like. Yet Orwell was no romantic socialist and recognised that what he had experienced was 'simply a temporary and local phase in an enormous game that is being played over the whole surface of the earth. But it lasted long enough to have its effect upon anyone who experienced it.' Repeatedly, he stresses these months were 'of great importance to me' and notes their 'curious vividness', concluding that this period 'so different from the rest of my life … has taken on a magic quality' (Orwell, 1938/1962: 101–103). The Spanish Civil War also gave him first-hand experience of the disillusioning course of revolutionary politics on the ground in the streets of Barcelona: 'few experiences', he says, 'could be more sickening, more disillusioning, or, finally, more nerve-racking than those evil days of street warfare' as the communists, anarchists and other factions fought for superiority. He marvelled 'at the folly of it all' and wondered 'What the devil was happening, who was fighting whom, and who was winning' (Orwell, 1938/1962: 125–126).

Taylor's account of these years necessarily draws heavily upon Orwell's own and is rightly sceptical of Raymond Williams's Marxist interpretation of events (Taylor, 2004: 242). Taylor stresses that 'Spain left an indelible mark on Orwell, quite apart from the bullet-hole in his throat'. He comments that 'many of the seeds of *Nineteen Eighty-Four* were sown in Catalonia' (Taylor, 2004: 238–239). Curiously, he does not say the same for *Animal Farm*, which, as indicated above, is more clearly prefigured, particularly in the atmosphere Orwell describes in Barcelona after his three and a half months at the front when he found the earlier revolutionary spirit was dissipating and 'things were returning to normal' (Orwell, 1938/1962: 110). 'Spain', Taylor says, 'both confirmed Orwell's belief in the indomitability of the human spirit' and made him 'a much more political animal, prepared for the first time to join a political party, to sign manifestoes, even – as the Second World War became inevitable – to take direct political action' (Taylor, 2004: 239–240). Rejected on health grounds for active service in the war, Orwell worked for two years for the BBC and then for a similar period as literary editor of *Tribune*. Behind these 'day jobs', he was more prolific than ever with essays and occasional writings, perhaps the most significant of which was 'The Lion and the Unicorn' (1941) with its arresting opening ('As I write, highly civilised human beings are flying overhead, trying to kill me'), its critical account of 'Englishness' and its six-point programme for English socialism (S. Orwell & I. Angus 1970, II: 74–99). This was 'incendiary stuff' in wartime, as Taylor remarks (p. 290). Orwell had embarked, too, upon writing *Animal Farm*, the result of his 'searching for a way to dramatise what he believed was the human betrayal practised by the Soviet regime in the twenty years since the Revolution' (Taylor, 2004: 322). Taylor plots the tortuous path of *Animal Farm* to eventual publication. Delayed by 'political squeamishness' from publishers, subverted by a government official later unmasked as a Soviet spy, criticised by T. S. Eliot at Faber, *Animal Farm* was finally published by Warburg in 1945 (pp. 333–340). Orwell's reaction to its success, as to any literary lionisation, was to duck out of the spotlight, which, in his case, meant planning his retreat to the remote Scottish island of Jura. But the winter of 1944–1945 also saw the death of his wife, Eileen, from a malignant tumour and his response was, Boxer-like, to work even harder, producing in the year following his bereavement around 130 pieces of literary journalism (p. 359). Much of Orwell's last major work, *Nineteen Eighty-Four*, was written on Jura when his health was deteriorating. Taylor situates the book in the context of Orwell's contemporary writing on 'Politics and the English Language', and argues that the connection between language and morality lies at its centre (p. 377). Winston Smith is yet another projection of the author, falsifying history in 'The Ministry of Truth' (aka University of London, Senate House) only a mile or two from 'Victory Square' (aka Trafalgar Square) where Nelson has been replaced by a statue of Big Brother (p. 388). The power of the book owes much to the immediacy of its topography; and the power of its message is that 'it is not exclusively anti-Communist but anti-totalitarian' (p. 402).

Given Taylor's sense of his subject's elusiveness, how successful is his search for 'Orwell'? It was hinted in the questions posed above that the mix of invention and documentation might favour the former. Because so much of the moral authority that first attracted Taylor to Orwell is grounded in the claims made by the apparent authenticity of his subject's experiences, readers look for reassurance from biography that Orwell's literary needs do not compromise his moral purpose. Similarly, we expect biography to clarify the relationship between the literary persona and the historical person, an issue of identity that Orwell complicated through changing his name. Taylor, as we have seen, is alert to these issues; and perhaps it was their special importance in Orwell's case that led him to include the ten interchapters that punctuate his biography, which 'still' the narrative momentum and give the reader pause for reflection on 'Orwell's Face', 'Orwell's Voice' and so on. These could be attempts, in Woolf's terms, to catch the 'rainbow' to complement the 'granite'; but do they? Opinion seems divided. For Paul Foot (*The Observer*, 1 June 2003), they are 'absurd parentheses'; for Piers Brendon (*The Guardian*, 7 June 2003), 'vivid snapshots'; for Stefan Collini (*TLS*, 20 June 2003), 'short inter-chapters on arresting topics'. In fact, they are a mixed bag. Some document surprising facts; for example, that there exists no record of Orwell's voice at the BBC, nor any sight of him on film. Others seem merely whimsical, such as 'Orwell's Dream' and 'Orwell's Things'. One, 'Orwell's Failure', usefully focuses on a lifelong obsession in his life and work. Another, 'The Case Against', plays devil's advocate in the guise of a Marxist critic demolishing Orwell's achievements and reputation. Taken in context, they do create Orwell as a more substantial figure in the mind's eye and help to compensate for the lacunae in the documentary record. These oblique glances are Taylor's way of trying to capture a subject who seems constantly to be slipping out of view.

Philip Larkin: A Writer's Life by Andrew Motion

Writing in 1975, ten years before his death, Larkin begins an essay-review of Jon Stallworthy's biography of Wilfred Owen with a typically controversial statement: 'A writer's reputation is twofold: what we think of his work, and what we think of him. What's more, we expect the two halves to relate: if they don't, then one or other of our opinions alters until they do' (Larkin, 1983: 228). Many of his fellow writers would dispute this intimacy of the life and works; but Larkin is hinting at the more subtle process of biographical hindsight in which, though 'the work is published, and will not be added to', the life, 'guarded by widow, family, friends, trustees', presents an incomplete picture. There is a measure of irony in these remarks in the light of the publishing history of Larkin's *Collected Poems* (1988), the *Letters* (1992) and Motion's biography (1993). For Thwaite's edition of the poems showed that the four published slim volumes could certainly be 'added to'; and the life, as revealed respectively by two of Larkin's literary executors in the *Letters* and the biography, was sufficiently 'unguarded' for a later biographer to comment that 'these new disclosures [were] seized upon with a frenzy hardly witnessed since the McCarthy era' (Bradford, 2005: 15). The analogy may be excessive but the point is sharply made: the relationship between Larkin's 'two halves', the man and the poet, became a much-debated issue. For the biographer, it was the central one.

Motion explains his dual role as biographer and literary executor: 'At no time during the nine years of our friendship did we discuss his biography. He did not ask me to write this book' (Motion, 1993: xv; all subsequent page numbers are to this edition unless otherwise stated). But, in 1983, he had asked Motion to join Monica Jones and Anthony Thwaite as one of his literary executors; and early in 1986, a few months after Larkin's death, it was Monica Jones, Larkin's long-time companion, who asked him to write the biography and who, inadvertently, provided the subtitle (p. 524). But in what sense was this 'a writer's life'? After all, Larkin's professional career as a librarian spanned forty years and his dedication to his day job and its demands, particularly in developing the new Brynmor Jones Library at Hull University, meant that his writing was, in the conventional sense, a part-time activity. Yet, as Seamus Heaney remarked on the publication of the *Collected Poems*, 'His [Larkin's] masquerade as a 9-to-5 man who occasionally hit one off is called into question by the evidence of a path followed over a lifetime in silence and in discipline' (Heaney, *The Observer*, 9 October 1988). Larkin knew he had talent and, more significantly, he knew that he needed to write to sustain himself. Motion summarises: 'The friends he made, the jobs he took, the habits he formed, the places he lived in, the people he loved – all were chosen so that he could concentrate on his writing, which is what mattered to him most. In the strictest sense, his was a writer's life' (p. xx). Motion's role is, in fact, a triple one – executor, biographer and, of course, fellow poet – one who is well placed to judge in just what ways we can read the life in the poetry. Two features characterise this authorised life: its insights into the poetry, and the involvement of the literary estate with the invention of the subject.

As Motion acknowledges, Larkin saw him coming; or, at least, anticipated his biographer in the guise of Jake Balokowsky in the poem 'Posterity'. Motion gives an early outing to the poet's description of himself as a biographer's subject – 'one of those old-type *natural* fouled-up guys' – a persona that Larkin could easily disown as a poetic exercise were it not for the fact that it is a self-image that is substantiated overtly in his letters, covertly in his poems and, despite the friendly care for his subject, in Motion's biography itself. For the portrait of Larkin that emerges is of a solitary, introverted man who was 'fouled-up' early in life by his sensitive awareness of the inadequacies of his parents' marriage. Motion quotes Larkin's account of family life as a grimly formative experience: '"When I try to tune into my childhood, the dominant emotions I pick up are, overwhelmingly, fear and boredom.... Certainly the marriage left me with two convictions: that human beings should not live together, and that children should be taken from their parents at an early age"' (pp. 13–15). This is the voice of the bitter, dogmatic, cynical Larkin (a voice notoriously translated into his poem 'This Be The Verse') made more curmudgeonly as he realised that he would never be free of his parents. He inherited his father's independent spirit, his bookishness and his uncompromising right-wing views, if not his Nazi sympathies; and he maintained regular visits to Eva, his mother ('an obsessive snivelling pest' as he called her), for over thirty years, feeling tied and resentful. On her death aged 91 in 1977 – pre-deceasing her son by just eight years – Motion comments that she 'had shaped his life more decisively than anyone else ... [she] ... was his muse – not a beauty to be won like Maud Gonne, but a misery which had to be both resisted and accepted' (pp. 467–468).

Motion's biography reflects the advantages of his position: as executor he had access to Larkin's papers (including rescuing over 200 letters from imminent destruction – see Motion, 2004); as a friend he could observe his subject at first hand; and as a poet he could contextualise the poems and assess them in relation to Larkin's life, letters and other writings. The biography moves deftly between Larkin's relationships with his parents and friends – particularly with Kingsley Amis and with the three main women in his life, Eva, Monica Jones and Maeve Brennan – and the ways in which his emotional life is transmuted into his poetry. He comments shrewdly on Larkin's non-theoretical stance, quoting him as saying that his 'poems owe their first responsibility to his own and his readers' feelings. They were all, he said, an attempt "to express or describe or to render or preserve emotions that people feel"' (p. 213). Yet emotions in life suffer a sea-change when they appear in poetry, nowhere more so than in poems inspired by his three women. Hence, tenderness as well as sorrow flows through one of his most beautiful poems, 'Love Songs in Age', even though it was prompted by one of his annual Christmas visits to his mother with all its attendant worries and irritations (p. 279). Or again, Motion shows how Larkin's love for Maeve intensified his 'imaginative contact' with the wider world: 'All experience, no matter what its nature, became charged and alluring because of his feeling about her' (p. 301). But the most telling instance of Larkin colouring his poems with the character of his emotional life is found in Motion's comments on 'An Arundel Tomb', a poem which arose out of his visit with Monica to Chichester Cathedral. Here they encountered the monument to the Earl of Arundel and his wife, two stone figures lying side by side, holding hands. Motion quotes the well-known final verse:

> Time has transfigured them into
> Untruth. The stone fidelity
> They hardly meant has come to be
> Their final blazon, and to prove
> Our almost-instinct almost true:
> What will survive of us is love.

The last line is beguiling, its assertiveness seeming to express a universal truth to which all can assent. Motion administers an immediate corrective by quoting Larkin's note on the MS draft: '"Love isn't stronger than death just because statues hold hands for 600 years"', and points to the 'sense of futility that hovers round the poem's conclusion' (p. 274). He could have gone further. All the positives are undermined: 'Time' has led to 'Untruth'; 'stone fidelity' amounts to no more than 'their final blazon'; and the triumph of love over death in the final line is subverted by the repeated 'almost' in the preceding one. The Arundel tomb becomes not a testament to the power of love but an emblem of the speaker's disbelief in its permanence and longevity. Larkin, the man, is looking on at these married figures admiring the 'sculptor's sweet commissioned grace' yet unconvinced by the faithfulness it represents. Larkin, the poet, fashions his thoughts in the most subtle language, clothing his doubts in a rich vocabulary ('transfigured', 'fidelity', 'blazon', 'true', 'survive', 'love') befitting his medieval subject. And also looking on is Monica. No doubt, by 1956, almost a decade into their relationship, she would recognise that Larkin's equivocal attitude permeated his personal life, too, one with which she would have to come to terms. 'An Arundel Tomb' illustrates themes that run through Larkin's poetry: as Motion points out, Larkin's 'obsession with death is inextricable from his fascination with love and marriage' (p. 291).

Motion singles out 'The Whitsun Weddings' as 'the poem which illustrates his [Larkin's] achievement better than any other'. He prefaces his commentary with Larkin's explanatory context given during an interview with Melvyn Bragg in 1981, and characterises the poem as combining 'a discursive novel-ish spread with the emotional intensity of a lyric'. He quotes the final verse when the trainload of newly-weds approaches London which concludes:

> ... and it was nearly done, this frail
> Travelling coincidence; and what it held
> Stood ready to be loosed with all its power
> That being changed can give. We slowed again,
> And as the tightened brakes took hold, there swelled
> A sense of falling, like an arrow-shower
> Sent out of sight, somewhere becoming rain.

Motion comments that 'All the paradoxes of the poem, and all those which govern Larkin's thoughts about love, are collected here in an image adapted ... from the arrows fired by the English bowmen in Laurence Olivier's film of *Henry V*'. He allows himself an apposite, if speculative, gloss on these lines, suggesting that Larkin 'reminds himself that the arrow-shower of love wounds as well as inspires' (p. 288). Motion's reading sees Cupid's arrows morphing into Olivier's arrows and, powered by Walton's accompanying music, raining down on the unseen futures of these couples, as likely to dampen their hopes as to stimulate their growth. His commentary gives us the Larkin music, an insight into the imagery, and the ambivalence of Larkin, the spectator, who simultaneously admires the vivifying effects of weddings on the couples and their families, and senses his own separateness and loss, while valuing his singular, onlooker role.

The judgements on both the poem and the man who made it flow directly from Motion's triple role as executor, biographer and poet. In fact, the whole biography gains considerable authority in this way. It substantiates what was already known of Larkin's early development from his mimicry of Keats and Tennyson in, say, 'Summer Nocturne' (1939); through his period of Auden-speak at Oxford in 'New Year Poem' (1940); his phase of 'Celtic fever' when Yeats's influence was supreme ('Mythological Introduction', 1943); until, in the mid-1940s, Hardy helped him to find his own voice. 'Instead of symbolism there was fidelity to familiar fact ... instead of a longing to transcend there was total immersion in everyday things.' Yet, as Motion argues (pp. 140–141), the Yeatsian influence continued to show, as is apparent in 'Going' (1946), the poem with which Thwaite begins *Collected Poems* and which is regarded as 'the first poem of his maturity which he [Larkin] chose to preserve' (Thwaite, 1988: xv). And echoes remain thirty years on in his last great poem, 'Aubade', which, like Hardy's 'Afterwards', reads like a valediction to the world.

Over the three post-war decades, despite a darkening in tone and a hardening in attitudes, Larkin's themes and characteristic ways of dealing with them remained remarkably consistent. Motion dates his 'transformation' into a mature poet around 1950 and shows that, during his five years in Belfast as a sub-librarian at Queen's University, he produced the poems that would bring him to public notice. They were eventually published in *The Less Deceived* (1955), 'the decisive turning-point in Larkin's career' (p. 270), and included 'Next, Please' with its intimations of death; 'Reasons For Attendance' in which he weighs up the 'the rival claims of self and society, sexual loneliness and sexual attachment' (p. 235); 'I Remember, I Remember', which recalls the emptiness of his 'unspent childhood' in Coventry and reflects that 'it's not the place's fault ... Nothing, like something, happens anywhere'; 'Toads', where 'he accepts that while he resents the daily grind in the library, he relies on it' (p. 236); and 'Church Going' with its 'self-mocking, detail-collecting, conversational manner' (p. 241) and in which Alvarez famously located, in the opening lines, 'the image of the post-war Welfare State Englishman: shabby and not concerned with his appearance; poor – he has a bike, not a car; gauche but full of agnostic piety; underfed, underpaid, overtaxed, hopeless, bored, wry' (Alvarez, 1962: 24–25). There is something if not everything of Larkin in Alvarez's description; it hints at both the personal image and the tone that has made 'Church Going' one of Larkin's best-known poems.

The move from Belfast to Hull in 1955 involved Larkin in a typically bleak search for convenient and consequently unpleasant lodgings – a quest that gave rise to the sardonic humour of 'Mr Bleaney' with its Prufrock echo 'That how we live measures our own nature', and the suspicion 'that his own life and Mr Bleaney's might be interchangeable' (p. 248). 'Mr Bleaney' was collected a decade later with, among others, the poetic still life 'Home Is So Sad', 'Ambulances', 'Afternoons' and the celebrated title poem in Larkin's second slim volume, *The Whitsun Weddings* (1965), which marked the high point of his career. Of the thirty-two poems, 'Dockery and Son' is, biographically speaking, the most significant, revisiting the chilling sentiment Larkin first coined in his family reminiscences quoted above: 'Life is first boredom, then fear.' Motion summarises: 'Bitterly funny and grievously melancholic, 'Dockery and Son' is a compressed autobiography. It encapsulates Larkin's views about the effect of his parents on his personality, it reports spiritedly on his undergraduate career, it grimly sketches the attitudes which dominated his adult life' (p. 334).

The mismatch between the reclusive, middle-aged bachelor and the culture of the swinging sixties played into Larkin's talent for irony and facetiousness about human relationships. Sex, love, death, society remained his themes but, in the poems that were collected in *High Windows* (1974), he contemplates them with the decade's greater sense of openness. The title poem sets the tone: 'a poem [that] grows out of rage: the rage of unsatisfied desire, the rage of "shame", the rage of having to persuade everyone that "the thought of high windows" guarantees happiness' (p. 355). But, by the end, the rage subsides into an image that is, at once, sad, resigned, beautiful and depressing. His eyes are lifted from the ironic paradise he depicts at the start to 'the deep blue air, that shows / Nothing, and is nowhere, and is endless'. The contrast between the plain idiom of the earlier verses and the symbolism of the ending expresses in miniature the character of the whole volume. He takes an archly sceptical glance at the mantras of 'sexual liberation' in 'Annus Mirabilis', a bitter, blunt line on the parents that fate deals you in 'This Be The Verse', and a solitary man's view of the awful necessity of the social round in 'Vers de Société', the poem which Motion sees as encapsulating the beliefs that dominated the last third of Larkin's life (pp. 411–412). Overall, he suggests, this final volume 'changed Larkin's life more decisively than any of his previous collections'. He summarises what could be called Larkin's early, middle and late periods: '*The Less Deceived* made his name; *The Whitsun Weddings* made him famous; *High Windows* turned him into a national monument' (p. 446).

A national monument? Well, maybe. But one that was tarnished. Moreover, it was tarnished both by Larkin himself and by his executors. Even those who could tolerate his love of Mrs Thatcher and his hatred of modernism, 'abroad' and the young found in the *Letters* and, to some extent, in the biography an unappealing, self-inflicted misery, a boringly puerile scatological vocabulary, and an intolerable racism. Neither Larkin's dark humour and verbal dexterity, nor the sardonic, lugubrious manner he cultivated, nor the element of self-parody in poems such as 'Annus Mirabilis' can nullify the less pleasant aspects of Larkin's life. He was a voyeur, not only in his liking for pornography and his habit of keeping a telescope on his windowsill to observe passing girls but, more fundamentally, in his relationships with women, especially with Monica. His self-regarding voyeurism entailed a refusal to commit, an inclination always to be the spectator, a tendency to project an appropriate persona as the occasion demanded rather than to engage. Even this could be humorous as well as sad. Motion catches this mix when he describes Larkin as 'a kind of sexually disappointed Eeyore' (p. 267). But there is no humour in his racism and, though his prejudice against non-white people is largely confined to his letters, if it leaked outside his private correspondence, he didn't care. 'Like his father before him, he felt proud of his right-wing isolation' (p. 411)

So, is this 'Life' a writer's life? Certainly, Motion succeeds in embedding the poems in their biographical contexts, in plotting Larkin's literary development, and in characterising the Larkin voice. One might quibble that spending seventy pages with Larkin at Oxford and his unpublished prose fictions is too generous; and that there are too many navel-contemplating letters which 'make diagnosis an end in itself' (p. 384). But perhaps a larger question mark sits over Motion's introductory image of Larkin's work and life which sees 'the beautiful flowers of his poetry … growing on long stalks out of pretty dismal ground' (p. xx). For, as Motion knows, the poems cannot be detached entirely from Larkin's life history. Cut flowers never last; and to sever Larkin's prejudices from his literary achievements would be an act of anti-biographical formalism. Motion's 'long stalks' are his attempt to distance the poems from the prejudices of the person. He defends his subject by arguing that Larkin assumed different personae in life and in poetry. He portrays him variously as dividing his life 'into compartments' (p. 332), as 'self-dramatising' (p. 280); and he shows how 'the integrity of his poems depended on his ability to draw on the whole range of his selves, and speak in all their voices' (p. 333). Whether any subtitle could capture the diversity of Larkin that his biography describes is doubtful. An alternative, perhaps, would be 'a singular life' with all the nuances this suggests: a life that was special, peculiar, even quirky; one that was solitary and placed high value on what he called in 'Best Society' 'uncontradicting solitude'; and one, above all, that was notable for the unique quality of poetry that combined quotidian subject matter, traditional poetic forms of expression and a sense of personal presence.

Contemporary Lives

The main differences, of course, between these twentieth-century 'Lives' and their predecessors are in the detailed accounts biographers give of their subjects' marriages, affairs and sexual proclivities – the intimacies that pre-war, and certainly pre-Stracheyean, biographies left out. But there is another difference. While we may experience a sense of the literary persona of many writers through their works, with these twentieth-century figures the personae are, in varying degrees, their own deliberate literary inventions. They are neither the tactical pseudonyms to ease publication like those of the Brontës or George Eliot, nor figures for the implied author, nor the explicit self-representations of Wordsworth and Joyce, but personae cultivated by the authors as an integral part of their literary selves. Their biographers have to work with these personae – to describe and account for their presence in the literary environment that surrounds them. So, here, along with Sherry, we are invited to become an observer and quasi-inhabitant of 'Greeneland'; Eliot's recurring label for himself as 'a resident alien' moves Ackroyd to present Eliot to us as a consciously constructed persona; according to Michael Holroyd, 'GBS' grew into a public carapace concealing the young 'Sonny'; 'Orwell', as we noted, has been seen as Eric Blair's most successful character, not merely a *nom de plume*; and Larkin's caricature persona as the Hermit of Hull (which he did nothing to discourage) is shown, as Motion implies, as more complex and varied in the range of selves and voices in the *Collected Poems*. One element of the biographer's task is to interrogate the persona in order to engage the reader with this aspect of their subject's self-invention. And part of the reason for the development of this self-consciousness about 'the literary life', in both the biographer and the subject, may well lie with the parallel development in the power of the literary estates.

Five 'Lives': two biographers known by their subjects, Sherry selected by Greene and operating uncomfortably alongside the literary estate, Motion writing from the position of a literary executor; two others coming to the task years after their subject's death, Holroyd appointed by the estate, Taylor benefiting from the relaxation of the estate's governance half a century on; and Ackroyd, turning his back on the estate and going his own way. At first sight, the official imprimatur conferred by the phrase 'the authorised life' suggests that the literary estate has appointed the biographer with care, sanctioned and supported the research, so that we can be confident in the probity and informed judgements in the resulting work. A second glance reveals evidence that things may be otherwise. Two brief examples indicate the sort of pitfalls that, unintentionally, authors or their executors can fall into: the ambiguities of Larkin's will, and the tangles that followed from Sonia Orwell's capriciousness over the appointment of an official biographer for her late husband.

Larkin's will demonstrates that the linguistic flair of the poet and the meticulous precision of the librarian do not easily translate into the language of the law. Despite Larkin's expressed concern that the wording should be clear and unambiguous, Motion quotes paragraphs of the will concerning the fate of Larkin's unpublished papers and manuscripts that are either opaque or plainly contradictory. He gives one commentator's summary: 'In three breaths Larkin gave his trustees the power to publish his unpublished work, instructed them to destroy it, and told them to discuss the matter with the literary executors' (Motion, 1993: xvi). According to Ian Hamilton, Motion subsequently took the view that such contradictions were unsurprising in that they were 'part of a much larger pattern of ambiguous feelings that he [Larkin] had about everything in his life – from women through work' (Hamilton, 1992: 309). Indecision came naturally to him and included devolving the issue of his papers on to his executors, leaving them with the problem of how to carry out one of their main responsibilities – how to implement what the dead author would have wished.

It was just this responsibility that led Sonia Orwell into her protracted vacillations over authorising a biography of her husband. Gordon Bowker plots the tortuous course over almost two decades, arguing that Muggeridge's 'official' appointment in 1955 was a calculated block to others because she knew he would not deliver. He quotes her distaste and uncertainty about the whole enterprise: 'I really hate the whole of this biography situation and just know that I really can't authorise one … I suppose one will be written as soon as I'm dead or the copyright expires, but quite honestly I cannot find it in myself to authorise one, even though I do see it might be sensible!' (Bowker, *TLS*, 15 September 2006: 15). But she changed her mind when, with Muggeridge having withdrawn, the unauthorised *The Unknown Orwell* by Stansky and Abrahams was published in 1972. She promptly authorised Bernard Crick, a Professor of Politics at London University, to write a full biography. It seems that she was too quick, for the first point Crick makes in his official thanks to her is that his is 'in no sense … an official biography' (Crick, 1980: ix); and his Introduction makes clear that his emphasis will be on Orwell as a 'political writer'. On seeing the final typescript, Sonia did not like what she read, changed her mind again, and insisted that the status of 'authorised' be rescinded. Within weeks she was dead and, according to Taylor (2004: 6), 'went to her grave believing that she had betrayed her late husband's memory'.

The authorised life, it transpires, may be more fully informed but is essentially no more stable than any other. 'Posterity' may be the judge, rather than authors or executors, but, even so, there is little evidence that such a *laissez-faire* attitude to history will lead to any truer sense of a subject's life. 'Lives', authorised or not, are true to the knowledge and perceptions of the period in which they are written.

11

Literary Lives: Scenes and Stories

> *Indeed I cannot conceive a more perfect mode of writing any man's life, than not only relating all the most important events of it in their order, but interweaving what he privately wrote, and said, and thought; by which mankind are enabled as it were to see him live, and to 'live o'er each scene' with him, as he actually advanced through the several stages of his life.*
>
> (Boswell, *The Life of Dr. Johnson*, 1791/1949: 8)

> *But whatever the reason may be, I find that scene making is my natural way of marking the past. A scene always comes to the top; arranged; representative.... In all the writing I have done (novels, criticism, biography) I almost always have to find a scene; either when I am writing about a person, I must find a representative scene in their lives; or when I am writing about a book, I must find the scene in their poems or novels.*
>
> (Woolf, 'Sketch of the Past', 1939–1940/2002: 145)

Imagining scenes and telling stories are primary acts of mind. Whether in factual or fictional lives, they are the substantive means by which we represent the past to ourselves. These two epigraphs return us to the major figures in literary biography discussed in Chapter 1 and to their key reflections on the genre. Boswell's remarks are from his Introduction to his *The Life of Dr. Johnson* in which he quotes copiously from his subject's essay in *The Rambler*, No. 60 and attempts to follow Johnson's recommendations, 'both in his precept and his example', so that Johnson 'will be seen as he really was'. Virginia Woolf's remarks come towards the end of her autobiographical reflections in 'Sketch of the Past' where she says that scenes are not merely a literary device; they are, for her, the way of conceiving 'reality' and, by extension, 'the origin of [her] writing impulse'. In both cases, 'scenes' are the coinage of biography, the means by which it tells its story. In enabling readers to 'live o'er each scene', Boswell conducts us through a sequence of stages in scenes which retain both the fleeting details of daily life and the character of Johnson's conversation. Behind Virginia Woolf's notion of 'representative' scenes lies her constant struggle to use them to reanimate the past, particularly her familial past, in an effort to understand it. In Boswell 'scene' connotes theatre; in Woolf it evokes painting.

How do such scenes and stories serve the literary lives they help to create? The prime issue for *literary* biography is the intimacy of life and literature. Ellmann noted this in writing Joyce's biography (see Chapter 8 above). It is no less true, if in different ways, of the lives and writings of Boswell, Johnson and Virginia Woolf. The implication for all literary biographers is the need to assess continuously 'the participation of the artist in two simultaneous processes', in Ellmann's phrase – the lived-through experiences of daily life and how, in turn, these contribute to and are shaped into artistic form. Such shaping is not just some simplistic recording of particular incidents; rather, it is to be found in the recurring images, the patterns of relationships, the emotional colouring, the narrative analogies that characterise an author's works. We have noted many such scenes and stories in earlier chapters. The purpose of this one is to scrutinise these aspects of biographical method further by close readings of two examples: two very different dinner parties, one occurring in the context of biography, the other in the context of a novel. The first, 'Dinner with Dr Johnson and John Wilkes', is an instance of a biographer engineering an event in actual life in order to be able to recreate it as a sequence of scenes in his biographical 'Life'; the second, 'Dinner with Mrs Ramsay', is an example of the fictionalisation of scenes derived from the author's own life in the novel in which Virginia Woolf is at her most painterly and temporally aware. Boswell's contrived scenes are biographical fictions; Woolf's scrupulously designed novel is fictional biography.

Dinner with Dr Johnson and John Wilkes

On Monday, 16 May 1763, two 'scenes' were enacted in London just a few streets apart. In one of those coincidences so beloved of biographers (though none seem to have noticed it), on the very day that Dr Johnson was observed through the glass door of Davies's Bookshop advancing towards the celebrated first meeting with James Boswell (Boswell, 1791/1949, I: 242), William Hogarth, whose pictures were equally famous with Londoners of the time, completed his satirical print of "John Wilkes Esq", dated 16 May

Figure 11.1 William Hogarth, *John Wilkes Esq.* (1763) Engraving, 31.8 × 22.2 cms. The British Museum

(Fig. 11.1), and available through the local print shops the following day (Uglow, 1997: 675). 'Four thousand copies were turned off at first printing, and the demand was so great that presses had to work day and night' (Paulson, 1993, III: 398). It was to be another thirteen years, almost to the day, before Boswell brought Wilkes and Johnson together at the famous dinner party.

Hogarth, who had been attacked by Wilkes in Issue 17 of his periodical the *North Briton*, shared Johnson's dislike of Wilkes but had no Boswell to bring about a reconciliation before he died the following year. Wilkes (1727–1797), a politician and journalist, had become an MP in 1757 but, as a consequence of an attack on King George III in Issue 45 of his periodical, was expelled from Parliament, briefly imprisoned in 1764 before being released to an adoring crowd, yet unable to take up his seat again for a further decade. Many poor people saw Wilkes as the champion of liberty; Hogarth saw him as a scheming demagogue. As Boswell points out, Johnson and Wilkes had 'attacked one another with some asperity in their writings'

(Boswell, 1791/1949, II: 45) and with his 'aversion to popular clamour' (II: 382), Johnson held a similarly low estimate of Wilkes, if not one fuelled with Hogarthian rancour. The picture is captioned as being 'Drawn from the Life' – to give added bite to what is a vicious caricature. The inclusion of the two offending issues of the *North Briton* make Hogarth's motives clear. The presentation of the figure of Wilkes is equally pointed. The traditional staff and cap of the figure of Liberty are replaced by an upturned vessel (uncomfortably similar to a chamber pot) balanced precariously on a pole above an ill-fitting wig drawn to resemble the devil's horns. The calculating eyes, leering expression and self-confident, unbuttoned posture are all devices to discredit the subject.

In his politics, values and rakish lifestyle, Wilkes was quite the opposite of the Tory and Christian Samuel Johnson. When Boswell brought them together on 15 May 1776, Wilkes's fortunes were high: he had served as Lord Mayor and was popular with many Londoners. Boswell had never written up the part of his Journal covering this famous dinner. His only record of the occasion was some brief notes, which he used as the basis for his retrospective account composed well over a decade later (II: 45–55). Paragraph by paragraph, scene by scene, we can observe Boswell constructing this episode as a domestic drama in which his own role is as central to the action as those of his protagonists. There are at least eight distinct phases in the development of Boswell's plot. Briefly, these are as follows.

(a) *The Problem*: Boswell begins by admitting his 'irresistible wish, if possible, to bring Dr Johnson and Mr Wilkes together. How to manage it, was a nice and difficult matter.' The biographer immediately casts himself as the puppet-master, making his readers feel the potential fun of a trick to be played on Johnson. The reader's expectations are raised but there is also the sense that a social risk is being taken.

(b) *The Plan*: Boswell uses his own invitation to dinner at Dilly's, a bookseller and friend, to engineer an invitation for Johnson in the knowledge that Wilkes will be present. He cleverly incorporates Dilly's alarm: '"Pray (said I), let us have Dr Johnson." – "What, with Mr Wilkes? Not for the world (said Mr Edward Dilly): Dr Johnson would never forgive me."' But when Boswell offers to negotiate and take the blame for any *faux pas* that might occur, Dilly acquiesces.

(c) *Baiting the Hook*: Boswell's self-congratulatory account of how he approached the topic indirectly is calculated to show himself in the best light as well as to heighten our comic sense of Johnson's social entrapment as he is inveigled into going to the dinner. 'I was persuaded that if I had come upon him with a direct proposal, "Sir, will you dine in company of Jack

Wilkes?" he would have flown into a passion'. So Boswell guilefully introduces his own imminent departure for Scotland and his general concern for the quality of the other guests to tempt Johnson's agreement to attend the dinner party. This highly dramatised scene, complete with capitalised speaking parts for himself and his subject, reaches its climax when Boswell delivers his *coup de théâtre*: 'BOSWELL: "I should not be surprised to find Jack Wilkes there." JOHNSON: "And if Jack Wilkes *should* be there, what is that to *me*, Sir?"

(d) *The Complication*: On the appointed day, Johnson has forgotten the invitation and arranged to have dinner at home! Boswell discovers him 'buffeting his books … and covered with dust'. Two minor characters are then introduced. Dr Johnson, a widower, was looked after by Mrs Anna Williams, his blind and potentially obstinate housekeeper to whose judgement on domestic matters Johnson tended to defer; and Francis Barber (Frank), his black manservant, a former slave whom Johnson took into his service. Boswell is again centre stage as we are able to observe how his charm and earnest entreaties work upon Mrs Williams until she agrees that Johnson should go.

(e) *Entering the Drawing Room*: Johnson finds himself 'in the midst of company he did not know'; Boswell adopts the role of silent spectator, watching Johnson's behaviour and supposedly recording snatches of conversation, including Johnson's enquiry, 'And who is the gentleman in lace?' only to learn that it is Mr Wilkes. Boswell continues his detached observation of Johnson's awkwardness at this information but intrudes himself into Johnson's thoughts, crediting himself with Johnson's self-composure as 'he [Johnson] no doubt recollected his having rated me for supposing that he could be at all disconcerted by any company'.

(f) *At the Dinner Table*: The scene shifts again: several minor characters are identified round the table; Johnson and Wilkes are seated next to each other. Boswell has some fun inventing dialogue exchanges between the two, with Wilkes taking the initiative with some appropriately banal lines about the meat and the sauces. '"Pray give me leave, Sir:– It is better here – A little of the brown – Some fat, Sir – A little of the stuffing – Some gravy – Let me have the pleasure of giving you some butter – Allow me to recommend a squeeze of this orange …"' and so on.

(g) *Conversation: Foote and Garrick*: The talk over dinner, reinvented in the next two paragraphs, focuses upon two well-known actors. Samuel Foote was a playwright and actor with a reputation for mimicry. David Garrick, Johnson's former pupil from Lichfield, was the most successful actor-manager of the century. There was no love lost between the two (see McIntyre, 1999: 135–137). Wilkes's mention of Garrick puts Boswell on tenterhooks: 'I knew that Johnson would let nobody attack Garrick but himself ...', and he contrives to feed Johnson a line on Garrick's liberal nature and so steer the conversation into safer waters. A topic with the potential to sink the whole dinner party is narrowly avoided.

(h) *Teasing Boswell*: After three or four paragraphs on literary matters, beginning with some fun at biography's expense, the conversation turns towards Scotland and its inhabitants. Boswell, to his credit, presents himself as the butt of the humour and the means through which Johnson and Wilkes can find common cause: 'JOHNSON: (to Mr Wilkes), "You must know, Sir, I lately took my friend Boswell and shewed him genuine civilised life in an English provincial town. I turned him loose at Lichfield, my native city, that he might see for once real civility: for you know he lives among savages in Scotland, and among rakes in London." WILKES: "Except when he is with grave, sober, decent people like you and me." JOHNSON (smiling): "And we ashamed of him."' The social sub-text of these exchanges is subtly orchestrated by Boswell: Johnson's double-edged phrase, 'rakes in London', indirectly associates Wilkes with such a lifestyle; Wilkes's rejoinder deftly deflects the implication and allies him with 'grave, sober, decent people like you and me'. The stage direction has Johnson smiling. The dinner party has been a success.

Boswell rounds off the sequence of scenes that make up this episode by patting himself on the back. He acknowledges that 'this record [is] by no means ... perfect' but serves as a reminder of an enjoyable occasion, one moreover that reconciled any animosity between the two men. Five years later, the effects could still be observed. In a scene again set at Edward Dilly's house, Boswell notes that 'no *negotiation* was now required to bring them together' (II: 385). With some heavy hints from Wilkes, Johnson gives him a copy of his recently published *Lives of the Poets* (1779–1781). Boswell records: 'I left the room for some time; when I returned, I was struck with observing Dr. Samuel Johnson and John Wilkes, Esq. literally *tête à tête* ... Such a scene of perfectly easy sociality between two such opponents in the war of political controversy, as that which I now beheld, would have been an excellent subject for a picture' (II: 389). Here, and more especially in the dinner party earlier, Boswell has in effect given us such a picture.

How was this achieved? Boswell's technique was to invent a little piece of theatre with all the principal elements in play: two strong characters in a potentially explosive situation, himself as the go-between whose strategy is put to the test, a carefully orchestrated plot development, swift changes of scene, variations in dialogue, and explicit or implied stage directions. The scenes shift in time and place: from (b) above, the initial proposal to Dilly at his premises in The Poultry some days before the dinner scheduled for

Wednesday 15 May; to (c), a subsequent quiet evening at Johnson's house where Boswell 'baits the hook'; to (d), the minor crisis on the day with Boswell scurrying upstairs and down between Johnson's study and Mrs Williams's room before finally getting Johnson into the hackney coach en route to Dilly's; to the scenes in the drawing room (e) and dining room (f–h) which conclude the evening. The structure of events is in classic style from an introduction, through intrigue and crisis, to climax and denouement, a development with which Boswell would be familiar from Molière's plays, Restoration comedies, the contemporary comedies of Sheridan and Goldsmith, and Hogarth's *Marriage à la Mode*. The dialogues range from Johnsonian bluntness with Boswell to Wilkes's silky playfulness at the dinner table. Stage directions are touched in to help us visualise the scenes, from the description of Johnson entering the drawing room, retreating to the window seat and taking refuge in a book in order to compose himself, to his final, conspiratorial smile at Boswell's discomfort as he remarks to Wilkes: 'And we ashamed of him.' Boswell's account in the *Life*, based on facts recorded over ten years earlier and embroidered with the vagaries of memory and a lively imagination, is not so much a piece of documentary biography as a comedy of manners.

Dinner with Mrs Ramsay

Virginia Woolf's painterly scenes are less animated, more densely textured than Boswell's theatricals. Her 'scene-making' grows from a reflective, not a dramatic, imagination. It is characterised by careful composition in which the weight of individual phrases and the density of descriptions are balanced like lines and masses in a painting to create an aesthetically satisfying form. Details are lit, colours touched in, as scene after scene steadily accumulates into the visual narrative of *To The Lighthouse*. While the book is classified as a novel, it is one which illustrates the ambiguities of semi-autobiographical fiction more subtly than either Joyce or Wordsworth since, unlike their egotistical self-representations, Virginia Woolf diffuses her sense of self into several characters (Lee, 1997: 480), into the landscapes of childhood memories of summers in North Cornwall, and into the nuances of family relationships, especially those with her parents. *To The Lighthouse* is a self-conscious experiment with form. Woolf herself was uncertain of the genre:

> I am making up *To The Lighthouse* – the sea is to be heard all through it. I have an idea that I will invent a new name for my books to supplant 'novel'. A new ——— by Virginia Woolf. But what? Elegy? (Diary, 27 June 1925, in Beja, 1970: 56)

Formally, *To The Lighthouse* consists of three unequal parts. Woolf envisaged the novel as 'Two blocks joined by a corridor', making a shape like a solid 'H' – two long episodes, 'The Window' and 'The Lighthouse', ten years apart, joined by a short corridor entitled 'Time Passes' at right angles, as it were, to the rest (Briggs, 2006a: 103). 'The Window' covers a few hours of one day, slowing down time and movement almost to stillness as Lily Briscoe paints a picture of the garden with Mrs Ramsay, seated in the window reading to her son James, represented by a triangular purple shape in the corner of the canvas (Woolf, 1928/2000: 72). The brief second part, 'Time Passes', spans ten years, shows the effects of time on the empty house, and disposes of her main character in an abrupt parenthesis. In the search for permanence and a sense of identity, Part One stills the external action and dwells on the minutiae of the characters' relationships, their momentary thoughts, feelings and perceptions – all framed, as it were, in the motif of the window. Part Two accelerates time and represents death as a moment in the flux, inconsequential almost, an afterthought dropped in between brackets. In Part Three, as throughout, the lighthouse acts as a viewfinder trained by Woolf, it seems, on the intractable issues of human identity in a temporal world which lie, she implies, beyond our horizon. Structurally, then, there are two pictorial accounts set in the same place, each covering part of a single day either side of the First World War, and each subject to the temporality of narrative. The modernist, painterly aesthetic that controls the overall design of the novel is reflected in its details, not least in Lily Briscoe's painting in which she constantly seeks a unity for her picture, finding it in the final sentences of the novel by drawing a line in its centre.

'The Window' constitutes over half the book. Of its nineteen sub-sections, number seventeen describing the dinner party is by far the longest and, at its centre, is Mrs Ramsay, a character based so intimately upon Julia Stephen that Vanessa Bell said, in a well-known letter to her sister, that 'It was like meeting her again [i.e. their mother] with oneself grown up and on equal terms and it seems to me the most astonishing feat of creation to have been able to see her such a way' (Lee, 1997: 480). At the dinner party as throughout, fiction is grounded in biography. Leonard Woolf described the book as 'a psychological poem' (Diary, 23 January 1927, in Beja, 1970: 62); Vanessa saw it as a supreme example of 'portrait painting': *To The Lighthouse* is a blend of genres. 'Scene-making', as the epigraph from 'Sketch of the Past' which heads this chapter suggests, is fundamental to this mix – indeed, it creates it by *stilling time* to focus us upon word-paintings, by *extending the time* of those epiphanic 'moments of being' through slow motion, and by *telescoping time* through vaulting over years to juxtapose present and past. Time follows the dictates of memory in *To The Lighthouse*.

The context for this dinner party – the setting, the story and the cast of characters – is profoundly biographical. Biographical memories are projected and transformed but exist as a palimpsest, their features showing through the fiction. Talland House in St Ives, where the Stephen family spent two months each summer for a decade, is transmuted to an unspecified island in the Hebrides; the germ of the plot is Virginia Woolf's childhood memory of her younger brother Adrian's desire to sail out to Godrevy lighthouse (Gordon, 2006: ix–x), visible from their holiday home; and Mr and Mrs Ramsay (aka Leslie and Julia Stephen) and their children bring alive the author's own family. The Stephens' frequent house guests are represented by the young and priggish philosopher Charles Tansley, the poet Augustus Carmichael, the botanist William Bankes, the young couple who become engaged, Paul Rayley and Minta Doyle, and the most important figure in this supporting cast, the painter Lily Briscoe. The imaginative centre of the book, the person around whom all else revolves, is Mrs Ramsay, the mother figure whom Virginia Woolf creates as a fiction in order to understand her as the presiding fact in her own life. Twelve years after the publication of *To The Lighthouse*, in her 'Sketch of the Past', Virginia Woolf was explicit about her 'obsession' with her mother, about coming to terms with the 'invisible presence' of her in her life, and about the role that writing *To The Lighthouse* played in exorcising her ghost.

> Until I was in the forties ... the presence of my mother obsessed me. I could hear her voice, see her, imagine what she would do or say about my day's doings. She was one of the invisible presences who after all play so important a part in every life ... she obsessed me, in spite of the fact that she died when I was thirteen, until I was forty-four. Then one day walking round Tavistock Square I made up, as I sometimes make up my books, *To The Lighthouse*; in a great, apparently involuntary rush. One thing burst into another. Blowing bubbles out of a pipe gives the feeling of the rapid crowd of ideas and scenes which blew out of my mind, so that my lips seemed syllabling of their own accord as I walked. What blew the bubbles? Why then? I have no notion. But I wrote the book very quickly; and when it was written, I ceased to be obsessed by my mother. I no longer hear her voice; I do not see her. (Woolf, 1939–1940/2002: 92–93)

The pages which follow give a moving and highly detailed picture of Julia Stephen as her daughter remembers her from childhood. She recalls, 'When I think of her spontaneously she is always in a room full of people' (p. 95); the constant factor was 'the common life of the family, very merry, very stirring, crowded with people; and she was the centre; it was herself' (p. 96). Mrs Ramsay's dinner party, a scene which she loved to create (Lee, 1997: 477), is the key 'representative scene' in both Virginia Woolf's art and life.

Unlike Boswell's scenes, Virginia Woolf's dinner party is literally a set piece: figures are seated around the dining table, the host and hostess at either end. The characters are physically still; the action is psychological. We begin with Mrs Ramsay 'taking her place at the head of the table', and end nearly forty pages later with her pausing 'a moment ... in a scene which was vanishing even as she looked'. In between, the scene is animated by a single incident (the late arrival of Paul and Minta who have been searching for the lost brooch); it is illuminated by one lighting change when the candles are lit; and it is focused by the arrival of the 'Bœuf en Daube', the 'perfect triumph', the centre piece of a three-course menu in which each element is invested with painterly significance. Hence, Charles Tansley lays down his soup spoon 'precisely in the middle of his plate', mirroring Lily Briscoe's constant need to balance her picture by putting 'the tree further in the middle' (Woolf, 1928/2000: 115). Mrs Ramsay peers into the dish 'and its confusion of savoury brown and yellow meats, and its bay leaves and its wine' and experiences conflicting emotions about the young lovers' feelings for each other (pp. 135–136). And, towards the end of the meal, she finds herself 'keeping guard over the dish of fruit (without realising it)', seeing it as a 'still life' of colours and shapes, experiencing the serenity it imparts, until 'a hand reached out, took a pear, and spoilt the whole thing' (pp. 146–147). Finding a balance, the simultaneous awareness of the real and the illusory in the same experience, the transcience of beauty – all read like biographical images which, having found their objective correlatives in a menu, are projected into the dinner party.

Although several hours must pass during the meal, the construction of Virginia Woolf's dinner party is better characterised as a number of overlapping circles than as a Boswellian sequence of discrete events, circles whose rings and eddies spread outwards from a fragment of conversation or a passing thought casually cast into the smooth social surface of the occasion. Yet, the chronological imperative that controls both fiction and biography dictates a temporal analysis of what is, essentially, a spatially conceived scene. Erich Auerbach's famous commentary identified the salient features of Woolf's novel: 'a multipersonal representation of consciousness, time strata, disintegration of the continuity of exterior events, shifting of the narrative viewpoint (all of which are interrelated and difficult to separate)' (Auerbach, 1953/2003: 525–553). The following analysis shows all these elements in a series of phases in the first half of the scene. Then the candles are lit, the scene changes, and that singular narrative voice – in which Woolf blurs the distinction between narrator and characters – records the rest of the occasion through the interpolated perceptions of Mrs Ramsay. (All page references are to the Oxford World's Classics edition of *To The Lighthouse*, ed. Margaret Drabble, 2000.)

The principal characteristic of Virginia Woolf's 'scene-making' is registered straight away as Mrs Ramsay directs her guests to their seats, begins to serve the soup, and thinks of herself as an outsider at her own table. 'Raising her eyebrows at the discrepancy – that was what she was thinking, this was what she was doing – ladling out soup ...' (p. 113). The interplay – and 'discrepancy' – between the external and internal lives that we all lead all the time is the basic feature. Virginia Woolf paints the consciousness of successive individuals' shifting thoughts and feelings as they register against objects, people and bits of dialogue that punctuate the surrounding, all-enveloping social atmosphere. The two quasi-biographical minds are those of Mrs Ramsay, based on Julia Stephen, and Lily Briscoe, whose perceptions are those of Woolf herself. Although Mrs Ramsay's consciousness is the dominant one, we are soon taken inside the mind of Lily Briscoe as she 'reads' the characters of Mrs Ramsay, William Bankes and Charles Tansley (pp. 114–115); we listen to the narrative voice as it interpolates Tansley's thoughts (p. 116); we eavesdrop on Lily Briscoe's annoyance at Tansley's earlier provocation, 'Women can't write, women can't paint', before her teasing request to him to take her to the Lighthouse leads into Tansley's own thought-track (p. 117); and we share in Bankes's self-questioning ('What does one live for?') as he preserves 'a demeanour of exquisite courtesy spreading the fingers of his left hand on the table-cloth' (pp. 120–121). Consciousness expands retrospectively, too, with twenty-year-old recollections of the Mannings and of a day by the Thames with Herbert Manning 'killing a wasp with a teaspoon on the bank!' Woolf's sense of mutability versus the fixity of memory permeates her scene-making: 'while she [Mrs Ramsay] had changed, that particular day, now become very still and beautiful, had remained there, all these years' (pp. 118–119). Mrs Ramsay is given the sense of a self then, both separate from yet intimate with the self now, like the memorial wasp preserved in amber. Mrs Ramsay's adoption of her 'social manner' with Bankes is observed by Tansley, whose mind is storing up the 'scraps and fragments' of the scene for a future satirical sketch on '"staying with the Ramsays"' (p. 122); while, simultaneously, Lily Briscoe observes him, projecting a gendered image to counter his earlier sneering comments on women (p. 123). Then follows a subtly orchestrated phase, a circle enclosing Tansley's egotistical thoughts, Mrs Ramsay's social anxieties, and Lily Briscoe's reading and rescue of her hostess from her social dilemma (pp. 124–125). Lily drifts back into a reverie about her painting, Mrs Ramsay back into the 'dream land ... of the Mannings' drawing-room at Marlow twenty years ago' (p. 126). This ebb and flow of consciousness both individualises each character and merges them into the overall scene, one that gains a painterly depth with Bankes and Tansley in the foreground arguing politics, while in the background, as it were, Lily continues to think about her painting and Mrs Ramsay's attention is turned towards her husband, whose barely suppressed anger at Carmichael's request for more soup is in danger of setting the children off into 'spasms of laughter' (pp. 127–130).

Mrs Ramsay's diversionary tactic to prevent this is the fulcrum of the scene. She asks the children to light the candles, thus signalling a change of atmosphere: it is both a social and a painterly technique – a change of light and a change of relationships: 'Some change at once went through them all ... and they were all conscious of making a party together' (p. 132). The much-heralded Bœuf en Daube is brought in, Paul and Minta arrive glowing with love for each other (pp. 132–134), and their happiness provokes ambivalent feelings in both Mrs Ramsay and Lily Briscoe. Mrs Ramsay experiences 'two emotions ... called up in her', one profound and serious in its respect for love, the other of 'lovers ... entering into illusion glittering-eyed [who] must be danced round with mockery' (pp. 135–136). Lily Briscoe, similarly, is 'made to feel violently two opposite things at the same time ... It is so beautiful, so exciting, this love ...; also it is the stupidest, the most barbaric of human passions' (pp. 138–139). But these ambivalences are not the same. For Mrs Ramsay, the celebration of the occasion outweighs the sense of illusion; for Lily Briscoe, the carrier of Woolf's personal feelings for her mother, the fissure in her response remains deep: 'that's what you feel ... that's what I feel ... fought together in her mind' (p. 138). Lily is given the author's response to and memories of her own mother, Julia Stephen; and it is significant that here, in the central phase of the dinner party where Mrs Ramsay is seen by Lily as 'irresistible', as having 'put a spell on them all', it is the subject of love that provokes Lily's psychological difficulties in coming to terms with her hostess's/mother's personality: 'So she listened again to what they were saying in case they should throw any light upon the question of love' (p. 139).

Thereafter, the second half of the dinner party is like 'celebrating a festival': Mrs Ramsay presides over the company, her presence touching everyone, serving up her 'tender piece[s] of eternity', her perceptions of her guests now taking over the narrative of the scene (pp. 140–141). Lily, self-contained and self-sufficient, is faded out ('One need never bother about Lily') and Virginia Woolf attributes two of her characteristic ideas, well known from her later 'Sketch of the Past', to Mrs Ramsay. First, she describes her experience of 'the coherence of things, a stability; something immune from change', a sense of peace and rest – the experience she later describes in her autobiographical memoir as one of those precious 'moments of being' (p. 142; 1939–1940/2002: 86). And, shortly afterwards, she gives Mrs Ramsay another 'moment [when] her eyes were so clear that they seemed to go round the table unveiling each of these people, and their thoughts and their feelings … as if what they said was like the movement of a trout when, at the same time, one can see the ripple and the gravel … and the whole is held together … For the moment she hung suspended' (p. 144). In the 'Sketch' (p. 92), Woolf uses the same metaphor of suspended animation to describe the 'invisible presences' that surround and press upon the individual life. If biography fails to analyse them, she says, 'how futile life-writing becomes'. In the novel, the displacement of these ideas into the consciousness of her fictionalised mother brings biography and fiction into compelling intimacy. The dinner closes with the narrative voice reporting a literary discussion (pp. 145–146), depicting a verbal still life in the description of the fruit bowl (pp. 146–147), and giving us Mrs Ramsay's perceptions of her four children (pp. 147–148). In an extended coda, Mr Ramsay brings the evening to an end by chanting the mysterious words of a poem, 'Luriana Lurilee', as the company prepares to leave this family festival which, in Mrs Ramsay's mind, invests this domestic ritual with the aura of a religious celebration (pp. 149–150).

'I wonder whether I … deal in autobiography and call it fiction?' (Diary, 14 January 1920, cited in Gordon, 2006: 7). The self-conscious intimacy that Virginia Woolf feels between these two genres, together with her painterly aesthetic that stresses stillness, silence and the insights of the concentrated gaze above the dynamism of actions and events in a developing plot, mean that not only do we come to know Woolf's characters from within but, more pertinently, we come to know more about her, too. By projecting aspects of herself directly into Lily Briscoe, we sense the daughter's mixture of admiration and fear, criticism and jealousy of the mother who always seemed centre stage, compared with her own quiet, inscrutable self looking on from the sidelines. And, in recording the unspoken thought-tracks of the other characters round the table, Woolf diffuses traits of her own inner life. Tansley's inner speech, a running commentary against women, reveals Woolf's feminism; Bankes's mixed feelings at being required to sit at the dinner table for hours suggest Woolf's ambivalence at the purpose, conduct and ambience of such social occasions; and Carmichael's self-possessed, insulated composure, which elicits Mrs Ramsay's respect, draws out Woolf's sympathetic understanding, too. The scene may be peopled by a variety of characters, but the stories of these inner lives read like the reflections of an autobiographical imagination. Her scene-making contains many 'looks', 'gazes' and 'glances' – Lily Briscoe's 'catching sight of the salt cellar' as she mentally works on her picture; the children 'gazing at [their] father' as he suppresses his annoyance at Carmichael; the host and hostess who 'looked at each other down the long table' – these cross-currents in the sightlines of the characters lend the depiction of this dinner party a curiously ambiguous painterly quality. The mingling gazes, the interactions caught in facial expressions, the body language of the guests, the effects of changing light upon the whole scene – Virginia Woolf's scene is rendered in a style quite different from Boswell's piece of theatre; yet, within a novel where the overall structure reflects post-impressionist principles, Mrs Ramsay's dinner party has many of the characteristics of a scrupulously painted, eighteenth-century conversation piece.

Biography and Fiction

It may seem odd to end a book on biography with discussion of a novel, but *To The Lighthouse* is no conventional fiction nor is its author a traditional storyteller. Virginia Woolf's Diary entry quoted above reminds us of the intimacy of life-writing and fiction, but it is her novel that offers a sophisticated illustration of how this intimacy operates. Autobiography and family biography dispersed into a diverse company of characters; factual places, objects and incidents transmuted into fictional scenes and a mythologised journey; portraiture that exposes the interior life of the mind behind the social mask – all are framed in a design that reworks the essential feature of life-writing and fiction – time – problematising its linear chronology by making it subject to the shifting strata of memory. To represent a person in either genre means to catch the living moment, not only the interplay of inner and outer life that characterises our continuous experience of being, but also the way in which both these elements reflect the aggregate of memories that form the unique history of each individual.

It is this unique history that biography attempts to record. We have seen, in the microcosm of Mrs Ramsay's dinner party, how biography may be filtered through fiction. We have seen, too, in the episode where Johnson dines with Wilkes, how fiction enters biography. We have noted how both scenes are grounded in memory, Boswell's partially supported by his Journal, Woolf's by her Diary. Both writers move from their primary memories to these recalled chronicles which, in turn, become the raw materials for narrativisation. Yet, the familiar vocabulary of scenes ('incidents', 'occurrences', 'events') and stories ('episodes', 'passages', 'phases') indicates that life is already structured in time *before* the biographer starts to refashion it into text. In saying that, for the biographer, the life is a 'given', we are also acknowledging that its ending and much of its significance are also known. The biographer generally comes to the life after it is over, considering it retrospectively, as it were, before shaping the details of its development to give readers the illusion of a life lived forwards. The ways in which narrative plays upon time and memory expose the differences between biographical fiction and fictional biography. Boswell has to stay close to chronology however much he embellishes memories with theatrical decoration; Woolf, on the other hand, can expand and contract time at will, elaborating Mrs Ramsay's dinner party with a depth of detail and psychological observation in order to represent the nature of familial memories. Ironically, with these two dinner parties, one is left with the sense that it is the biographer who is keen to tell a good story, whereas the novelist is searching for the truth. As Peter Ackroyd, novelist and biographer, is quoted as saying: 'The only difference' between the two genres 'is that the biographer can make things up, but the novelist is compelled to tell the truth' (*Guardian Review*, 15 September 2007). But to dismiss these genre differences with such an aphorism would be glib and unjust to Boswell. A fairer comparison is with Virginia Woolf's biographer.

Hermione Lee's biography (1997) already has claims to be a modern classic by a writer who, by her own account, has a special affinity with her subject. In her first chapter, 'Biography', she incorporates a clause from Virginia Woolf's Diaries, and points to biography's need to get behind the mask to the face: 'The life-writer must explore and understand the gap between the outer self ("the fictitious V.W. whom I carry like a mask about the world") and the secret self' (Lee, 1997: 6). Lee takes her cue from her subject, explicitly associating herself with the Boswellian approach to her task (p. 7), and produces a multi-faceted portrait, contextualised and detailed in ways that her subject would approve through copious quotation from and reference to letters, diaries, essays and novels, and reconstructions of 'scenes' in which Virginia Woolf figured. The masks are there in Woolf's social charm, witty conversation and her roles within the Bloomsbury clan. So, too, is the person behind them: the 13-year-old who was devastated by her mother's death (p. 79ff.); the sexual molestation she suffered from her half-brother (pp. 126–127, 158–159); her lifelong sibling rivalry with her older sister, Vanessa (pp. 118–120); and the personal importance to her, psychologically and emotionally, of her reading and writing (pp. 402–417). The 'secret self' that Lee presents is fundamentally a 'literary self' – a sense of identity defined by the subject and represented by her biographer (Lee, 1997: 481). The same could be said of Boswell's Dr Johnson whose character, as Boswell is at pains to stress, is to be largely defined by Johnson himself – by 'his own minutes, letters, or conversation', since Boswell is 'convinced that this mode is more lively, and will make my readers better acquainted with him, than even most of those were who actually knew him'

(Boswell, 1791/1949, I: 7–8). Both biographers provide what Boswell calls the 'minute particulars' of their subject's behaviour, which is why Lee admires Boswell's inexhaustible ability to record Johnson's talk, opinions and reactions. Ackroyd's remark is a useful reminder of the relative nature of 'truth', discussed in Chapter 2, and of the different ways in which biography and fiction try to be 'true to life'. But, as far as biography is concerned, the best definition of the genre is caught in Lyndall Gordon's (1994: 329) description of Mrs Gaskell's *The Life of Charlotte Brontë* cited in Chapter 3: 'a lasting imaginative truth based on a selection of facts'.

12

Biography and the Future

Many of the issues discussed in this book lead back to the concept of biography's generic dualism (Chapter 3). Art versus craft, fictional narrative versus historical narrative, imaginative empathy versus verifiable data and, extrapolating from these aesthetic tensions, reading the life in the works versus the works in the life – literary biography is a hybrid genre. It treats its subjects not merely as historical figures to be observed and documented and whose existence is confirmed through the memories of contemporaries, but as conscious beings whose living presences can be evoked and explored through recreating a sense of their psychological states, their motives and feelings. Keeping the balance of biography's twofoldness is the key, which is why my preferred definition of the genre is that given at the end of the previous chapter. It is an expression of biography as an art whose imaginative truth is relative to the choice of data with which it works to tell its story. The problem for biography lies in the selection, representation and reception of its factual data. For readers tend to accept facts literally, overlooking, during the process of reading, that the representation of the life is always figurative. Recent developments in literary biography which have moved the genre on from tracing the chronology of a single life from cradle to grave have gone some way to meeting the problem. Variations on this traditional model have been apparent for some time: group biographies of the Romantics or Bloomsbury have widened the focus; pair biographies of the Stephen sisters, Wordsworth and Coleridge, or the Hughes–Plath marriage have explored the personal and creative relationships between authors; and there have been short biographies written in a personal and freer style such as Carol Shields's *Jane Austen* or Claire Tomalin's *Shelley and His World*. The 'old' *Dictionary of National Biography* has been mined for a hundred entries on literary lives (Sutherland, 2001), while the *New DNB* (2004) has given a boost to what its editor calls 'capsule' biography to distinguish it from the 'tombstone' or multi-volume 'Lives' that, in inexpert hands, can seem like heavy hangovers from Victorian times (Harrison, 2004: 85). But these indicators are less significant than those offered by four biographies, all published since the turn of the new century, each exemplifying a fresh and invigorating approach to literary biography and suggesting models for the future.

First, *the snapshot*. Charles Nicholl's *The Lodger: Shakespeare on Silver Street* takes the episode in Shakespeare's life when he was lodging with a family of Huguenot refugees, the Mountjoys, in their house on Silver Street in the Cripplegate area of London. The period of his tenancy, and the focus of Nicholl's book, are the years 1603–1605 during which Shakespeare reached the age of 40. The episode owes its unique significance to the fact that, in May 1612, Shakespeare gave evidence and made a signed statement in a lawsuit over a contested dowry between his former landlord and his apprentice, Stephen Belott, who had married Mary, the Mountjoys' daughter. For once, Shakespeare moves from invisibility into the shadows, although his role as a witness gives little away, mainly focusing on his sworn testimony 'that some time in 1604 he "persuaded" Stephen Belott to marry Mary Mountjoy' (Nicholl, 2008: 251). Around this episode, Nicholl paints a compelling picture of Jacobean London, its society, its commerce, the court, the theatre; and he suggests how the plays written during Shakespeare's time as the lodger in the upstairs room – *Othello*, *Measure for Measure*, *King Lear* and especially *All's Well That Ends Well* – may have been influenced by living with a French family. He argues that, given the plays are part of the cultural circumstances of the time, it would be perverse to ignore the connections between Shakespeare's life and writing in the name of academic correctness when one of them, *All's Well*, is about a young Frenchman being pressed reluctantly into marriage (p. 34). By narrowing the biographical focus in time and place and composing his picture with vivid details, Nicholl provides a rich context; and by giving us the only record of Shakespeare's spoken words and the sense of his presence in Silver Street, he brings us as close to Shakespeare the man as we are ever likely to get.

Second, *the dossier*, to use Jonathan Coe's own term for his book *Like a Fiery Elephant: The Story of B. S. Johnson*. It 'has the look … more of a dossier than a conventional literary biography', he tells us. 'It contains its fair share of guesswork, and was compiled with plenty of selectivity; but my guiding principle … has been to tell the story as much as I can in Johnson's own words' (Coe, 2004: 8–9). His apology for the 'fragmentary, unpolished' result is scarcely necessary for Coe's book is not only highly readable and entertaining, it is also a rigorously developed compilation of tape-recorded conversations, letters, drafts of unfinished pieces, summaries of his subject's seven novels, reflections on the writing process – all presented in a very 'Johnsonian' way. In fact, it is the style and organisation, mirroring that of his subject's works, that make the first impact. Structurally, it is divided up as 'A Life in Seven Novels', 'A Life in 160 Fragments' and 'A Life in 44 Voices', plus a 'Coda' to investigate the mysterious circumstances of Johnson's suicide, a bit of detective work that clearly appeals to the novelist in the biographer. It is also confessional, with an Introduction about biography stemming from how he first came to Johnson as a 10-year-old, together with periodic expressions of frustration with a genre that cannot honestly describe what writers actually do since the essential 'life' goes on inside the head (p. 35). Coe's oppositional stance towards literary biography parallels Johnson's towards the traditional novel: he has learned 'what it is like to force yourself to work within a set of assumptions that you fundamentally distrust' (p. 7). His ambivalence towards the genre is pervasive: he recognises the impossible position of the biographer between history and creative art (p. 35); when he adopts the biographical voice, he does so with an engaging self-consciousness (p. 42); he wonders whether a novel about B. S. Johnson would have been a better option (p. 64), admits to getting bored with some of the detail (p. 83), and to feeling frustrated with the form (pp. 203–204). But the most revealing moment comes when Coe reproduces one of the graphs Johnson kept to measure his productivity. Coe notes that on 17 August 1965, Johnson 'sat at his desk for six and a quarter hours, and wrote 1700 words of *Trawl*. Boring, or what? *But this is what writers do*.' And he adds: 'It is the one thing I cannot write about ... It shows up the whole process I am engaged upon for the potentially dishonest enterprise that it is' (p. 194). The most challenging aspect of *Like a Fiery Elephant* is that, taking his cue from his subject, Coe's biography is not only an adventurous approach to life-writing but also a subtle interrogation of the nature of writing itself.

Third, *the thematic biography*. *Knowing Dickens* by Rosemarie Bodenheimer operates from the premise that 'chronology is the great limitation of biography, at once the spinal column that holds the story together and the straitjacket that prevents its freedom of motion' (Bodenheimer, 2007: 15). Accordingly, she dispenses with conventional chronology and organises her chapters in five themes, an eclectic collection that aims to connect Dickens's inner world and its exterior manifestations: language, memory, male friendships and rivalry, houses and their management, and writing and walking. Each chapter 'juxtaposes letters, stories, articles, and sections of novels that bear on its subject area, discovering patterns that are common to the life and the writing' (p. 14). The overtly speculative interpretation that this entails is unusual in biography. It produces a form of biographical criticism that throws fresh light on familiar matters. For example, Dickens's use of 'defensive language' is attributed in part to his own father's language and 'highly elaborated patterns of denial' (p. 29) which reappear in fictional fathers such as Mr Micawber, Harold Skimpole and Mr Dorrit (pp. 39–50). Similarly, in a section on 'The Christiana Weller Affair' (pp. 101–105), Bodenheimer explores the subtle interactions between Dickens and nubile young women, both his fictional creations and his actual acquaintances. Again, this is well-trodden ground but Bodenheimer shows how the interplay of life and literature works both ways. In a description analogous to Buss's painting (Chapter 6, vii), we are invited to imagine the figure of Christiana playing the piano in a public celebration of Dickens's success surrounded by other images – memories of his description of Little Nell, of his traumatic reaction to the death of Mary Hogarth, and of his mixed feelings of 'pride and resentment he had felt about [his sister] Fanny's special status during the miserable period of their youth' (p. 102). But Bodenheimer does not leave the matter at the level of Dickensian fantasy. She extends its reach into the lives of Christiana's father and future husband, exploring all these relationships as offering insights into how far Dickens was knowing, or unknowing, about the patterns of his own behaviour.

A third example is the most familiar of all. Bodenheimer introduces a discussion of 'The Autobiographical Fragment' (pp. 68–73) that Dickens wrote for Forster with a battery of questions that have been raised about its status and implications. She identifies three kinds of writing, each geared to enabling Dickens 'to take rhetorical command' of the memories and the feelings that had become attached to them over the quarter of a century between the events of his boyhood and his retrospective account: 'first, highly detailed memories of places, food, and people; second, moments of specular drama when the narrator in the present watches the child being watched by others in the past; and, finally, the interpolated passages of anger and outrage in which the present narrator heats up the emotional temperature of the piece' (p. 69). The sharply recalled sign, COFFEE-ROOM, on the door of one of the coffee-shops, seen differently from outside and inside, is vividly evoked, suggestive of Dickens's child and adult identities, and, as Bodenheimer says, provides some of the details that 'form the "factual" basis of every subsequent biographical account' (p. 70). The 'implicit split between the retrospective narrator and the child-character becomes explicit' when the child-Dickens goes into a pub and demands a glass of '"your very best – the VERY *best* – ale" and the landlord calls his wife, who "joined him in surveying me. Here we stand, all three, before me now, in my study in Devonshire terrace".' And the anger and resentment of the adult-Dickens, Bodenheimer points out, are apparent in 'the mantra-like repetition of sentence beginnings and the build up of clause on clause that Dickens uses when he is going for a direct assault on his reader's emotions'. This heightened language is typical of the passages most often quoted: '"It is wonderful to me how I could have been so easily cast away at such an age"; "No words can express ..."; "I know that I do not exaggerate ..."' (p. 71). Bodenheimer argues that, in writing 'The Autobiographical Fragment', Dickens realised the impossibility of autobiographical recall as a means of coming to terms with his past – 'the critical disconnect between trauma and language' – and that it was this that 'may well have turned him towards the fiction of *David Copperfield*, where he could re-bury ... his story within a context he invented and controlled' (p. 72). *Knowing Dickens* is a cunning title for a sophisticated book that explores its subject's self-knowledge, his projection of aspects of himself into his fictions, and the 'Dickens' we come to know from reading him.

Fourth, *the inside-out biography. Being Shelley: The Poet's Search for Himself* by Ann Wroe is an experiment in trying 'to write the life of a poet from the inside out'; that is, she explains, 'from the perspective of the creative spirit struggling to discover its true nature. It is a book about Shelley the poet, rather than Shelley the man' (Wroe, 2008: ix). In attempting this, she is providing one sort of answer to Jonathan Coe's frustrations with literary biography. As in his case, her sources are predominantly the subject's own words – 'poetry, prose, letters, recorded conversations and especially his notebooks'. The search for the creative spirit in this data necessitates a startlingly original form. Out goes the conventional life story with its predictable chronology; in comes a 'narrative track' which aims to represent 'the poet's quest for truth'. Instead of a developing history of events, the quest is organised around a loose structure of the four elements of ancient cosmology, 'the steadily rarefying elements of earth, water, air and fire' (p. x). The result is a book that has more the texture of a collage than the smooth finish of a representational portrait. How does this experiment work in practice?

Shelley's sense that all matter shares the same substance – the earth, himself, the smallest animalculae that he could see only through his microscope – is Wroe's starting-point in the opening section, 'Earth'. Her detailed 'Notes', here as throughout, indicate her main sources as she, too, puts her subject under the microscope. So, we first see him as a starer at things being stared at himself by his biographer: 'as closely as was feasible, he stared at things. He got right down beside the plate to study pink fatty slabs of bacon or the jutting crag of a teacake. Pressed against fir trees, he inspected and licked the oozy runnels of resin. He read with his face only inches from the page, and watched tiny insects in the palm of his hand with fervent dedication'

(p. 10) His senses 'were the ultimate and only source of knowledge about the world'. Everything in Nature was animated:

> I tell thee that those viewless beings,
> Whose mansion is the smallest particle
> Of the impassive atmosphere,
> Think, feel and live like man …
> (Quoted in Wroe, 2008: 11)

And in 'Queen Mab', Shelley developed his notion of 'creation' as an arrangement and organisation of matter operating according to the laws of its own nature. 'Unending mutability was the nature of existence' (pp. 11–12). Wroe's Shelley has a keen excitement with the Earth and all its creatures, but is anything but Earth-bound.

Shelley's affinity with water was a fateful passion. 'Water', Wroe tells us, 'marked the first escape from densest matter, slippery and quick and translucent' (p. 114). She records a host of instances and anecdotes about his boyhood love of boats and moving water, his curious inability to swim, and his visionary voyages in 'Adonais' and other poems. There is humour – his celebrated appearance as a naked merman at a dinner party at Villa Magni (pp. 116–117) – and there is the tragedy of his drowning when his dangerously unstable yacht, *Don Juan*, sank in the Bay of Spezia (p. 187). Wroe interprets these diverse aspects of Shelley's life, and even his death, as metaphors for his ways of thinking: 'Water in all its guises, then, was thought in all its modes of expression' (p. 169). In this section, particularly, Wroe's penchant for figurative descriptions is sometimes overdone ('eddying ideas') or over the top ('tumultous thought … burst through in his letters, spraying out ink'), but, generally, the poetic Shelleyean voice she adopts in order to blend her diverse materials keeps such rhetorical indulgences under control, enabling her to avoid the parody to which her style is vulnerable.

If Shelley 'could not cope in water, in air he imagined he could move like a swimmer' (p. 201). The third section gives us the 'Ariel Shelley', perhaps the most familiar image of the poet (p. 215). It offers, too, detailed accounts of two of Shelley's most famous poems, 'To a Skylark' and 'Ode to the West Wind', which, interpolated with passages from *A Defence of Poetry*, explore the source of the poet's creative spirit and come as close as anywhere to fulfilling Wroe's biographical agenda.

Shelleyean 'Fire', like the other elements, is recreated in Wroe's book from sources as different as the unintended domestic dramas of his boyhood when he set the butler alight with a blazing stove and terrified his sisters with electric shocks (p. 299), to her account of his realisation that his revolution should be waged with words, not guns. 'His pen, therefore, was his fire-weapon' and his 'exemplar' was Prometheus who stole fire from the gods (p. 330).

In its leaning away from history, this is a biography that inclines not towards fiction but towards poetry. Its organisation may have been suggested by Trelawny's supposed incantation at Shelley's cremation. '"I restore to nature through fire the elements of which this man was composed, earth, air and water"' (p. 388). In its language, Wroe's biography deliberately fuses her own voice with that of her subject, producing a poetic prose that echoes and extends Shelley's style. The combined effect is to establish Shelley even more firmly as a major figure in literary biomythography.

All four approaches are innovative in different ways but share a common purpose: to get closer to their subjects. Nicholl gives us a 'blow-up' of the image of Shakespeare on Silver Street; Coe writes an *avant-garde* biography of an *avant-garde* writer; Bodenheimer cuts across familiar storylines in Dickens biography in the search for new perspectives on familiar issues; and Wroe, as her subtitle signals, appropriates this common notion of 'the search' and applies it to the biographee. Whether their approaches are transferable to other subjects is the challenge they throw down to future biographers. Distinguished biographies along conventional lines continue to be written (Jonathan Bate, *John Clare*, 2003; John Stubbs, *Donne*, 2006), but, as Michael Holroyd has remarked: 'Biography will continue to change, will become more personal, more idiosyncratic, imaginative, experimental, more hybrid, and will move further from the comprehensive "Life and Letters" structure' (Holroyd, 2003: 30). Perhaps the underlying change is hinted at in the titles of the two most recent books: the participles 'Knowing' and 'Being' indicate biographies which abandon the chronological imperative and replace it with a narrative of the writer's creative life. They take an inclusive view of the works, seeking the patterns in all of the subject's writings; and they recognise that an understanding of the story of a literary life requires imaginative energy to capture it in action.

Select Bibliography

Further Reading

The aim of this part of the Bibliography is to be of use to students and general readers wanting to follow up on particular authors without feeling daunted by the size and number of biographies available. I have exercised, therefore, a self-imposed limitation of two titles per author. Usually, one gives the standard life, the other a distinctive line on the subject's life and works. The losses here are less than might be supposed: biographers build upon what has gone before, so that I have generally chosen recent biographies knowing that they refer to their predecessors. Anyone wanting a historical view of how the genre treats a particular author should be able to identify the main sources from the General Bibliography.

I have distinguished between writers before and after 1900, an arbitrary yet commonly used watershed in literary history. Initially, I restricted the list to six novelists/prose writers and six poets either side of this date but, having done so, this seemed too severe. The character of the genre, like those of its subjects, is best understood from a variety of perspectives; hence, I have included six additional biographies which, for the treatment of their subjects, should not be missed, plus short lists of other related literature. On occasions where the lives of authors seem inseparable (Johnson and Boswell; the Brontës; Ted Hughes and Sylvia Plath), I have left them together. Inevitably there are omissions which I regret – Chaucer, Coleridge, the Brownings, Tennyson, Wilde ... the list seems endless; but the Internet provides easily accessible information and, in an introductory book, I judged it more important to make the Further Reading digestible rather than exhaustive.

Some Major Prose Writers and Novelists, pre-1900

Samuel Johnson: Samuel Johnson, 'Life of Savage' (1744), reprinted in *Lives of the English Poets* (1779–1781), Oxford University Press, 1906. Reissued in Classic Biographies, ed. Richard Holmes, HarperCollins, 2005.

	Peter Martin, *Samuel Johnson: A Biography*, Weidenfeld & Nicolson, 2008.
James Boswell:	James Boswell, *The Life of Dr. Johnson* (1791), Dent Everyman (2 vols), 1949.
	Adam Sisman, *Boswell's Presumptuous Task: Writing the Life of Dr. Johnson*, Hamish Hamilton, 2000; Penguin, 2001.
Jane Austen:	Park Honan, *Jane Austen: Her Life*, revised edition, Phoenix, 1997.
	Claire Tomalin, *Jane Austen: A Life*, revised edition, Penguin, 2000.
Charlotte Brontë:	Elizabeth Gaskell, *The Life of Charlotte Brontë*, 1857; Penguin, 1975.
	Lyndall Gordon, *Charlotte Brontë: A Passionate Life*, Chatto & Windus, 1994.
The Brontës:	Juliette Barker, *The Brontës*, Weidenfeld & Nicolson, 1994.
	Lucasta Miller, *The Brontë Myth*, Jonathan Cape, 2001.
George Eliot:	Rosemary Ashton, *George Eliot: A Life*, Penguin, 1996.
	Kathryn Hughes, *George Eliot: The Last Victorian*, Fourth Estate, 1998.
Charles Dickens:	Edgar Johnson, *Charles Dickens: His Tragedy and Triumph*, 1953; Penguin, 1986.
	Peter Ackroyd, *Dickens*, Sinclair-Stevenson, 1990; Vintage, 1999.
Thomas Hardy:	Michael Millgate, *Thomas Hardy: A Biography Revisited*, Oxford University Press, 2006.
	Claire Tomalin, *Thomas Hardy: The Time-Torn Man*, Viking, 2006.

Some Major Poets, pre-1900

William Shakespeare:	Park Honan, *Shakespeare: A Life*, Oxford University Press, 1999.
	James Shapiro, *1599: A Year in the Life of William Shakespeare*, Faber, 2005.
John Milton:	Anna Beer, *Milton: Poet, Pamphleteer and Patriot*, Bloomsbury, 2008.
	Barbara K. Lewalski, *The Life of John Milton*, Blackwell, 2001.
William Blake:	Peter Ackroyd, *Blake*, Sinclair-Stevenson, 1995.
	G. E. Bentley, Jr, *The Stranger from Paradise: A Biography of William Blake*, Yale, 2001.
William Wordsworth:	Juliet Barker, *Wordsworth: A Life*, Viking, 2000.

Kenneth R. Johnston, *The Hidden Wordsworth*, Pimlico, 2000.

Lord Byron: Benita Eisler, *Byron: Child of Passion, Fool of Fame*, Hamish Hamilton, 1999; Penguin, 2000.

Fiona MacCarthy, *Byron: Life and Legend*, Faber, 2003.

John Keats: Robert Gittings, *John Keats*, Heinemann, 1968; Penguin, 2001.

Andrew Motion, *Keats*, Faber, 1997.

Some Twentieth-Century Novelists

Joseph Conrad: Jeffrey Meyers, *Joseph Conrad: A Biography*, Charles Scribner's Sons, 1991.

John Stape, *The Several Lives of Joseph Conrad*, Heinemann, 2007.

Virginia Woolf: Hermione Lee, *Virginia Woolf*, Vintage, 1997.

Virginia Woolf, *Moments of Being: Autobiographical Writings*, ed. J. Schulkind, Pimlico, 2002.

James Joyce: Richard Ellmann, *James Joyce*, 1959; new and revised edition, Oxford University Press, 1983.

Stanislaus Joyce, *My Brother's Keeper*, ed. Richard Ellmann, Faber, 1958.

D. H. Lawrence: John Worthen, *D. H. Lawrence: The Life of an Outsider*, Allen Lane, 2005; Penguin, 2008.

Harry T. Moore, *The Life and Works of D. H. Lawrence*, Unwin Books, 1951.

George Orwell: D. J. Taylor, *Orwell: The Life*, Vintage, 2004.

G. Bowker, *George Orwell*, Little, Brown, 2004.

Graham Greene: Norman Sherry, *The Life of Graham Greene* (3 vols), Viking, 1989, 1995, 2004.

Graham Greene, *A Sort of Life* (1971) and *Ways of Escape* (1980), Vintage, 1999.

Some Twentieth-Century Poets

Wilfred Owen: Dominic Hibberd, *Wilfred Owen: A New Biography*, Weidenfeld & Nicolson, 2002.

Jon Stallworthy, *Wilfred Owen: A Biography*, Oxford, 1974.

T. S. Eliot: Peter Ackroyd, *T. S. Eliot*, Abacus, 1985.

Lyndall Gordon, *T. S. Eliot: An Imperfect Life*, Vintage, 1998.

W. B. Yeats: Richard Ellmann, *Yeats: The Man and The Masks*, Norton, revised edition, 1979.

	Roy Foster, *W. B. Yeats: A Life* (2 vols), Oxford University Press, 1997, 2000.
W. H. Auden:	Humphrey Carpenter, *W. H. Auden: A Biography*, Houghton Mifflin, 1981.
	Charles Osborne, *W. H. Auden: The Life of a Poet*, M. Evans, new edition, 1995.
Ted Hughes:	Elaine Feinstein, *Ted Hughes: The Life of a Poet*, Phoenix, 2002.
and	Anne Stevenson, *Bitter Fame: A Life of Sylvia Plath*, Viking, 1989; Penguin, 1998.
Sylvia Plath:	Janet Malcolm, *The Silent Woman: Sylvia Plath and Ted Hughes*, Vintage, 1995.
	Erica Wagner, *Ariel's Gift: Ted Hughes, Sylvia Plath and the Story of 'Birthday Letters'*, Faber, 2001.

Six Biographies, Not Discussed Earlier, But Not To Be Missed

Richard Holmes, *Shelley the Pursuit*, Penguin, 1987.
Jonathan Bate, *John Clare: A Biography*, Picador, 2003.
John Stubbs, *Donne: The Reformed Soul*, Viking, 2006.
Richard Ellmann, *Oscar Wilde*, Hamish Hamilton, 1987.
Jenny Uglow, *Elizabeth Gaskell: A Habit of Stories*, Faber, 1993/1999.
Hermione Lee, *Edith Wharton*, Vintage, 2008.

Fiction on the Dilemmas of Biography

Henry James, *The Aspern Papers* (1888), Penguin, 1994.
Oscar Wilde, *The Portrait of Mr. W. H.* (1921), Hesperus, 2003.
Virginia Woolf, *Orlando: A Biography* (1928), Oxford World's Classics, 1998.
William Golding, *The Paper Men*, Faber, 1985.
Julian Barnes, *Flaubert's Parrot*, Picador, 1985.
A. S. Byatt, *Possession*, Vintage, 1991.

Biofictions and Others

Richard Holmes, *Dr. Johnson and Mr. Savage*, Hodder & Stoughton, 1993; Flamingo, 1994. [On Dr Johnson]
Beryl Bainbridge, *According to Queeney*, Abacus, 2002. [On Dr Johnson]
Michael Cunningham, *The Hours*, Fourth Estate, 1999. [On Virginia Woolf]
David Lodge, *Author, Author*, Penguin, 2005. [On Henry James]
Colm Toibin, *The Master*, Picador, 2005. [On Henry James]
Julian Barnes, *Arthur and George*, Jonathan Cape, 2005. [On Arthur Conan Doyle]

General Bibliography

Ackroyd, P. (1985) *T. S. Eliot*, London: Abacus.

Ackroyd, P. (1995) *Blake*, London: Sinclair-Stevenson.

Ackroyd, P. (1999) *Dickens*, London: Vintage.

Ackroyd, P. (2005) *Shakespeare: The Biography*, London: Chatto & Windus.

Alexander, P. (2003) *Rough Magic: A Biography of Sylvia Plath*, 2nd edition, New York: Da Capo Press.

Alperson, P. (ed.) (1992) *The Philosophy of the Visual Arts*, New York and Oxford: Oxford University Press.

Altick, R. D. (1965/1979) *Lives and Letters: A History of Literary Biography in England and America*, New York: Greenwood Press.

Alvarez, A. (1962) *The New Poetry*, Harmondsworth: Penguin.

Alvarez, A. (1974) *The Savage God: A Study of Suicide*, Harmondsworth: Penguin.

Anderson, L. (2001) *Autobiography*, London: Routledge.

Anderson, M. (2005) *'Shakespeare' by Another Name*, New York: Gotham Books.

Aubrey, J. (1681/1965) *Brief Lives*, Harmondsworth: Penguin.

Auden, W. H. (1963/1975) *The Dyer's Hand*, London: Faber.

Auerbach, E. (1953/2003) 'The Brown Stocking', in *Mimesis: The Representation of Reality in Western Literature*, trans. W. R. Trask, Princeton and Oxford: Princeton University Press.

Austen-Leigh, J. E. (1870/2002) *A Memoir of Jane Austen and Other Family Recollections*, Oxford: Oxford World's Classics.

Backscheider, P. (1999) *Reflections on Biography*, Oxford: Oxford University Press.

Bainbridge, B. (2002) *According to Queeney*, London: Abacus.

Barker, J. (1994) *The Brontës*, London: Weidenfeld & Nicolson. Reprinted, Phoenix, 1995.

Barker, J. (2000) *Wordsworth: A Life*, London: Viking.

Barnes, J. (1985) *Flaubert's Parrot*, London: Picador.

Bate, J. (1997) *The Genius of Shakespeare*, London: Picador.

Bate, J. (2003) *John Clare: A Biography*, London: Picador.

Bearman, R. (1994) *Shakespeare in the Stratford Records*, Stroud: Alan Sutton Publishing, in association with the Shakespeare Birthplace Trust.

Beja, M. (ed.) (1970) *Virginia Woolf: To The Lighthouse*, Basingstoke: Palgrave Macmillan.

Beja, M. (ed.) (1973) *James Joyce: Dubliners and A Portrait of the Artist as a Young Man*, Basingstoke: Palgrave Macmillan.

Bell, C. (1850/1965) 'Preface to *Wuthering Heights*', in E. Brontë, *Wuthering Heights*, ed. D. Daiches, Harmondsworth: Penguin.

Bentley, G. E., Jr (1969/1988) *Blake Records*, Oxford: Clarendon Press.

Bentley, G. E., Jr (2001) *The Stranger from Paradise: A Biography of William Blake*, New Haven and London: Yale University Press.

Bloom, H. (1995) *The Western Canon*, London: Macmillan.

Bloom, H. (1998) *Shakespeare: The Invention of the Human*, New York: Riverhead.

Bodenheimer, R. (2007) *Knowing Dickens*, Ithaca and London: Cornell University Press.

Booth, W. C. (1961) *The Rhetoric of Fiction*, Chicago: Chicago University Press.

Borges, J. L. (1992) 'Everything and Nothing', in *Labyrinths*, London: Picador.

Bostridge, M. (ed.) (2004) *Lives for Sale: Biographers' Tales*, London: Continuum.

Boswell, J. (1791/1949) *The Life of Dr. Johnson* (2 vols), London: J. M. Dent & Sons.

Bowlby, R. (1998) 'Introduction', in Virginia Woolf, *Orlando*, Oxford: World's Classics.

Bradbury, M. (1988) 'The Telling Life: Some Thoughts on Literary Biography', in E. Homberger and J. Charmley (eds.), *The Troubled Face of Biography*, London: Macmillan.

Bradford, R. (2005) *First Boredom, Then Fear: The Life of Philip Larkin*, London: Peter Owen.

Brigden, S. (2001) *New Worlds, Lost Worlds: The Rule of the Tudors 1485–1603*, Harmondsworth: Penguin.

Briggs, J. (2006a) *Virginia Woolf: An Inner Life*, London: Penguin.

Briggs, J. (2006b) *Reading Virginia Woolf*, Edinburgh: Edinburgh University Press.

Brilliant, R. (1997) *Portraiture*, London: Reaction Books.

Bryson, B. (2008) *Shakespeare*, London: Harper Perennial.

Burgess, A. (1964) *Nothing Like the Sun: A Story of Shakespeare's Love Life*, London: Heinemann.

Byatt, A. S. (1991) *Possession: A Romance*, London: Vintage.

Cecil, D. (1936) 'Introduction', in *An Anthology of Modern Biography*, London: Thomas Nelson & Sons. Reprinted in Clifford (1962).

Cecil, D. (1978) *A Portrait of Jane Austen*, London: Constable & Co. Reprinted as a Classic Penguin, 2000.

Chambers, E. K. (1923/1951) *William Shakespeare: A Study of Facts and Problems*, revised edition (2 vols). Oxford: Clarendon Press.

Chesterton, G. K. (1906/1975) *Charles Dickens*, London: Burns & Oates.

Christiansen, R. (1989) *Romantic Affinities: Portraits from an Age 1780–1830*, London: Sphere Books.

Clifford, J. L. (ed.) (1962) *Biography as an Art: Selected Criticism, 1590–1960*, London and New York: Oxford University Press.

Clifford, J. L. (1970) *From Puzzles to Portraits: Problems of a Literary Biographer*, Chapel Hill: University of North Carolina Press and Oxford University Press.

Coe, J. (2004) *Like a Fiery Elephant: The Story of B. S. Johnson*, London: Picador.

Cooper, T. (2006) *Searching for Shakespeare*, London: National Portrait Gallery.

Crick, B. (1980) *George Orwell: A Life*, London: Secker & Warburg.

de Man, P. (1979) 'Autobiography as De-Facement', *Modern Language Notes*, 94: 919–930.

de Man, P. (1987/1993) 'Time and History in Wordsworth', in C. Chase (ed.), *Romanticism*, London: Longman.

Denzin, N. K. (1989) *Interpretive Biography* (Qualitative Research Methods, Vol. 17), London: Sage Publications.

Dickens, M. (1885/1911) *Charles Dickens: By His Eldest Daughter*, London: Cassell & Co.

Dolby, G. (1885) *Charles Dickens as I Knew Him: The Story of the Reading Tours*, London: T. Fisher Unwin.

Dowden, E. (1875) *Shakespeare: His Mind and Art*, London.

Duncan-Jones, K. (2001) *Ungentle Shakespeare: Scenes from his Life*, London: Thomson Learning.

Dunn, J, (2000) *Virginia Woolf and Vanessa Bell: A Very Close Conspiracy*, London: Virago.

Edel, L. (1957) *Literary Biography*, Toronto: University of Toronto Press. Reprinted, Doubleday Anchor, 1959.

Edel, L. (1984) *Writing Lives: Principia Biographia*, New York and London: Norton.

Eisler, B. (2000) *Byron: Child of Passion, Fool of Fame*, Harmondsworth: Penguin.

Eliot, T. S. (1957) 'The Frontiers of Criticism', in *On Poetry and Poets*, London: Faber.

Ellis, D. (2000) *Literary Lives: Biography and the Search for Understanding*, Edinburgh: Edinburgh University Press.

Ellmann, R. (1973) 'Literary Biography', in *Golden Codgers: Biographical Speculations*, London: Oxford University Press.

Ellmann, R. (1959/1983) *James Joyce*, new and revised edition, Oxford: Oxford University Press.

Feinstein, E. (2002) *Ted Hughes: The Life of a Poet*, London: Phoenix.

Fielding, J. K. (1966) *Charles Dickens*, London: Longmans, Green & Co.

Fleishman, A. (1983) *Figures of Autobiography: The Language of Self-Writing in Victorian and Modern England*, Berkeley, Los Angeles and London: University of California Press.

Forster, J. (1872–1874/1969) *The Life of Charles Dickens* (2 vols), London: J. M. Dent.

France, P. & St Clair, W. (eds) (2002) *Mapping Lives: The Uses of Biography*, Oxford: Oxford University Press.

Frye, N. (1957) *The Anatomy of Criticism*, Princeton: Princeton University Press.

Gaskell, E. (1857/1975) *The Life of Charlotte Brontë*, Harmondsworth: Penguin.

Gilbert, S. M. & Gubar, S. (1979) *The Madwoman in the Attic: The Woman Writer and the Nineteenth-Century Literary Imagination*, New Haven and London: Yale University Press.

Gilchrist, A. (1863/2005) *The Life of William Blake, 'Pictor Ignotus'*, London: Macmillan. Reprinted as *Gilchrist on Blake*, ed. R. Holmes (2005), London and New York: Harper Perennial.

Gill, S. (1990) *William Wordsworth: A Life*, Oxford: Oxford University Press.

Gittings, R. (1978) *The Nature of Biography*, London: Heinemann.

Gittings, R. (1968/2001) *John Keats*, London: Classic Penguin.

Gittings, R. (1975/2001) *Thomas Hardy*, London: Classic Penguin.

Gombrich, E. H. (1960) *Art and Illusion: A Study in the Psychology of Pictorial Representation*, London: Phaidon.

Gooding, M. (ed.) (1998) *Painter as Critic. Patrick Heron: Selected Writings*, London: Tate Gallery Publications.

Gordon, L. (1994) *Charlotte Brontë: A Passionate Life*, London: Chatto & Windus. Reprinted, Vintage, 1995.

Gordon, L. (1998) *T. S. Eliot: An Imperfect Life*, London: Vintage.

Gordon, L. (2006) *Virginia Woolf: A Writer's Life*, revised edition, London: Virago.

Greenblatt, S. (2004) *Will in the World: How Shakespeare Became Shakespeare*, London: Jonathan Cape.

Greene, G. (1971/1999) *A Sort of Life*, London: Vintage.

Greene, G. (1980/1999) *Ways of Escape*, London: Vintage.

Gross, J. (1992) *Shylock: Four Hundred Years in the Life of a Legend*, London: Chatto & Windus.

Gruetzner Robins, A. (1997) *Modern Art in Britain 1910–1914*, London: Merrell Holberton.

Gurr, A. (1970) *The Shakespearean Stage, 1574–1642*, Cambridge: Cambridge University Press.

Hagstrum, J. (1958) *The Sister Arts: The Tradition of Literary Pictorialism and English Poetry from Dryden to Gray*, Chicago: Chicago University Press.

Halperin, J. (1984/1996) *The Life of Jane Austen*, Baltimore and London: Johns Hopkins University Press.

Hamilton, I. (1992) *Keepers of the Flame: Literary Estates and the Rise of Biography*, London: Hutchinson.

Hamilton, I. (2003) *Against Oblivion: Some Lives of the Twentieth-Century Poets*, Harmondsworth: Penguin.

Hardy, B. (2006) *George Eliot: A Critic's Biography*, London and New York: Continuum.

Hardy, F. E. (1928/1994) *The Life of Thomas Hardy*, London: Studio Editions.

Harrison, B. (2004) 'The Dictionary Man', in Bostridge (2004).

Hartman, G. (1962/1993) 'Romanticism and Anti-Self-Consciousness', in C. Chase (ed.), *Romanticism*, London: Longman.

Hayman, R. (2003) *The Death and Life of Sylvia Plath*, Stroud: Sutton Publishing.

Hibberd, D. (ed.) (1973) *Wilfred Owen: War Poems and Others*, London: Chatto & Windus.

Hibberd, D. (1986) *Owen the Poet: A Critical Study*, London: Palgrave Macmillan.

Hibberd, D. (1992) *Wilfred Owen: The Last Year*, London: Constable.

Hibberd, D. (2001) *Harold Monro: Poet of the New Age*, Basingstoke: Palgrave.

Hibberd, D. (2002) *Wilfred Owen: A New Biography*, London: Weidenfeld & Nicolson.

Hibberd, D. & Onions, J. (2007) *The Winter of the World: Poems of the First World War*, London: Constable & Robinson.

Holden, A. (1999) *William Shakespeare: His Life and Work*, London: Abacus.

Holmes, R. (1985) *Footsteps: Adventures of a Romantic Biographer*, London: Hodder & Stoughton. Reprinted, Flamingo, 1995.

Holmes, R. (1987) *Shelley: The Pursuit*, Harmondsworth: Penguin.

Holmes, R. (1994) *Dr. Johnson and Mr. Savage*, London: Flamingo.

Holmes, R. (1995) 'Inventing the Truth', in J. Batchelor (ed.), *The Art of Literary Biography*, Oxford: Clarendon Press.

Holmes, R. (2002) 'The Proper Study?', in France & St Clair (2002).

Holmes, R. (2004) 'Death and Destiny', in *The Guardian Review*, 24 January.

Holmes, R. (ed.) (2005) *Johnson on Savage*, London and New York: Harper Perennial.

Holroyd, M. (1988–1992) *Bernard Shaw* (4 vols), London: Chatto & Windus.

Holroyd, M. (1997) *Bernard Shaw: The One-Volume Definitive Edition*, London: Vintage.

Holroyd, M. (2003) *Works on Paper: The Craft of Biography and Autobiography*, London: Abacus.

Homberger, E. & Charmley, J. (eds.) (1988) *The Troubled Face of Biography*, London: Macmillan.

Honan, P. (1997) *Jane Austen: Her Life*, revised edition, London: Phoenix.

Honan, P. (1999) *Shakespeare: A Life*, Oxford: Oxford University Press.

Honigman, E. A. J. (1985/1998) *Shakespeare: The 'Lost Years'*, Manchester: Manchester University Press.

House, H. (1941/1960) *The Dickens World*, London: Oxford University Press.

Howarth, P. (2006) *British Poetry in the Age of Modernism*, Cambridge: Cambridge University Press.

Hughes, T. (1994) *Winter Pollen: Occasional Prose*, London: Faber.

Hughes, T. (1998) *Birthday Letters*, London: Faber.

Iser, W. (1978) *The Act of Reading: A Theory of Aesthetic Response*, London: Routledge & Kegan Paul.

Jackson, R. (2005) *Shaker of the Spears*, Sussex: Book Guild Publishing.

James, B. with Rubenstein, W. D. (2005) *The Truth Will Out: Unmasking the Real Shakespeare*, Harlow: Pearson Longman.

James, H. (1866) 'The Novels of George Eliot', *The Atlantic Monthly*, Vol. 18, issue 108 (October), p. 485.

James, H. (1888/1994) *The Aspern Papers*, Harmondsworth: Penguin.

Jay, P. (1984) *Being in the Text: Self-Representation from Wordsworth to Roland Barthes*, Ithaca and London: Cornell University Press.

Johnson, B. S. (2004) *Omnibus: Albert Angelo, Trawl, House Mother Normal*, London: Picador.

Johnson, E. (1953/1986) *Charles Dickens: His Tragedy and Triumph*, Harmondsworth: Penguin.

Johnson, S. (1744) *An Account of the Life of Mr. Richard Savage, Son of Earl Rivers.* Reprinted in Holmes (2005).

Johnson, S. (1750, 1759, 1760) 'On Biography', *The Rambler*, No. 60; 'Autobiography', *The Idler*, No. 84; 'Literary Biography', *The Idler*, No. 102. All reprinted in Holmes (2005).

Johnson, S. (1779–1781/1906) *Lives of the English Poets* (2 vols). London: Oxford University Press.

Johnston, K. R. (2000) *The Hidden Wordsworth*, London: Pimlico.

Joyce, J. (1904/1973) 'A Portrait of the Artist', in Beja (1973).

Joyce, J. (1904–1906/1956) *Stephen Hero*, ed. T. Spencer, Rev. J. J. Slocum & H. Cahoon. London: Jonathan Cape.

Joyce, J. (1916/1960) *A Portrait of the Artist as a Young Man*, Harmondsworth: Penguin.

Kaplan, F. (1988) *Dickens: A Biography*, London: Hodder & Stoughton.

Keats, J. (1817/2002) *Selected Letters*, ed. R. Gittings. Oxford: World's Classics.

Kermode, F. (2000) *Shakespeare's Language*, London: Allen Lane.

Keynes, G. (ed.) (1956) *Poetry and Prose of William Blake*, London: Nonesuch Library.

Kitton, G. F. (1899) *Dickens and his Illustrators*, London: G. Redway. Reprinted, AMS Press, New York, 1975.

Lamarque, P. & Olsen, S. H. (1996) *Truth, Fiction, and Literature*, Oxford: Clarendon Press.

Larkin, P. (1983) *Required Writing: Miscellaneous Pieces 1955–1982*, London: Faber.

Leavis, F. R. & Leavis, Q. D. (1972) *Dickens the Novelist*, Harmondsworth: Penguin.

Lee, H. (1997) *Virginia Woolf*, London: Vintage.

Lee, H. (2002) 'Introduction', in Virginia Woolf, *Moments of Being: Autobiographical Writings*, ed. J. Schulkind, London: Pimlico.

Lee, H. (2005) *Virginia Woolf's Nose: Essays on Biography*, Princeton and Oxford: Princeton University Press.

Lee, H. (2008) *Body Parts: Essays on Life-Writing*, London: Pimlico.

Lindop, G. (2001) 'A Palace of his Own', *The Times Literary Supplement*, 31 August.

Lodge, D. (2005) *Author, Author*, Harmondsworth: Penguin.

MacCarthy, F. (2002) 'Poet of all the Passions', *The Guardian Review*, 9 November.

MacCarthy, F. (2003) *Byron: Life and Legend*, London: Faber.

McIntyre, I. (1999) *Garrick*, London: Penguin.

Malcolm, J. (1995) *The Silent Woman: Sylvia Plath and Ted Hughes*, London: Vintage.

Mengham, R. (2001) *Charles Dickens*, Tavistock, Devon: Northcote House.

Miller, L. (2001) *The Brontë Myth*, London: Jonathan Cape.

Millgate, M. (1984) *The Life and Work of Thomas Hardy*, London: Macmillan.

Millgate, M. (2006) *Thomas Hardy: A Biography Revisited*, Oxford: Oxford University Press.

Motion, A. (1993) *Philip Larkin: A Writer's Life*, London: Faber.

Motion, A. (1997) *Keats*, London: Faber.

Motion, A. (2000) *Wainewright the Poisoner*, London: Faber.

Motion, A. (2004) 'Breaking In', in Bostridge (2004).

Newman, C. (ed.) (1971) *The Art of Sylvia Plath: A Symposium*, Bloomington and London: Indiana University Press.

Nicholl, C. (2008) *The Lodger: Shakespeare on Silver Street*, London: Penguin.

Norman, M. & Stoppard, T. (1998) *Shakespeare in Love* (screenplay).

Nuttall, A. D. (2007) *Shakespeare the Thinker*, New Haven and London: Yale University Press.

O'Connor, G. (1992) *William Shakespeare: A Life*, London: Hodder & Stoughton, Sceptre.

Orwell, G. (1938/1962) *Homage to Catalonia*, Harmondsworth: Penguin.

Orwell, S. & Angus, I. (eds.) (1970) *The Collected Essays, Journalism and Letters of George Orwell* (4 vols), Harmondsworth: Penguin.

Owen, H. (1963–1965) *Journey from Obscurity* (3 vols), Oxford: Oxford University Press.

Parke, C. N. (2002) *Biography: Writing Lives*, New York and London: Routledge.

Paulson, R. (1993) *Hogarth* (3 vols), Cambridge: Lutterworth Press.

Piper, D. (1982) *The Image of the Poet: British Poets and their Portraits*, Oxford: Clarendon Press.

Plath, S. (1965) *Ariel*, London: Faber.

Pointon, M. (1993) *Hanging the Head: Portraiture and Social Formation in Eighteenth-Century England*, New Haven and London: Yale University Press.

Prince, G. (1982) *Narratology: The Form and Function of Narrative*, The Hague: Mouton.

Reynolds, Sir Joshua (1770/1975) *Discourses on Art*, ed. R. R. Wark, New Haven and London: Yale University Press.

Rose, J. (1992) *The Haunting of Sylvia Plath*, Cambridge, MA: Harvard University Press.

Rosenblatt, L. (1978) *The Reader, the Text, the Poem: The Transactional Theory of the Literary Work*, Carbondale: Southern Illinois University Press.

Rowse, A. L. (1973) *Shakespeare the Man*, London: Macmillan.

Runyan, W. M. (1984) *Life Histories and Psychobiography: Explorations in Theory and Method*, New York and Oxford: Oxford University Press.

Salwack, D. (ed.) (1996) *The Literary Biography: Problems and Solutions*, London: Macmillan.

Saumarez Smith, C. (1997) *The National Portrait Gallery*, London: National Portrait Gallery Publications.

Schoenbaum, S. (1987) *William Shakespeare: A Compact Documentary Life*, Oxford: Oxford University Press.

Schoenbaum, S. (1993) *Shakespeare's Lives*, revised edition, New York and London: Oxford University Press.

Scholes, R. (1981) 'Language, Narrative and Anti-Narrative', in W. J. T. Mitchell, *On Narrative*, Chicago and London: University of Chicago Press.

Seymour-Jones, C. (2001) *Painted Shadow: A Life of Vivienne Eliot*, London: Constable.

Shakespeare, W. (1955) *The Merchant of Venice*, ed. J. R. Brown, Arden edition, London: Methuen.

Shakespeare, W. (1967) *King Henry V*, ed. J. H. Walter, Arden edition, London: Methuen.

Shakespeare, W. (1969) *The Tempest*, ed. F. Kermode, Arden edition, London: Methuen.

Shakespeare, W. (1982) *Hamlet*, ed. H. Jenkins, Arden edition, London: Methuen.

Shakespeare, W. (1986) *The Sonnets and A Lover's Complaint*, ed. J. Kerrigan, London: Penguin.

Shakespeare, W. (1997) *Shakespeare's Sonnets*, ed. K. Duncan-Jones, Arden edition, London: Thomson Learning.

Shakespeare, W. (2002) *The Complete Sonnets and Poems*, ed. C. Burrow, Oxford: World's Classics.

Shapiro, J. (2005) *1599: A Year in the Life of William Shakespeare*, London: Faber.

Sherry, N. (1989, 1995, 2004) *The Life of Graham Greene* (3 vols), London: Viking.

Shields, C. (2001) *Jane Austen*, London: Phoenix.

Shone, R. (1999) *The Art of Bloomsbury*, London: Tate Gallery Publishing.

Slater, M. (1983) *Dickens and Women*, London: J. M. Dent.

Slater, M. (2004) 'Dickens: Charles John Huffam, 1812–1870', in H. C. G. Matthews & B. Harrison (eds.), *Oxford Dictionary of National Biography*, 16: 75–76. Oxford: Oxford University Press.

Sisman, A. (2001) *Boswell's Presumptuous Task: Writing the Life of Dr. Johnson*, Harmondsworth: Penguin.

Spurling, H. (2002) *The Girl From the Fiction Department: A Portrait of Sonia Orwell*, London: Hamish Hamilton.

Stansky, P. & Abrahams, W. (1972) *The Unknown Orwell*, London: Constable.

Stauffer, D. A. (1941) *The Art of Biography in Eighteenth-Century England*, London: Russell & Russell.

Stevenson, A. (1989) *Bitter Fame: A Life of Sylvia Plath*, London: Viking.

Storey, G. (1939) *Dickens and Daughter*, London: Frederick Mueller.

Strachey, L. (1918/1986) *Eminent Victorians*, Harmondsworth: Penguin.

Stubbs, J. (2006) *Donne: The Reformed Soul*, London: Penguin.

Sutherland, J. (ed.) (2001) *Literary Lives*, Oxford: Oxford University Press.

Sutherland, K. (2002) 'Introduction', in Austen-Leigh (1870/2002).

Taylor, D. J. (2004) *Orwell: The Life*, London: Vintage.

Tennant, E. (1999) *Burnt Diaries*, London: Canongate.

Tennant, E. (2001) *The Ballad of Sylvia and Ted*, New York: Henry Holt.

Thomson, P. (1999) *Shakespeare's Professional Career*, Cambridge: Cambridge University Press.

Thwaite, A. (ed.) (1988) *Philip Larkin: Collected Poems*, London: Marvell Press and Faber.

Thwaite, A. (ed.) (1992) *Selected Letters of Philip Larkin, 1940–1985*, London: Faber.

Tomalin, C. (1991) *The Invisible Woman: The Story of Nelly Ternan and Charles Dickens*, Harmondsworth: Penguin.

Tomalin, C. (1992) *Shelley and His World*, London: Penguin.

Tomalin, C. (2000) *Jane Austen: A Life*, revised edition, London: Penguin.

Tomalin, C. (2003) *Samuel Pepys: The Unequalled Self*, London: Penguin.

Tomalin, C. (2006) *Thomas Hardy: The Time-Torn Man*, London: Viking Penguin.

Uglow, J. (1997) *Hogarth: A Life and a World*, London: Faber.

Uglow, J. (1999) *Elizabeth Gaskell: A Habit of Stories*, London: Faber.

Wagner, E. (2001) *Ariel's Gift: Ted Hughes, Sylvia Plath and the Story of 'Birthday Letters'*, London: Faber.

Wagner-Martin, L. (1987) *Sylvia Plath: A Biography*, London: Chatto & Windus.

Wagner-Martin, L. (2003) *Sylvia Plath: A Literary Life*, London: Macmillan.

Walton, I. (1670) *The Lives of Dr. John Donne [&] ... Mr. George Herbert*, London.

Wells, S. (1995) *Shakespeare: A Life in Drama*, New York and London: Norton.

Wendorf, R. (1990) *The Elements of Life: Biography and Portrait-Painting in Stuart and Georgian England*, Oxford: Clarendon Press.

West, S. (2004) *Portraiture* (Oxford History of Art), Oxford: Oxford University Press.

Wilde, O. (1921/2003) *The Portrait of Mr. W. H.*, London: Hesperus Press.

Williams, J. (1980) *The Practical Princess and Other Liberating Fairy Tales*, London: Scholastic.

Williams, R. (1971) *Orwell*, London: Fontana Collins.

Wood, M. (2003) *In Search of Shakespeare*, London: BBC Books.

Woolf, V. (1928/1998) *Orlando: A Biography*, Oxford: World's Classics.

Woolf, V. (1928/2000) *To The Lighthouse*, ed. M. Drabble. Oxford: World's Classics.

Woolf, V. (1933/1998) *Flush*, Oxford: World's Classics.

Woolf, V. (1939–1940/2002) 'Sketch of the Past', in *Moments of Being: Autobiographical Writings*, ed. J. Schulkind, London: Pimlico.

Woolf, V. (1940/1969) *Roger Fry: A Biography*, London: Hogarth Press.

Woolf, V. (1967) 'The New Biography' (1927), 'The Art of Biography' (1939) and 'I Am Christina Rossetti', in *Collected Essays*, Vol. 4, London: Hogarth Press.

Wordsworth, W. (1802/1968) 'Preface' to *Lyrical Ballads*, ed. R. L. Brett & A. R. Jones, London and New York: Methuen.

Wordsworth, W. (1805/1960) *The Prelude or Growth of a Poet's Mind*, ed. E. de Selincourt, London: Oxford University Press.

Wordsworth, W. (1979) *The Prelude 1799, 1805, 1855*, ed. J. Wordsworth, M. H. Abrams & S. Gill, New York: Norton.
Wordsworth, W. (1807/1983) *Poems, in Two Volumes and Other Poems 1800–1807*, ed. J. Curtis, Ithaca: Cornell University Press.
Wright, T. (1935) *The Life of Charles Dickens*, London.
Wroe, A. (2008) *Being Shelley: The Poet's Search for Himself*, London: Vintage.

Index

Note: page numbers in italics denote figures or illustrations

Printed and bound by CPI Group (UK) Ltd, Croydon, CR0 4YY

07/07/2026

14916222-0005